# The Machine Shed Roots

We opened the Iowa Machine Shed Restaurant in 1978 in rural Davenport, Iowa with just over 100 seats. Our location wasn't great and much of the equipment was old (but clean) and broke too often.

We were all pretty young and green, but we started with a powerful commitment. That commitment was a simple five word constitution- "Dedicated to the Iowa Farmer." That dedication meant that we worked to have a restaurant that wasn't just "farm" themed but would be something that farmers could be proud of. That meant using only the best pork and beef, real whipped cream on the pies, hearty soups, fresh baked goods made from scratch, and little things like genuine mashed potatoes and real butter. Although we still had a lot to learn, that dedication guided us through the early days. Even though money was tight, we were never tempted to take a cheaper route.

Thanks to folks like you, the Machine Shed has been popular from the very start. The original Machine Shed has been expanded and improved many times. Now, other Machine Sheds have sprung up in Des Moines, Iowa; Olathe, Kansas; Rockford and Aurora, Illinois; Pewaukee and Appleton, Wisconsin and Lake Elmo, Minnesota. Along the way we have been delighted to have received a bushel basket full of honors from farm groups like the Pork Producers and the Beef Industry Council. We're constantly trying to live up to those honors in the food we prepare and the service we provide.

*Mike Whalen*

Thanks for your help

# Heart of America
### Restaurants & Inns

**Iowa Machine Shed**
7250 Northwest Blvd.
Davenport, IA 52806
▶

**Comfort Inn**
7222 Northwest Blvd.
Davenport, IA 52806
▶

**Thunder Bay Grille**
6511 Brady Street
Davenport, IA 52806
▶

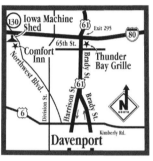

**Gramma's Kitchen/
The Checkered Flag**
I-80 / Exit 284
Walcott, IA 52773
▶

**Iowa Machine Shed**
11151 Hickman Road
Urbandale, IA 50322
▶

**Comfort Suites at
Living History Farms**
11167 Hickman Road
Urbandale, IA 50322
▶

**Wildwood Lodge**
11431 Forest Avenue
Clive, IA 50325
▶

**Sleep Inn**
11211 Hickman Rd.
Urbandale, IA 50322
▶

**Wingate Inn**
6800 Fleur Dr.
Des Moines, IA 50321
▼

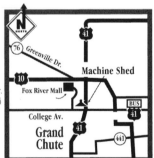

**Wisconsin Machine Shed**
Interstate 94 & Hwy J
Pewaukee, WI 53072
▶

**Comfort Suites
Lake Country**
Interstate 94 & Hwy J
Pewaukee, WI 53072
▶

**Thunder Bay Grille**
Interstate 94 & Hwy J
Pewaukee, WI 53072
▶

**Wisconsin
Machine Shed**
220 North Fox River Dr.
Grand Chute, WI 54914
▶

ISBN# 1-57166-18

# True Midwestern hospitality

## Visit all of Heart of America's properties throughout the Midwest

**Planted Earth Cafe**
1300 River Dr.
Moline, IL 61265
▶

**Illinois Machine Shed**
Interstate 88 &
Orchard Rd.
Aurora IL
▶

**Marriot Courtyard**
Interstate 88 &
Orchard Rd.
Aurora, IL
▶

**Illinois Machine Shed**
7475 Potawatomi Trail
Rockford, IL 61108

**Thunder Bay Grille**
7652 East State St.
Rockford, IL 61107
▶

**Minnesota Machine Shed**
Interstate 94 &
Radio Drive
Lake Elmo, MN 55042
▶

**Comfort Suites**
Interstate 94 &
Radio Drive
Lake Elmo, MN 55042
▶

**Kansas Machine Shed**
12080 South Strang Line Rd.
Olathe, KS 66062
▶

**Comfort Suites Olathe Station**
12070 South Strang Line Rd.
Olathe, KS 66062
▶

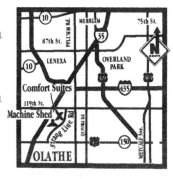

# About Low-Fat Dieting & Cooking

Fat, like protein and carbohydrate, is a principal and essential component of the diet. Fat is the body's most concentrated source of energy. Some dietary fat is vital to enable the body to function properly. Fat is responsible for transporting fat-soluble vitamins A, D, E and K.

Dietary fats also are a source of fatty acids, including essential fatty acids which are necessary to assure good health. Essential fatty acids must be obtained from dietary sources (primarily vegetable oil) because the body cannot make them. Fatty acids are separated by their structure as either saturated, monounsaturated, or polyunsaturated. Although naturally occurring fats in food are a mixture of many different fatty acids, fats can be characterized by their origin.

SATURATED fats are mainly found in foods of animal origin. These include the fats in whole milk, cream, cheese, butter, meat and poultry. Saturated fats also can be found in large amounts in some vegetable products, such as cocoa butter, coconut oil, and palm oil. Saturated fats are usually solid at room temperature.

MONOUNSATURATED fats are found primarily in plants, but also are found in animals. Olive, peanut and canola oil are common examples of fats high in monounsaturated fatty acids. Also, most margarines and hydrogenated vegetable shortenings tend to be high in monounsaturated fatty acids. Monounsaturated fats are liquid at room temperature.

POLYUNSATURATED fats are found mostly in plants. Sunflower, corn, soybean, cotton seed and safflower oils are vegetable fats that contain a relatively high proportion of polyunsaturated fats. Margarines with vegetable oil as the primary ingredient, and some fish, also are sources of polyunsaturated fats. Polyunsaturated fats usually are liquid at room temperature.

By using low-fat alternatives in preparing your meals, and eating foods lower in fat, plus eating a balanced diet in moderation, you've found a great way to eat healthy and lose weight all at the same time.

FAST FAT FIGURING FOR YOUR DIET

1.) To quickly estimate your daily allotment of fat in grams, divide your ideal weight by 2.

2.) Calorie needs are based on a variety of factors: age, size, gender, overall health and activity level. But for a quick estimate of your daily allotment, multiply your current weight by 10 if you are unactive---by 12 if you are moderately active----and by 15 if you are very active.

3.) Experts recommend that no more than 30% of daily caloric intake come from fat. A quick way to figure this: multiply the grams of fat by 9--divide that number by the total number of calories--then multiply that number by 100.

# Acknowledgement

Comfort food is a nurturing and nostalgic popular food phenomenon. While this style of food is important to all of us, it doesn't always fit into our nutritional requirements.

In this cookbook, Mary Schneckloth has worked her magic to create recipes for the foods we crave, in a lighter, more healthful version. Mary's recipes also include for your convenience the nutritional values for calories, protein, fat, cholesterol and carbohydrates.

A well balanced diet eaten in moderation is always your best choice. Fats, as well as proteins and carbohydrates, are essential components to a healthy diet. Keep in mind, if you deprive yourself of good food, you will end up eating the wrong foods when your willpower is weak.

This book's over 300 recipes will delight your senses and make you comfortable enjoying comfort food.

Recipes shown on cover:
Sesame Ginger Chicken - page 107
Grilled Shiitake Mushrooms - page 173
Mustard and Herb Marinated Vegetables - page 181

# Table of Contents

# List Your Favorite Recipes

**Recipes**                                        **Page**

_____    _____

_____    _____

_____    _____

_____    _____

_____    _____

_____    _____

_____    _____

_____    _____

_____    _____

_____    _____

_____    _____

_____    _____

_____    _____

_____    _____

_____    _____

_____    _____

_____    _____

# Appetizers and Drinks

# List Your Favorite Recipes

**Recipes**                                    **Page**

_____          _____

_____          _____

_____          _____

_____          _____

_____          _____

_____          _____

_____          _____

_____          _____

_____          _____

_____          _____

_____          _____

_____          _____

_____          _____

_____          _____

_____          _____

_____          _____

_____          _____

_____          _____

_____          _____

# Banana Brunch Punch

6 medium ripe bananas
1 (12-ounce) can frozen orange juice
   concentrate, thawed
1 (6-ounce) can frozen lemonade
1 (6-ounce) can frozen lemonade
   concentrate, thawed
2 cups warm water, divided
2 cups sugar, divided
1 (46-ounce) can pineapple juice
3 bottles (2 liters each) lemon-
   lime soda
Orange slices (optional)

IN a blender or food processor, blend bananas and concentrates until smooth.
REMOVE half of the mixture and set aside.
ADD 1 1/2 cups of warm water and 1 cup sugar to mixture in blender; blend until smooth. PLACE in freezer container.
REPEAT with remaining banana mixture, water and sugar; add to container.
COVER and freeze until solid.
ONE hour before serving, take punch base out of freezer.
JUST before serving, place in a large punch bowl.
ADD pineapple juice and soda; stir until well blended. Garnish with orange slices if desired.
YIELD: 10 quarts

PER 1/2-cup serving:
CALORIES 79
(1% from fat)
FAT trace
(saturated trace)
CARBOHYDRATE 20g
CHOLESTEROL 0mg
SODIUM 9mg

# Cappuccino Mix

PER 3/4-cup serving
CALORIES 106
(4% from fat)
FAT trace
(saturated trace)
PROTEIN 1g
CARBOHYDRATE 25g
CHOLESTEROL 0mg
SODIUM 28mg

1  cup powdered fat-free nondairy creamer
1  cup instant chocolate drink mix
1/2 cup sugar
2/3 cup instant coffee granules
1/2 teaspoon ground cinnamon
1/4 teaspoon ground nutmeg

COMBINE all ingredients; mix well.
STORE in an airtight container.
TO serve, add 3 tablespoons mix to 3/4 cup boiling water, stir.
YIELD: 16 (3/4-cup) servings

# Hot Apple Cider

2/3 cup packed brown sugar
1   teaspoon whole cloves
1   teaspoon ground allspice
3   (3-inch) cinnamon sticks, broken
1 gallon apple cider

FILL the filter-lined basket of a large automatic percolator with the brown sugar, cloves, allspice, and cinnamon sticks.
PREPARE as you would coffee, according to manufacturer's directions, but substitute cider for water.
YIELD: 16 servings

DO NOT use a drip-style coffee maker.

PER 1-cup serving:
CALORIES 154
(0% from fat)
FAT trace
(saturated trace)
PROTEIN trace
CARBOHYDRATE 39g
CHOLESTEROL 0mg
SODIUM 29mg

# Hot Chocolate Mix

PER 3/4-cup serving:
CALORIES 99
(4% from fat)
FAT trace
(saturated trace)
PROTEIN 6g
CARBOHYDRATE 19g
CHOLESTEROL 3mg
SODIUM 103mg

1   (8-quart) package nonfat dry milk
1   (6-ounce) jar fat-free nondairy coffee
      creamer
1   (16-unce) container instant chocolate drink
      mix
1/2 cup confectioners' sugar

PLACE all ingredients in a very large bowl or kettle.
STIR until well blended.
STORE in airtight containers or pack into small
gift containers.
TO serve, add 1/4 cup instant chocolate mix to 2/3
cup hot water.
YIELD: 48 servings (3 quarts dry mix)

# Hot Ginger Coffee

6   tablespoons ground coffee (not instant)
1   tablespoon grated orange peel
1   tablespoon chopped crystallized or
      candied ginger
1/2 teaspoon ground cinnamon
6   cups cold water
Light whipped topping (optional)

COMBINE the coffee, orange peel, ginger and cinnamon; pour into a coffee filter.
ADD water to coffeemaker and brew according to manufacturer's directions.
POUR into mugs; garnish with whipped topping if desired.
YIELD: 6 servings

PER 1-cup serving:
CALORIES 5
(1% from fat)
FAT trace
(saturated 0g)
PROTEIN trace
CARBOHYDRATE 1g
CHOLESTEROL 0mg
SODIUM 5mg

# Hot Mocha

6   cups brewed coffee
1/2 cup sugar
1/2 cup unsweetened cocoa
1/4 cup plus 2 tablespoons Kahlua (coffee-
        flavored liqueur)

COMBINE brewed coffee, sugar and cocoa in a medium saucepan; stir well.
COOK coffee mixture over medium heat until hot (Do Not Boil).
REMOVE coffee mixture from heat, and stir in Kahlua.
YIELD: 13 servings

PER 1/2-cup serving:
CALORIES 69
(6% from fat)
FAT 0.5g
(saturated 0.3)
PROTEIN 1.2g
CARBOHYDRATE 11.8g
FIBER 0g
CHOLESTEROL 0mg
SODIUM 4mg

# Iced Strawberry Tea

1  pint fresh strawberries
4  cups cold tea
1/3 cup sugar
1/4 cup lemon juice
     Ice cubes

SET aside five whole strawberries.
PURÉE the rest in a blender; strain into a pitcher.
STIR in tea, sugar and lemon juice until sugar dis-
solves; chill.
SERVE over ice; garnish with whole strawberries.
YIELD: 5 servings

PER 1-cup serving:
CALORIES 78
(3% from fat)
FAT trace
(saturated trace)
PROTEIN trace
CARBOHYDRATE 20g
CHOLESTEROL 0mg
SODIUM 7mg

# Lime Punch

1   (46-ounce) can lime citrus drink
2   (12-ounce) cans frozen limeade
        concentrate, thawed
1/4 cup sugar
1/4 cup lime juice
1   (1-quart) carton lime sherbet, softened
1   (2-liter) bottle lemon-lime soda, chilled
Lime slices (optional)

IN a punch bowl, combine citrus drink, limeade, sugar, lime juice and sherbet; stir until smooth and dissolved.
ADD soda; stir to mix.
FLOAT lime slices on top of punch if desired.
SERVE immediately.
YIELD: 32 servings (1 gallon)

# Mocha Punch

1   (2-ounce) jar instant coffee granules
1   cup boiling water
3/4 cup sugar
1   gallon skim milk
1/2 gallon chocolate nonfat frozen yogurt,
        softened
1/2 gallon vanilla nonfat frozen yogurt,
        softened
1   cup frozen reduced-calorie whipped
        topping, thawed

COMBINE coffee granules and boiling water, stirring until coffee dissolves.
ADD sugar, stirring until sugar dissolves; cover and chill.
COMBINE coffee mixture and milk in a large punch bowl; gently stir in frozen yogurts.
SPOON whipped topping on top.
YIELD: about 2 1/2 gallons

PER 1-cup serving:
CALORIES 124
(3% from fat)
FAT 0..4g
(saturated 0.1g)
PROTEIN 6.3g
CARBOHYDRATE 24.7g
FIBER 0.0g
CHOLESTEROL 2mg
SODIUM 98mg

# Pineapple Eggnog

3   cups buttermilk
1   (8-ounce) can crushed pineapple
       with juice, chilled
1/4 cup sugar
1   tsp. vanilla extract
5   ice cubes
Fresh mint sprigs (optional)

IN a blender container, combine buttermilk, pineapple, sugar and vanilla.
COVER and blend for 30 seconds, or until combined.
WITH blender running, add ice cubes, one at a time, through opening in lid.
BLEND until mixture is frothy and nearly smooth.
POUR into chilled glasses.
IF desired, garnish with a sprig of mint.
YIELD: 6 servings

# Pineapple Wassail

2 1/2 cups water
2   regular-size orange pekoe tea bags
3/4 cup unsweetened pineapple juice
1/2 cup frozen orange juice concentrate,
      thawed
2   tablespoons honey
1/2 teaspoon lemon juice
3   whole cloves
1   (3-inch) cinnamon stick

BRING water to a boil; pour over tea bags.
COVER; let stand 10 minutes.
DISCARD bags.
COMBINE tea, pineapple juice and remaining in-
gredients in a saucepan; cook over medium-low
heat 15 minutes, or until heated.
DISCARD whole spices.
POUR into mugs.
YIELD: 7 servings

PER 1/2-cup serving:
CALORIES 66
(1% from fat)
FAT 0.1g
PROTEIN 0.6g
CARBOHYDRATE 16.5g
FIBER 0.2g
CHOLESTEROL 0mg
SODIUM 1mg

# Raspberry Tea

PER 1-cup serving:
CALORIES 37
(0% from fat)
FAT 0.0g
(saturated 0.0g)
PROTEIN 0.0g
CARBOHYDRATE 9.5g
FIBER 0.0g
CHOLESTEROL 0mg
SODIUM 18mg

2   cups boiling water
4   raspberry zinger herb tea bags
3   tablespoons sugar
2   cups reduced-calorie ginger ale, chilled

POUR boiling water over tea bags; cover and steep for 5 minutes.
REMOVE tea bags from water, squeezing gently.
STIR in sugar, and let tea mixture cool.
STIR in chilled ginger ale; pour over ice.
YIELD: 4 cups

# Sparkling Punch

3   cups water
2   cups cranberry juice
1   (6-ounce) can frozen orange juice
       concentrate, thawed
1   (6-ounce) can frozen lemonade
       concentrate, thawed
1/2 cup sugar
1 1/2 liters lemon-lime soda, chilled

IN a large bowl, combine the first 5 ingredients;
mix until sugar is dissolved.
CHILL for 1 to 2 hours.
JUST before serving, stir in soda.
YIELD: 24 servings

PER 1/2-cup serving:
CALORIES 87
(0% from fat)
FAT trace
(saturated 0)
PROTEIN 0
CARBOHYDRATE 23g
CHOLESTEROL 0
SODIUM 13mg

# Spice Lemonade

6  cups water, divided
3/4 cup sugar
2  cinnamon sticks (3 to 4 inches)
6  whole cloves
1  large lime, thinly sliced
1  lemon, thinly sliced
3/4 cup fresh lemon juice

IN a large saucepan, bring 4 cups water, sugar, cinnamon and cloves to a boil.
REDUCE heat; simmer for 10 minutes.
REMOVE from the heat; discard cinnamon and cloves; cool.
POUR into a large pitcher.
STIR in lime, lemon, lemon juice and remaining water.
CHILL at least 1 hour.
CAN also be served warm.
YIELD: 8 servings (2 quarts)

# Spicy Tomato Warm-Up

1 (46-ounce) can no-salt-added tomato juice
1 (14 1/4-ounce) can no-salt-added beef broth
3 tablespoons lemon juice
3 tablespoons low-sodium Worcestershire
    sauce
1/2 teaspoon salt
1/2 teaspoon pepper
1/2 teaspoon celery seeds
1/2 teaspoon hot sauce
1/4 teaspoon garlic powder
1/4 teaspoon onion powder

COMBINE all ingredients in a large saucepan; cook
over medium heat until thoroughly heated.
SERVE warm.
YIELD: 8 cups

PER 1-cup serving:
CALORIES 45
(0% from fat)
FAT 0.0g
(saturated 0.0g )
PROTEIN 1.8g
CARBOHYDRATE 10.4g
FIBER 0.1g
CHOLESTEROL 0mg
SODIUM 189mg

# Wassail Punch

2 quarts apple cider
2 cups orange juice
2 cups pineapple juice
1/2 cup lemon juice
1/2 cup sugar
12 whole cloves
4 cinnamon sticks (3 to 4 inches)
Orange slices and additional cloves
    (optional)

IN a large kettle, bring the first 7 ingredients to a boil.
REDUCE heat; simmer for 10 to 15 minutes.
REMOVE cinnamon and cloves; serve warm.
IF desired, stud orange slices with cloves and float in punch bowl.
YIELD: 18 servings

PER 3/4-cup serving:
CALORIES 104
(1% from fat)
FAT trace
(saturated trace)
PROTEIN trace
CARBOHYDRATE 26g
CHOLESTEROL 0mg

# Baked Artichoke Dip

2   (14-ounce) cans quartered artichoke hearts,
       drained and chopped
1   cup nonfat mayonnaise
3/4 cup grated Parmesan cheese
1   clove garlic, minced
1/4 teaspoon reduced-sodium Worcestershire
       sauce
1/8 teaspoon hot sauce
Vegetable cooking spray

COMBINE first 6 ingredients; spoon evenly into a 1-
quart casserole coated with cooking spray.
BAKE uncovered, at 350 degrees for 25 minutes, or
until thoroughly heated.
SERVE with melba toast rounds.
YIELD: 3 1/2 cups

PER 1-tablespoon serving:
CALORIES 14
(32% from fat)
FAT 0.5g
(saturated 0.3g)
PROTEIN 0.9g
CARBOHYDRATE 1.8g
FIBER 0.1g
CHOLESTEROL 1mg
SODIUM 89mg

# Baked Swiss-Onion Dip

PER 1-tablespoon serving:
CALORIES 28
(35% from fat)
FAT 1.1g
(saturated 0.6g)
PROTEIN 2.3g
CARBOHYDRATE 2.1g
FIBER 0.0g
CHOLESTEROL 4mg
SODIUM 103 mg

1 (10-ounce) package frozen chopped onion, thawed
2 cups (8 ounces) shredded reduced-fat Swiss cheese
1 cup nonfat mayonnaise
1 tablespoon coarse-ground Dijon mustard
1/8 teaspoon pepper

DRAIN onion on paper towels.
COMBINE onion and remaining ingredients.
SPOON mixture into a 1-quart baking dish.
BAKE at 325 degrees for 25 minutes or until bubbly and lightly browned.
SERVE dip with melba toast rounds.
YIELD: 2 1/4 cups

# Bean Dip with Browned Garlic

1   tablespoon olive oil
4   garlic cloves, minced
2   tablespoons fresh lemon juice
1   tablespoon sesame seed paste
1   tablespoon water
1   teaspoon minced fresh rosemary
1/4 teaspoon salt
1/4 teaspoon pepper
1   (9-ounce) can cannellini beans or
      other white beans, drained

HEAT oil in a small nonstick skillet over medium
heat until hot.
ADD minced garlic, and sauté 1 minute, or until
lightly browned.
PLACE garlic mixture, lemon juice and remaining
ingredients in a blender; cover and process until
smooth.
SERVE with toasted pita wedges or carrot sticks.
YIELD: 1 1/2 cups

PER 1-tablespoon serving:
CALORIES 27
(33% from fat)
FAT 1g
(saturated 0.1g)
PROTEIN 1.3g
CARBOHYDRATE 3.6g
FIBER 0.6g
CHOLESTEROL 0mg
SODIUM 26mg

# Black Bean Dip

1 (15-ounce) can black beans, drained
1 (8-ounce) can no-salt-added tomato sauce
1/2 cup (2 ounces) shredded reduced-fat
    sharp Cheddar cheese
1 teaspoon chili powder

COMBINE beans and tomato sauce in a small sauce-pan; bring to a boil over medium heat, stirring occasionally.
REMOVE from heat.
MASH beans with potato masher or back of spoon.
ADD cheese and chili powder; cook, stirring constantly, until cheese melts.
SERVE dip warm with toasted pita triangles and fresh vegetables.
YIELD: 2 cups

PER 1-tablespoon serving:
CALORIES 19
(19% from fat)
FAT 0.4g
(saturated 0.2g)
PROTEIN 1.3g
CARBOHYDRATE 2.6g
FIBER 0.5g
CHOLESTEROL 1mg
SODIUM 37mg

# Blue Cheese Spread

1   (8-ounce) package nonfat cream
        cheese, softened
1/2 cup crumbled blue cheese
1/4 cup chopped pecans, toasted

POSITION knife blade in food processor bowl; add cheeses and process 20 seconds, or until well blended.
LINE a 1-cup bowl with plastic wrap, and press cheese mixture into bowl.
COVER and chill at least 8 hours.
UNMOLD cheese spread, and remove plastic wrap.
ROLL outside edges of cheese mold in chopped pecans.
SERVE cheese spread with apple slices.

PER 1-tablespoon serving:
CALORIES 37
(56% from fat)
FAT 2.3g
(saturated 0.8g)
PROTEIN 2.9g
CARBOHYDRATE 0.9g
FIBER 0.1g
CHOLESTEROL 5mg
SODIUM 134mg

# Sherry Cheese Paté

6 ounces nonfat cream cheese, softened
1/2 cup (2 ounces) shredded reduced-fat
    sharp Cheddar cheese
2 tablespoons dry sherry
1/2 teaspoon curry powder
1/3 cup chutney
2 green onions, sliced

COMBINE first 4 ingredients; shape into a 5-inch circle on a serving plate and chill.
JUST before serving, spread chutney over cheese, and sprinkle with green onions.
SERVE with low-fat crackers.
YIELD: 1 cup

PER 1-tablespoon serving:
CALORIES 36
(18% from fat)
FAT 0.7g
(saturated 0.4g)
PROTEIN 2.6g
CARBOHYDRATE 4.2g
FIBER 0.1g
CHOLESTEROL 4mg
SODIUM 1.1mg

# Cheese-Garlic-Stuffed Bread

2   cloves garlic
1   (8-ounce) package light process
      cream cheese, softened
1   cup loosely-packed fresh parsley
1/2 cup (2 ounces) shredded reduced-
      fat Swiss cheese
2   tablespoons skim milk
1   (16-ounce) round loaf pumpernickel
      bread

PER serving:
CALORIES: 208
(3% from fat)
FAT 10.0g
(saturated 5.8)
PROTEIN 11.5g
CARBOHYDRATE 19.0g
FIBER 1.8g
CHOLESTEROL 34mg
SODIUM 440mg

POSITION knife blade in food processor bowl.
DROP garlic through food chute with processor running; process 3 seconds, or until garlic is minced.
ADD cream cheese and next 3 ingredients.
PROCESS until smooth, stopping once to scrape down sides; set aside.
SLICE off top third of bread loaf, leaving a 2-inch-deep bowl and 1-inch shell.
SET bread shell aside.
CUT inside bread pieces into 1 1/2-inch cubes; set aside.
SPOON cheese mixture into bread shell, and re-place bread top.
WRAP filled bread in heavy-duty aluminum foil, and place on a baking sheet.
BAKE at 350 degrees for 45 minutes, or until bread is thoroughly heated.
REMOVE bread top and cut into 1 1/2-inch cubes.
SERVE cheese mixture with bread cubes.
YIELD: 5 appetizer servings

# Cheese and Ham Bread Bowl Dip

2 (16-ounce) loaves French bread
1 (8-ounce) package light process cream cheese, softened
1 (8-ounce) carton nonfat sour cream
2 cups (8 ounces) shredded reduced-fat Cheddar cheese
1/2 cup chopped, cooked lean ham
1/3 cup chopped green onions
1/3 cup finely-chopped green bell pepper
1/4 teaspoon low-sodium Worcestershire sauce
Paprika

SLICE top off top fourth of 1 bread loaf.
HOLLOW out bottom section, leaving a 1-inch shell.
RESERVE bread top for another use; set shell aside.
CUT remaining bread loaf into 1 1/2-inch cubes; place bread shell and cubes on two large baking sheets.
BAKE at 350 degrees for 12 minutes, or until lightly browned.
BEAT cream cheese at medium speed with an electric mixer until smooth; add sour cream, beating until creamy.
STIR in Cheddar cheese and next 4 ingredients.
SPOON cheese mixture into bread shell, wrap in heavy-duty aluminum foil, and place on a baking sheet.
BAKE at 350 degrees for 30 minutes; unwrap and place on a serving platter.
SPRINKLE with paprika, and serve with toasted bread cubes.
YIELD: 13 appetizer servings

# Cheese Wafers

1/4 cup margarine, softened
1   cup (4 ounces) shredded reduced-fat
        extra-sharp Cheddar cheese
1/4 cup nonfat buttermilk
1 1/2 cups crisp rice cereal
1   cup all-purpose flour
1/8 teaspoon salt
1/8 teaspoon ground red pepper
Dash of paprika

POSITION knife blade in food processor bowl; add margarine, cheese and buttermilk
PROCESS until blended, stopping once to scrape down sides.
ADD cereal and remaining 4 ingredients; process until mixture forms a ball, stopping often to scrape down sides.
SHAPE dough into 1/2-inch balls, and place about 2 inches apart on ungreased baking sheets.
FLATTEN each ball in a crisscross pattern with a fork dipped in flour.
BAKE at 350 degrees for 15 minutes, or until lightly browned.
REMOVE to wire racks to cool.
YIELD: 4 1/2 dozen

PER wafer:
CALORIES 26
(45% from fat)
FAT 1.3g
(saturated 0.5g)
PROTEIN 0.9g
CARBOHYDRATE 2.5g
FIBER 0.1g
CHOLESTEROL 2mg
SODIUM 40mg

# Chicken Balls

6   ounces fat-free cream cheese, softened
2   tablespoons orange marmalade
2   teaspoons curry powder
1/4 teaspoon salt
1/4 teaspoon pepper
3   cups finely-minced cooked chicken
3   tablespoons minced celery
1   cup finely-chopped fresh parsley
3   tablespoons minced green onion

IN a mixing bowl, combine the first five ingredi-
ents.
BEAT until smooth.
STIR in chicken, onions and celery.
SHAPE into 10-inch balls; roll in parsley.
COVER and chill until firm.
YIELD: 5 dozen

# Chicken Spread

1 1/2 cups chopped, cooked chicken
1   (8-ounce) package fat-free cream
      cheese, softened
1/2 cup chopped celery
1/2 cup fat-free mayonnaise
2   tablespoons chopped onion
1   teaspoon onion powder

PLACE all ingredients in a food processor until coarsely chopped.
YIELD: 2 1/2 cups

PER 2-tablespoon serving:
CALORIES 34
(14% from fat)
FAT trace
(saturated trace)
PROTEIN 5g
CARBOHYDRATE 2g
CHOLESTEROL 9mg
SODIUM 155 mg

# Crab Mousse

2   teaspoons unflavored gelatin
1/4 cup cold water
1   cup skim milk
3   tablespoons lemon juice
1   tablespoon grated onion
1   teaspoon dry mustard
1/2 teaspoon salt
1/4 teaspoon paprika
1/4 teaspoon hot sauce
1   (8-ounce) package Neufchatel cheese,
       softened
8   ounces fresh crabmeat, drained
Vegetable cooking spray

SPRINKLE gelatin over cold water in a 1-cup liquid measuring cup; let stand 1 minute
COMBINE gelatin mixture, milk and next 6 ingredients in a heavy saucepan; cook over low heat, stirring constantly, until gelatin dissolves (mixture may appear curdled).
ADD cheese, stirring until blended.
CHILL until consistency of unbeaten egg white.
FLAKE crabmeat, removing any bits of shell; gently fold crabmeat into gelatin mixture, and spoon into a 4-cup mold coated with cooking spray.
COVER and chill at least 8 hours.
UNMOLD and serve with low-fat crackers.
YIELD: 3 1/2 cups

■ ■ ■ ■ ■ ■ ■

# Crab Purses

24 green onion tops, cut into 3-inch
    julienne strips
6 ounces lump crabmeat, shell pieces removed
1 (4-ounce) block fat-free cream cheese
1/4 cup minced green onions
2 teaspoons fresh lemon juice
1/2 teaspoon hot sauce
1/4 teaspoon salt
1/8 teaspoon pepper
24 won ton wrappers
1 egg white, lightly beaten
Vegetable cooking spray
2 tablespoons low-sodium soy sauce
1 tablespoon water
1 tablespoon fresh lemon juice

PER 2-appetizer serving:
CALORIES 126
(7% from fat)
FAT 0.9g
(saturated 0)
PROTEIN 10g
CARBOHYDRATE 18.4g
FIBER 1.2g
CHOLESTEROL 26mg
SODIUM 566mg

DROP green onion strips in boiling water; cook 10 seconds or until limp; drain onion strips and set aside.

COMBINE crabmeat and next 6 ingredients in a bowl; stir well.

WORKING with 1 won ton wrapper at a time (cover remaining wrappers with a damp towel to keep them from drying out), spoon 2 teaspoons crabmeat mixture into center of wrapper, and crimp to seal, forming a purse.

TIE 1 green onion strip around crimped top of purse. Brush with beaten egg white.

REPEAT procedure with remaining won ton wrappers, crabmeat mixture, egg white and green onion strips.

ARRANGE half of won ton purse in a single layer in a vegetable steamer coated with cooking spray.

STEAM purses, covered, 8 minutes or until tender.

CAREFULLY remove purses from steamer; set aside and keep warm.

REPEAT process with remaining half of purses.

COMBINE soy sauce, water and 1 tablespoon lemon juice in a small bowl; stir well.

SERVE with purses.

YIELD: 2 dozen appetizers

# Cranberry Meatballs

Egg substitute equivalent to 2 eggs
1  cup corn flake crumbs
1/3 cup ketchup
2  tablespoons light soy sauce
1  tablespoon dried parsley flakes
2  tablespoons dehydrated onions
1/4 teaspoon pepper
2  pounds ground turkey breast

SAUCE:
1  (16-ounce) can jellied cranberry sauce
1  cup ketchup
3  tablespoons brown sugar
1  tablespoon lemon juice

IN a mixing bowl, combine the first eight ingredients.
SHAPE into 72 meatballs, 1-inch each.
PLACE in a 10x15x1-inch baking pan coated with nonstick cooking spray.
BAKE at 350 degrees for 20 to 25 minutes, or until done.
IN a large saucepan, combine sauce ingredients.
COOK, stirring frequently, until cranberry sauce is melted.
ADD the meatballs and heat through.
YIELD: 6 dozen

# Curried Chicken Mousse

1   envelope unflavored gelatin
1   cup cold water, divided
2   teaspoons chicken-flavored bouillon
      granules
1/4 teaspoon ground red pepper
1   teaspoon curry powder
2   teaspoons minced onion
1 1/4 cup finely-chopped cooked chicken
      breast, skinned before cooking and
      cooked without salt
1/4 cup finely-chopped celery
1   (2-ounce) jar diced pimento, drained
1   tablespoon chopped fresh parsley
1   (8-ounce) carton nonfat sour cream
Vegetable cooking spray

PER 1-tablespoon serving:
CALORIES 11
(16% from fat)
FAT 0.2g
(saturated 0.1g)
PROTEIN 1.7g
CARBOHYDRATE 0.5g
FIBER 0.0g
CHOLESTEROL 3mg
SODIUM 45mg

SPRINKLE gelatin over 1/2 cup cold water in a small saucepan; let stand 1 minute.

COOK over low heat, stirring until gelatin dissolves (about 2 minutes).

ADD bouillon granules, red peppers and curry powder, stirring until bouillon granules dissolve; remove from heat.

ADD remaining 1/2 cup cold water and minced onion, stirring well; chill until consistency of unbeaten egg white.

STIR in chicken and next four ingredients; spoon mixture into a 4-cup mold coated with cooking spray.

COVER and chill at least 8 hours.

UNMOLD and serve with low-fat crackers.

YIELD: 2 3/4 cups

# Gazpacho Dip

PER 1-tablespoon serving:
CALORIES 7
(51% from fat)
FAT 0.4g
(saturated 0.1g)
PROTEIN 0.1g
CARBOHYDRATE 0.7g
FIBER 0.2g
CHOLESTEROL 0mg
SODIUM 8mg

8   green onions, thinly sliced
2   large tomatoes, chopped
1   firm avocado, chopped
1/2 cup diced green pepper
1   (4.5-ounce) can chopped green chilies,
      undrained
1/2 (4.5-ounce) can chopped ripe olives,
      drained
2   cloves garlic, minced
3   tablespoons apple cider vinegar
1/4 teaspoon pepper
Lime slices, for garnish

COMBINE all ingredients except the garnish, toss-
ing gently.
COVER and chill up to 4 hours.
GARNISH, if desired.
SERVE dip with baked tortilla chips.
YIELD: 5 cups

YOU may use this dip as a salad dressing; spoon
mixture over shredded lettuce, and top with shredded reduced-fat Cheddar cheese and nonfat sour
cream.

# Hot Crabmeat Dip

2 (8-ounce) packages light process
    cream cheese
1/2 cup nonfat mayonnaise
1/4 cup grated onion
1/2 teaspoon garlic powder
1/4 teaspoon salt
1/2 teaspoon pepper
3 tablespoons dry white wine or
    dry vermouth
2 teaspoons prepared mustard
2 teaspoons prepared horseradish
1/2 pound fresh lump crabmeat, drained
2 tablespoons chopped fresh chives
2 tablespoons chopped fresh parsley

PER 1-tablespoon serving:
CALORIES 25
(54% from fat)
FAT 1.5g
(saturated 0.8g)
PROTEIN 1.7g
CARBOHYDRATE 1.2g
FIBER 0.1g
CHOLESTEROL 9mg
SODIUM 97mg

COMBINE first 9 ingredients in a medium saucepan; stir well.
COOK over low heat, stirring constantly, until cream cheese melts and mixture is smooth.
STIR in crabmeat and remaining ingredients.
TRANSFER to a chafing dish, and keep warm.
YIELD: 3 1/2 cups

# Marinated Cheese

■ ■ ■ ■ ■ ■ ■ ■
PER appetizer:
CALORIES 52
(35% from fat)
FAT 2.0g
(saturated 1.2g)
PROTEIN 3.5g
CARBOHYDRATE 5.2g
FIBER 0.1g
CHOLESTEROL 7mg
SODIUM 163mg

1/2 pound part-skim Mozzarella cheese
1/2 pound reduced-fat Cheddar cheese
1   cup fat-free Italian salad dressing
1/4 teaspoon freshly-ground pepper
1   (12-ounce) French baguette
Fresh basil leaves, for garnish

CUT cheeses into 1/4-inch-thick slices (for variety,
cut the cheese with a crinkle-edged cutter.)
ALTERNATE cheeses in a 13x9x2-inch dish, overlap-
ping slightly.
COMBINE dressing and pepper; pour over cheese.
COVER and chill 8 hours.
CUT baguette into 1/4-inch slices.
PLACE on baking sheets.
BAKE at 350° for 8 to 10 minutes, or until lightly
toasted, turning once.
DRAIN cheeses.
PLACE 1 cheese slice on each bread slice.
GARNISH, if desired.
SERVE immediately.
YIELD: 44 appetizers

'YOU may make these appetizers ahead, marinate
the cheese overnight in the refrigerator. You can
also toast the bread a day ahead and store it at
room temperature wrapped in cloth towels;. AS-
SEMBLE the appetizers right before the party.

# Meatballs

1 pound ground round
Egg substitute equivalent to 1 egg
1/2 cup soft bread crumbs
1/4 cup skim milk
1/3 cup finely-chopped onion
1/2 teaspoon Worcestershire sauce

SAUCE:
1/2 cup ketchup
1/2 cup chopped onion
1/3 cup sugar
1/3 cup vinegar
1 tablespoon Worcestershire sauce
1/8 teaspoon pepper

COMBINE the first 6 ingredients; mix well.
SHAPE into 1-inch balls.
IN a skillet over medium heat, brown meatballs;
drain.
PLACE in a 2 1/2-quart baking dish.
COMBINE sauce ingredients.
POUR over meatballs.
BAKE, uncovered, at 350 degrees for 50 to 60 minutes, or until meatballs are done.
YIELD: 4 dozen

PER 3-meatball
    serving size:
CALORIES 85
(26% from fat)
FAT 3g
(saturated 1g)
PROTEIN 8g
CARBOHYDRATE 9g
CHOLESTEROL 24mg
SODIUM 199mg

# Mexican Crab Dip

PER 1-tablespoon
serving size:
CALORIES 24
(49% from fat)
FAT 1.3g
(saturated 0.8g)
PROTEIN 2.3g
CARBOHYDRATE 0.5g
FIBER 0.1g
CHOLESTEROL 9mg
SODIUM 80mg

1   (8-ounce) package Neufchatel cheese
1   (8-ounce) block nonfat cream cheese
1   (6-ounce) can lump crabmeat, undrained
1/2 cup salsa

PLACE cheeses in a microwave-safe bowl, and cover with waxed paper.

MICROWAVE at MEDIUM POWER for 2 to 3 minutes, or until softened, stirring with a wire whisk until smooth.

DRAIN crabmeat through a sieve into a bowl, reserving 1 tablespoon liquid.

ADD reserved liquid, crabmeat and salsa to cheese; stir well.

SERVE warm or at room temperature with baked tortilla chips, raw vegetables, or breadsticks.

YIELD: 2 1/2 cups

# Oregano Cheese Puffs

2/3 cup skim milk
2 tablespoons reduced-calorie stick
    margarine
3/4 cup all-purpose flour
1/4 teaspoon salt
1/8 teaspoon pepper
3/4 cup egg substitute
1/2 cup (2 ounces) shredded reduced-fat
    Swiss cheese, divided
2 teaspoons dried oregano
Vegetable cooking spray

PER appetizer:
CALORIES 27
(30% from fat)
FAT 0.9g
(saturated 0.3g)
PROTEIN 1.8g
CARBOHYDRATE 3.0g
FIBER 0.1g
CHOLESTEROL 1mg
SODIUM 43mg

BRING milk and margarine to a boil in a medium saucepan.
REDUCE heat to low; add flour, salt and pepper all at once, stirring vigorously, until mixture leaves sides of pan and forms a smooth ball.
REMOVE from heat; cool 5 to 10 minutes.
ADD egg substitute, 1/4 cup at a time, beating with a wooden spoon after each addition.
STIR in 1/4 cup cheese and oregano.
DROP by level tablespoonfuls onto baking sheets coated with cooking spray.
BAKE at 400 degrees for 16 to 18 minutes.
SPRINKLE with remaining 1/4 cup cheese, and bake 1 to 2 additional minutes.
SERVE immediately.
YIELD: 29 appetizers

# Oven-Baked Tomatoes
## Appetizers

PER appetizer:
CALORIES 52
(16% from fat)
FAT 0.9g
(saturated 0.3)
PROTEIN 1.8g
CARBOHYDRATE 8.9g
FIBER 0.6g
CHOLESTEROL 1mg
SODIUM 156mg

1   (12-ounce) French baguette
Olive oil-flavored vegetable cooking spray
12   small Roma tomatoes (1 pound)
1/2 teaspoon sugar
1/2 teaspoon salt
1   teaspoon dried thyme
1/3 cup crumbled reduced-fat Feta cheese

CUT 24 (1/2-inch) slices from baguette; place on a baking sheet.
COAT lightly with cooking spray.
BAKE at 400 degrees for 5 minutes; cool.
CUT tomatoes in half lengthwise; scoop out seeds and pulp and reserve for another use.
PLACE tomato halves, cut-side up, on a rack in broiler pan; sprinkle evenly with sugar, salt and thyme.
BAKE at 350 degrees for 30 minutes.
PLACE tomato halves, cut-side up, on bread; sprinkle with cheese.
SERVE immediately.
YIELD: 2 dozen

# Parmesan-Coated Brie

1 large egg, lightly beaten
1 tablespoon water
1/4 cup fine, dry bread crumbs
1/4 cup grated nonfat Parmesan cheese
1 1/2 teaspoon dried Italian seasoning
1 (15-ounce) mini Brie with herbs
Vegetable cooking spray
Fresh rosemary sprigs, for garnish

COMBINE egg and water in a shallow dish.
COMBINE bread crumbs, cheese and seasoning in another shallow dish.
DIP Brie into egg mixture, turning to coat top and sides (do not coat bottom).
PLACE Brie in bread crumb mixture, turning to coat top and sides; repeat procedure.
PLACE on a baking sheet coated with cooking spray; chill at least 1 hour.
BAKE at 375 degrees for 10 minutes.
GARNISH, if desired.
SERVE with French baguette slices or low-fat crackers.
YIELD: 15 appetizer servings

PER serving:
CALORIES 110
(65% from fat)
FAT 8.0g
(saturated 5.0g)
PROTEIN 6.4g
CARBOHYDRATE 2.9g
FIBER 0.1g
CHOLESTEROL 28mg
SODIUM 228mg

# Potato Skins

PER 4-shell serving size:
CALORIES 40
(1% from fat)
FAT trace
(saturated trace)
PROTEIN 1g
CARBOHYDRATE 9g
CHOLESTEROL 0mg
SODIUM 5mg

4   large baking potatoes, baked
1   teaspoon salt (optional)
1   teaspoon garlic powder
1   teaspoon paprika
Nonfat sour cream (optional)
Chives (optional)

CUT potatoes in half lengthwise; scoop out pulp, leaving a 1/4-inch-thick shell (save pulp for another use).

CUT shells lengthwise into quarters and place on a baking sheet coated with nonstick cooking spray.

MIST shells with nonstick cooking spray.

COMBINE salt if desired, garlic powder and paprika; sprinkle over skins.

BROIL until golden brown, 5 to 8 minutes.

IF desired, combine sour cream and chives; serve with potato skins.

YIELD: 32 shells

# Salmon Appetizers

1  (15-ounce) can salmon, or 2 cups
     cooked salmon, drained, boned and
     flaked
1  (8-ounce) package fat-free cream cheese,
     softened
4  tablespoons salsa
2  tablespoons chopped fresh parsley or
     cilantro
1/4 teaspoon ground cumin
8  (8-inch) flour tortillas

IN a small bowl, combine salmon, cream cheese,
salsa, parsley and cumin.
SPREAD about 2 tablespoons over each tortilla.
ROLL up tightly and wrap individually with plastic
wrap.
REFRIGERATE for 2 to 3 hours.
SLICE into bite-size pieces.
YIELD: 4 dozen

PER 2-piece serving:
CALORIES 74
(26% from fat)
FAT 2g
(saturated trace)
PROTEIN 6g
CARBOHYDRATE 7g
CHOLESTEROL 8mg
SODIUM 227mg

# Spicy Buffalo Wings

3   pounds chicken wings
Vegetable cooking spray
1/2 cup hot sauce
1/4 cup water
1   (1-ounce) package dry onion soup mix
1 to 3 teaspoons ground red pepper
1   (8-ounce) bottle nonfat blue cheese
       salad dressing

CUT off and discard wing tips; cut wings in half at joint.
PLACE chicken on a rack of broiler pan coated with cooking spray; set aside.
COMBINE hot sauce, water, soup mix and red pepper.
BRUSH chicken with half of hot sauce mixture.
BAKE, uncovered, at 375 degrees for 30 minutes.
REMOVE from oven; turn chicken and brush with remaining hot sauce mixture.
BAKE 10 to 15 additional minutes, or until tender.
SERVE warm with salad dressing.
YIELD: 3 dozen

# Sweet and Spicy Popcorn

1   tablespoon sugar
1   teaspoon chili powder
1/2 teaspoon ground cinnamon
1/4 teaspoon salt (optional)
Dash of cayenne pepper
6   cups plain popped popcorn


PLACE sugar, chili powder, cinnamon, salt if desired, and cayenne pepper in a resealable plastic bag or other 2-quart airtight container; mix.
ADD popcorn; mist popcorn with nonstick cooking spray.
CLOSE bag and shake.
REPEAT one or two times, until popcorn is coated.
YIELD: 6 cups

PER 1 1/2-cup serving
(without salt):
CALORIES 78
(14% from fat)
FAT 1g
(saturated trace)
PROTEIN 2g
CARBOHYDRATE 16g
CHOLESTEROL 0mg
SODIUM 7mg

# Tomatillo Salsa

PER 1-tablespoon serving:
CALORIES 7
(13% from fat)
FAT 0.1g
(saturated 0.0g)
PROTEIN 0.3g
CARBOHYDRATE 1.3g
FIBER 0.1g
CHOLESTEROL 0mg
SODIUM 14mg

2 1/2 pounds fresh tomatillos
6   cloves garlic, unpeeled
4   large jalapeño peppers
2   large onions, quartered
1/2 cup nonfat sour cream
1/2 cup chopped fresh cilantro
1/2 teaspoon salt
1/2 teaspoon freshly-ground pepper

REMOVE and discard tomatillo husks; rinse tomatillos.

PLACE tomatillos and next 3 ingredients in a single layer in a 15x10x1-inch jellyroll pan.

BAKE at 500 degrees for 15 to 20 minutes, or until vegetables are charred; cool completely.

REMOVE and discard stems (but not seeds) from peppers.

PEEL garlic, discarding skins.

DRAIN tomatillos, discarding any liquid.

POSITION knife blade in food processor bowl; add half of roasted vegetables and pulse 10 to 12 times, or until vegetables are coarsely chopped.

REPEAT procedure with remaining roasted vegetables.

POUR mixture into a bowl; stir in sour cream and remaining ingredients.

SERVE with baked tortilla chips or grilled chicken.

YIELD: 6 cups

# Turkey Meatballs

1 pound ground turkey breast
1 egg, lightly beaten
3/4 cup crushed reduced-fat butter-
    flavored crackers
1/2 cup shredded part-skim Mozzarella
    cheese
1/4 cup chopped onion
1/2 teaspoon ground ginger
6 tablespoons Dijon mustard, divided
1 1/4 cups unsweetened pineapple juice
1/4 cup chopped green pepper
2 tablespoons honey
1 tablespoon cornstarch
1/4 teaspoon onion powder

PER 3-meatball serving:
CALORIES 176
(40% from fat)
FAT 8g
(saturated 2g)
PROTEIN 11g
CARBOHYDRATE 14g
CHOLESTEROL 48mg
SODIUM 337mg

IN a bowl, combine turkey, egg, cracker crumbs, cheese, onion, ginger and three tablespoons mustard.
FORM into 30 balls, 1-inch each.
PLACE in a greased 13x9x2-inch baking dish.
BAKE, uncovered, at 350 degrees for 20 to 25 minutes, or until juices run clear.
IN a saucepan, combine pineapple juice, green pepper, honey, cornstarch and onion powder; bring to a boil, stirring constantly.
COOK and stir 2 minutes more; reduce heat.
STIR in remaining mustard until smooth.
BRUSH meatballs with about 1/4 cup sauce and return to the oven for 10 minutes.
SERVE remaining sauce as a dip for meatballs.
YIELD: 2 1/2 dozen

# Turkey Sausage Turnovers

1/2 pound ground turkey sausage
1/2 cup finely-chopped onion
1  tablespoon all-purpose flour
1  tablespoon dry sherry
1  (10-ounce) can refrigerated pizza
     crust dough
Olive oil-flavored vegetable cooking spray
Paprika
1  cup fat-free spaghetti sauce

COOK sausage and onion in a large skillet over high heat, stirring until sausage crumbles.
REMOVE from heat; drain.
RETURN sausage and onion to skillet.
STIR in flour and sherry; cool.
ROLL pizza crust into a 12-inch square on a lightly-floured surface.
CUT into 16 (3-inch) squares.
PLACE 1 tablespoon sausage mixture on half of each square.
MOISTEN edges of squares with water, and fold in half, pressing edges to seal; crimp with a fork.
PLACE on baking sheets coated with cooking spray.
COAT tops with cooking spray.
CUT 3 small slits in top of each turnover.
BAKE at 375 degrees for 16 to 18 minutes, and sprinkle with paprika.
SERVE warm with spaghetti sauce.
YIELD: 16 turnovers

# White Bean Spread

1   (2-ounce) can anchovies, drained
     and chopped
9   cloves garlic, minced
3   tablespoons chopped fresh rosemary
2   teaspoons olive oil
4   (15-ounce) cans cannellini beans, drained
1/4 cup lemon juice
1/2 teaspoon white pepper

COOK anchovies, garlic and rosemary in olive oil in
a small skillet, over medium heat for 2 to 3 min-
utes, stirring constantly.
REMOVE from heat; set aside.
POSITION knife blade in food processor bowl; add
cannellini beans.
PROCESS until beans are smooth, stopping once to
scrape down sides.
ADD anchovy mixture, lemon juice and pepper;
process until smooth, stopping once to scrape
down sides.
SPOON bean mixture into a serving bowl.
SERVE with fresh vegetables or low-fat crackers.
YIELD: 5 cups

PER 1-tablespoon serving:
CALORIES 16
(11% from fat)
FAT 0.2g
(saturated 0.0g)
PROTEIN 0.9g
CARBOHYDRATE 2.5g
FIBER 0.5g
CHOLESTEROL 0mg
SODIUM 41mg

# Notes & Recipes

# Main Dishes

# List Your Favorite Recipes

**Recipes**                                          **Page**

_____     _____

_____     _____

_____     _____

_____     _____

_____     _____

_____     _____

_____     _____

_____     _____

_____     _____

_____     _____

_____     _____

_____     _____

_____     _____

_____     _____

_____     _____

_____     _____

_____     _____

# Barbecued Chicken

4   skinless, boneless chicken breast halves
(4 ounces each)

FOR THE SAUCE:
1/4 cup reduced-sodium ketchup
3   tablespoons cider vinegar
1   tablespoon ready-made white horseradish
2   teaspoons firmly-packed dark brown sugar
1   clove garlic, minced
1/8 teaspoon thyme
1/4 teaspoon black pepper

PREHEAT broiler, heat a charcoal grill until coals form white ash, or preheat a gas grill to medium. TO PREPARE sauce, in a small saucepan, combine ketchup, vinegar, horseradish, brown sugar, garlic and thyme; mix well. Bring to a boil over medium-low heat. Cook, stirring frequently, until thickened, about 5 minutes. Remove from heat; stir in pepper. BRUSH tops of chicken pieces lightly with sauce. Place chicken, sauce-side down, on a foil-lined broiler pan or grill rack. Brush other sides lightly with sauce.
BROIL or grill 3 inches from heat, basting with remaining sauce and turning until no longer pink in center, about 5 to 7 minutes per side. Let chicken stand for 5 minutes before serving.
YIELD: 4 servings

TO prevent foods from sticking to the grill, scrub the grill rack with a wire brush, and then spray with a vegetable cooking spray.
CHICKEN must be seared over a hot grill before turning or the skin will stick to the grill. Turn several times throughout the cooking time and baste with each turn.
IT is best to use tongs to turn chicken as a fork will pierce the meat and allow the flavorful juices to escape.

PER serving:
CALORIES 146
(9% from fat)
FAT 1g
PROTEIN 26g
CARBOHYDRATE 5g
CHOLESTEROL 66mg
SODIUM 188mg

# Baked Penne with Veal

1   pound ground veal
Vegetable cooking spray
4   cups chopped onion
1   teaspoon salt
1   teaspoon ground cinnamon
1/2 teaspoon sugar
1/2 teaspoon pepper
1/4 teaspoon ground cloves
4   garlic cloves, minced
3   (14 1/2-ounce) cans diced tomatoes, undrained
2   tablespoons margarine
2   tablespoons all-purpose flour
3   cups 1% low-fat milk
1 1/2 cups egg substitute
1/2 teaspoon salt
1/8 teaspoon pepper
6   cups hot cooked penne (about 12 ounces
      uncooked pasta)
1/2 cup (2 ounces) grated fresh Romano cheese
1/4 teaspoon ground cinnamon

COOK veal in a large nonstick skillet over medium heat until browned, stirring to crumble. Drain in colander; set aside.
COAT skillet with cooking spray, and place over medium-high heat until hot.
ADD onion; sauté 10 minutes.
ADD 1 teaspoon salt and next 6 ingredients; bring to a boil.
REDUCE heat and simmer, uncovered, 20 minutes, stirring occasionally.
RETURN veal to skillet; simmer an additional 10 minutes. Set mixture aside.
MELT margarine in a medium saucepan over medium heat. Add flour, stirring constantly with wire whisk until blended.

Continued on following page.

Continued from preceding page.

GRADUALLY add milk, stirring constantly. BRING to a boil; reduce heat and simmer 10 minutes or until slightly thickened, stirring constantly.
REMOVE from heat and set aside.
PLACE egg substitute in a medium bowl; beat at high speed on an electric mixer until doubled in volume.
GRADUALLY add hot milk mixture to egg substitute, stirring constantly with a wire whisk.
STIR in 1/2 teaspoon salt and 1/8 teaspoon pepper.
PREHEAT oven to 350 degrees.
COMBINE veal mixture and pasta in a large bowl; stir well.
SPOON veal mixture evenly into 2 (11x7-inch) baking dishes coated with cooking spray.
POUR sauce evenly over each dish of veal mixture (poke with a fork in several places to allow the sauce to run to the bottom of the dish).
COMBINE cheese and 1/4 teaspoon cinnamon, stirring well. Sprinkle evenly over each dish of veal mixture.
COVER and bake at 350°for 30 minutes.
UNCOVER and bake an additional 15 minutes.
LET stand 15 minutes before serving.
YIELD: 12 servings (6 servings per baking dish)

PER serving:
CALORIES 276
(36% from fat)
FAT 10.9g
(saturated 2.9g)
PROTEIN 18.9g
CARBOHYDRATE 33.7g
FIBER 2.7 g
CHOLESTEROL 38mg
SODIUM 615mg

# Beef with Peppercorn Rub

1   tablespoon drained brine-packed green
      peppercorns, crushed (place
      peppercorns in a zip-top bag
      and crush with a meat mallet)
2   teaspoons ground coriander
1 1/2 teaspoons Hungarian sweet paprika
1/2 teaspoon dried thyme
1/2 teaspoon pepper
1/4 teaspoon salt
4   (4-ounce) beef tenderloin steaks (3/4-inch
      thick)
2   teaspoons olive oil
Vegetable cooking spray
1/4 cup cognac and 1/4 cup water

COMBINE first 6 ingredients in a small bowl; stir
well.
RUB steaks with spice mixture; let stand 5 minutes.
HEAT oil in a nonstick skillet, coated with cooking
spray, over medium heat until hot.
ADD steaks; cook 4 minutes on each side or until
desired degree of doneness.
REMOVE steaks from skillet; set aside.
ADD cognac and water to skillet, scraping skillet to
loosen browned bits; cook over medium-high heat
15 seconds or until reduced to 1/4 cup, stirring constantly.
SPOON cognac mixture over steaks.
YIELD: 4 servings (serving size: 1 steak and 1 tablespoon sauce)

NOTE: This meal is a little higher than the recom-
mended 30% calories from fat. You need to add
healthy side dishes to keep it within the fat guide-
lines.

# Blue Cheese-Walnut Stuffed Fillets

1/4 cup crumbled blue cheese
1   tablespoon finely-chopped walnuts, toasted
1   tablespoon nonfat sour cream
4   (1-inch-thick) beef tenderloin steaks, (4 ounces each)
2   tablespoons reduced-fat margarine
2   cloves garlic, minced
4   green onions, finely chopped
1/2 cup Madeira wine

COMBINE first 3 ingredients.
CUT a pocket into side of each steak.
SPOON blue cheese mixture evenly into steak pockets; set aside.
MELT margarine in a large nonstick skillet over medium-high heat; add garlic and green onions, stirring constantly, until tender. Remove garlic mixture and set aside.
COOK steaks in skillet over medium heat 7 minutes on each side or to desired degree of doneness.
REMOVE steaks, reserving drippings in skillet; add wine to drippings and cook 1 to 2 minutes or by half.
STIR in garlic mixture; spoon over steaks.
YIELD: 4 servings

PER serving:
CALORIES 252
(52% from fat)
FAT 14.6g
(saturated 4.9g)
PROTEIN 26.3g
CARBOHYDRATE 3.0g
FIBER 0.4g
CHOLESTEROL 76mg
SODIUM 222mg

# Casserole Spaghetti

1 1/2 pounds ground round
1/4 teaspoon salt
1 1/2 cups chopped onion
1   cup chopped bell pepper
1/2 cup chopped celery
2   cloves garlic, crushed
1   (10 3/4-ounce) can low-fat, reduced-sodium
       cream of mushroom soup, undiluted
1   (14 1/2-ounce) can no-salt-added whole
       tomatoes, undrained and chopped
3/4 cup water
2   tablespoons chili powder
1/4 teaspoon pepper
1   (8-ounce) package spaghetti
2 ounces reduced-fat sharp Cheddar cheese,
       cut into 1/2-inch cubes
2   tablespoons chopped pimiento-stuffed
       olives
Vegetable cooking spray
1/2 cup (2 ounces) shredded reduced-fat sharp
       Cheddar cheese

COOK first 6 ingredients in a Dutch oven, stirring
until meat crumbles; drain well, and return to
Dutch oven.
STIR in soup and add next 4 ingredients.
BRING mixture to a boil over medium heat.
COVER, reduce heat, and simmer 1 hour, stirring
occasionally.
COOK spaghetti according to package directions,
omitting the salt and fat; drain.
STIR spaghetti, cheese cubes, and olives into meat
sauce.
SPOON mixture into a 13x9x2-inch baking dish
coated with cooking spray.
COVER and bake at 325 degrees for 20 minutes, or
until thoroughly heated.
SPRINKLE with 1/2 cup shredded cheese and bake,
uncovered, 10 additional minutes.
YIELD: 8 servings

# Cheddar Chicken

8  (4-ounce) skinned and boned chicken breast halves
8 ounces reduced-fat sharp Cheddar cheese,
    cut into 8 equal pieces
1/2 cup egg substitute
3/4 cup fine, dry bread crumbs
1/4 cup reduced-calorie margarine
Vegetable cooking spray
1  cup sliced fresh mushrooms
1/2 cup chopped green bell pepper
1  cup canned reduced-sodium chicken broth
2  tablespoons all-purpose flour
1/2 teaspoon salt
1/2 teaspoon pepper
3  cups cooked long-grain rice, cooked
    without salt or fat
1  (2-ounce) jar diced pimiento, drained
Garnish: fresh oregano sprigs

PER serving:
CALORIES 382
(27% from fat)
FAT 11.4g
(saturated 4.2g)
PROTEIN 40.0g
CARBOHYDRATE 28.6g
FIBER 1.3g
CHOLESTEROL 85mg
SODIUM 664 mg

PLACE chicken between two sheets of heavy-duty plastic wrap, and flatten to 1/4-inch thickness, using a meat mallet or rolling pin.

PLACE a piece of cheese in center of each breast; fold over all sides of breast, enclosing cheese, and secure with wooden picks.

DIP chicken in egg substitute, draining excess; dredge in bread crumbs, coating all sides.

MELT margarine in a large nonstick skillet coated with cooking spray. Cook chicken bundles on both sides over medium-high heat until browned; remove from skillet. Set aside, and keep warm.

ADD mushrooms and bell pepper to skillet; cook, stirring constantly, until tender.

GRADUALLY add broth to flour, stirring until smooth. ADD broth mixture, salt and pepper to skillet; cook, stirring constantly, until thickened.

ADD rice and pimiento; pour into a 13x9x2-inch baking dish, coated with cooking spray. Place bundles on top.

BAKE, uncovered, at 400 degrees for 20 minutes.

REMOVE wooden picks before serving.

GARNISH, if desired.

YIELD: 8 servings

# Chicken Biscuit Stew

2   tablespoons reduced-calorie stick
      margarine
1/2 cup all-purpose flour
1/4 teaspoon salt
1/4 teaspoon pepper
1/2 cup skim milk
1   (10 1/2-ounce) can low-salt chicken broth
1 1/2 cups cubed, cooked chicken breasts
1/3 cup chopped onion
1   (8 1/2-ounce) can green peas, drained
1   (8 1/4-ounce) can sliced carrots, drained
1   (4 1/2-ounce) can refrigerated buttermilk
      biscuits

PREHEAT oven to 375 degrees.
MELT margarine in a 9-inch cast iron skillet over medium-high heat.
STIR in flour, salt and pepper.
GRADUALLY add milk and broth, stirring with a whisk until blended.
COOK milk mixture 4 minutes or until thick and bubbly, stirring constantly.
ADD chicken, onion, peas and carrots; cook 1 minute.
REMOVE from heat.
CAREFULLY split biscuits in half horizontally; place over chicken mixture.
BAKE at 375 degrees for 20 minutes, or until biscuits are golden brown.
YIELD: 5 servings (serving size: 3/4 cup stew and 2 biscuit halves)

# Chicken and Dumplings

1/2 cup self-rising flour
1/2 teaspoon pepper
6   chicken leg-thigh combinations (3 pounds), skinned
Vegetable cooking spray
2   tablespoons vegetable oil
1   medium onion, chopped
2   cloves garlic, minced
1   tablespoon self-rising flour
5   cups canned reduced-sodium chicken broth
2   tablespoons chopped fresh basil
2   tablespoons chopped fresh thyme
1   tablespoon chopped fresh rosemary
1/2 teaspoon grated lemon rind
2   tablespoons lemon juice
2   cups self-rising flour
1   cup nonfat buttermilk
1/4 cup reduced-fat sour cream

PER serving:
CALORIES 476
(25% from fat)
FAT 13.0g
(saturated 3.4g)
PROTEIN 39.7g
CARBOHYDRATE 46.9g
FIBER 0.8g
CHOLESTEROL 123mg
SODIUM 1253mg

COMBINE 1/2 cup flour and pepper in a large heavy-duty zip-top plastic bag.
ADD chicken; seal bag securely; shake gently to coat.
COAT a Dutch oven with cooking spray.
ADD oil; place over medium heat until hot.
ADD chicken; cook until golden, turning once.
REMOVE chicken from pan, reserve drippings in pan.
COOK onion and garlic in drippings, stirring constantly, until tender.
ADD 1 tablespoon flour, and cook 1 minute, stirring constantly; gradually add broth, stirring constantly.
ADD basil and next 4 ingredients; bring to a boil.
RETURN chicken to Dutch oven; cover, reduce heat, and simmer 30 minutes.
REMOVE chicken from Dutch oven and keep warm; reserve broth mixture in Dutch oven.
COMBINE 2 cups flour and buttermilk in a large bowl, stirring with a fork.
BRING reserved broth mixture to a rolling boil.
DROP dough by heaping tablespoonfuls into broth.
COVER, reduce heat and simmer, without stirring, 7 to 10 minutes or until dumplings are firm in center.
REMOVE from heat, stir in sour cream.
SERVE over chicken.
YIELD: 6 servings

# Chicken Lasagna

6 lasagna noodles, uncooked
1 (10-ounce) package frozen chopped spinach, thawed
2 cups chopped cooked chicken breast (skinned before cooking and cooked without salt)
1 1/2 cups (6 ounces) shredded reduced-fat sharp Cheddar cheese
1 cup sliced mushrooms
1/3 cup finely-chopped onion
1 (10 3/4-ounce) can reduced-fat cream of mushroom soup, undiluted
1 (8-ounce) carton nonfat sour cream
1/3 cup nonfat mayonnaise
1 tablespoon corn starch
1 tablespoon low-sodium soy sauce
1/4 teaspoon freshly-ground nutmeg
1/4 teaspoon pepper
Butter-flavored vegetable cooking spray
3 tablespoons reduced-calorie margarine
1/4 cup finely-chopped pecans
1/2 cup fine, dry bread crumbs
1/2 cup grated Parmesan cheese

COOK noodles according to package directions, omitting salt and fat; drain and set aside.
DRAIN spinach well, pressing between layers of paper towels to remove excess mixture.
COMBINE spinach, chicken and next 10 ingredients in a large bowl; stir well.
ARRANGE 2 noodles in an 11 x 7 x 1 1/2-inch baking dish, coated with cooking spray.
SPREAD half of chicken mixture over noodles.
REPEAT procedure with remaining noodles and chicken mixture; set aside.
MELT margarine in a medium-size nonstick skillet over medium heat; add pecans and cook 1 minute.
REMOVE from heat; stir in bread crumbs and cheese.
SPRINKLE topping over casserole; coat with cooking spray.
COVER and bake at 350 degrees for 55 to 60 minutes, or until hot and bubbly.
LET stand 15 minutes before serving.
YIELD: 8 servings

# Chicken with Potatoes and Rosemary

Vegetable cooking spray
3   (6-ounce) skinned chicken breast halves
3   chicken thighs (about 9 ounces), skinned
1   medium onion, halved lengthwise and
       thinly sliced (about 1 cup)
2   garlic cloves, minced
1   (10 1/2-ounce) can low-salt chicken broth
1 1/2 tablespoons chopped fresh rosemary
3/4 teaspoon salt
1/8 teaspoon pepper
2   bay leaves
1 1/2 pounds baking potato, cut in 1/4-inch slices
1   cup water
2   teaspoons cornstarch

PER serving:
CALORIES 267
(22% from fat)
FAT 6.4g
(saturated 1.7g)
PROTEIN 28.3g
CARBOHYDRATE 23.1g
FIBER 2.4g
CHOLESTEROL 75mg
SODIUM 390mg

COAT a large Dutch oven with cooking spray. Place over medium-high heat until hot.
ADD half of chicken pieces, browning on all sides.
REMOVE chicken from pan; set aside.
REPEAT with remaining chicken.
ADD onion and garlic; sauté 3 minutes.
ADD broth, rosemary, salt, pepper and bay leaves; stir well.
RETURN chicken to pan; top with potatoes.
COVER and cook 30 minutes or until done, stirring occasionally.
REMOVE chicken and vegetables from pan with a slotted spoon; set aside; and keep warm.
DISCARD bay leaves.
COMBINE water and cornstarch in a small bowl; stir well.
ADD cornstarch mixture to broth mixture in pan; cook 1 minute or until thick and bubbly, stirring constantly with a wooden spoon to loosen browned bits.
SPOON broth mixture over chicken and vegetables.
YIELD: 6 servings (serving size: 1 chicken breast or thigh and 1 drumstick, 2/3 cup vegetables, and about 3 tablespoons sauce)

# Chicken Parmesan

6   (4-ounce) skinned and boned chicken
      breast halves
1   egg white, lightly beaten
2   tablespoons water
1/2 cup fine, dry bread crumbs
1/4 cup grated nonfat Parmesan cheese
1   teaspoon dried Italian seasoning
2   tablespoons vegetable oil
1   (27 1/2-ounce) jar low-fat spaghetti sauce
1   (12-ounce) package spaghetti
1   cup (4 ounces) shredded part-skim
      Mozzarella cheese
2   teaspoons grated nonfat Parmesan cheese
Garnish: fresh basil sprigs, or parsley sprigs

PLACE each chicken breast half between two
sheets of heavy-duty plastic wrap; flatten to 1/4-
inch thickness, using a meat mallet or rolling pin.
COMBINE egg white and water in a bowl.
COMBINE bread crumbs, 1/4 cup Parmesan cheese
and Italian seasoning in a separate bowl.
DIP chicken in egg white mixture; dredge in bread
crumb mixture.
BROWN chicken in oil in a large nonstick skillet
over medium heat.
ADD spaghetti sauce; cover and simmer 10 min-
utes.
COOK spaghetti according to package directions,
omitting salt and fat.
PLACE spaghetti on a serving platter.
SPOON chicken and sauce over spaghetti; sprinkle
with Mozzarella cheese and 2 teaspoons Parmesan
cheese.
COVER and let stand until cheese melts.
GARNISH, if desired.
YIELD: 6 servings

# Chicken Pot Pie

2   tablespoons reduced-calorie margarine
1/3 cup all-purpose flour
1   (12-ounce) can evaporated skimmed milk
1   cup canned reduced-sodium chicken broth
1/2 teaspoon freshly-ground pepper
Vegetable cooking spray
1   (8-ounce) package presliced fresh
      mushrooms
1   small onion, chopped
3   stalks celery, sliced
3 1/2 cups chopped, cooked chicken breast
      (skinned before cooking and cooked
      without salt)
3   hard-cooked egg whites, chopped
1/2 (15-ounce) package refrigerated pie crusts

PER serving:
CALORIES 443
(34% from fat)
FAT 16.6g
(saturated 5.3g)
PROTEIN 36.9g
CARBOHYDRATE 35.5g
FIBER 1.4g
CHOLESTEROL 78mg
SODIUM 669mg

MELT margarine in a heavy saucepan over low
heat.
COMBINE flour and evaporated milk, stirring until
smooth.
ADD milk mixture and chicken broth to saucepan;
cook over medium heat, stirring constantly, until
thickened and bubbly.
STIR in pepper; set sauce aside.
COAT a large nonstick skillet with cooking spray;
place over medium-high heat until hot.
ADD mushrooms, onion and celery; cook, stirring
constantly, until tender. Stir vegetable mixture,
chicken and egg whites into sauce.
COAT a 2-quart round casserole with cooking spray.
SPOON filling into casserole; top with pie crust.
TRIM off excess pastry; fold edges under and flute;
cut slits in top.
BAKE, uncovered, at 375 degrees for 40 to 50 min-
utes, or until golden.
YIELD: 6 servings

# Crab Cakes

PER serving:
CALORIES 206
(57% from fat)
FAT 13.1g
(saturated 1.9g)
PROTEIN 16.3g
CARBOHYDRATE 5.2g
FIBER 0.1g
CHOLESTEROL 86mg
SODIUM 819mg

1   egg white, lightly beaten
4   low-sodium saltine crackers, crushed
1 1/2 tablespoons chopped, fresh parsley
3/4 teaspoon garlic powder
1/2 teaspoon low-sodium Worcestershire sauce
4   drops hot sauce
1/8 teaspoon freshly-ground pepper
3   tablespoons reduced-fat mayonnaise
1   lb. fresh lump crabmeat, drained
Vegetable cooking spray
2   tablespoons reduced-fat mayonnaise
1/4 teaspoon garlic powder
Paprika
Tartar sauce (see below)
Garnishes: fresh oregano sprigs, lemon
slices

COMBINE   first 8 ingredients in a bowl; stir in crabmeat.
SHAPE into 6 (3-inch) patties; place on a baking sheet coated with cooking spray.
COMBINE 2 tablespoons mayonnaise and 1/4 teaspoon garlic powder; spread evenly on crab cakes. Sprinkle with paprika.
BAKE, uncovered, at 350 degrees for 20 minutes, or until crab cakes are golden. (Do not overbake.)
SERVE with Tartar Sauce.

TARTAR SAUCE:
3/4 cup reduced-fat mayonnaise
1   tablespoon finely-chopped fresh parsley
2   teaspoons chopped fresh chives
2   teaspoons sweet pickle relish
1   teaspoon capers, chopped
3/4 teaspoon Dijon mustard
1   hard-cooked egg white, finely chopped

COMBINE all ingredients; cover and chill.
YIELD: 6 servings

# Crab Imperial

1   tablespoon reduced-calorie margarine
2   tablespoons chopped onion
2   tablespoons chopped green bell pepper
2   tablespoons all-purpose flour
1/2 cup skim milk
1   pound fresh lump crabmeat, drained
1/2 teaspoon garlic powder
1/4 teaspoon ground black pepper
1/4 cup reduced-fat mayonnaise
1   tablespoon dry sherry
1/4 teaspoon low-sodium Worcestershire
       sauce
Vegetable cooking spray
Paprika

PER serving:
CALORIES 138
(36% from fat)
FAT 5.5g
(saturated 0.8g)
PROTEIN 16.4g
CARBOHYDRATE 4.2g
FIBER 0.2g
CHOLESTEROL 79mg
SODIUM 510mg

MELT margarine in a large nonstick skillet over medium-high heat.
ADD onion and bell pepper; cook, stirring constantly, until tender.
COMBINE flour and milk, stirring well.
ADD to vegetable mixture, and cook 2 minutes or until thickened, stirring often.
ADD crabmeat and next 5 ingredients.
SPOON into baking shell or ramekins coated with cooking spray; sprinkle with paprika.
BAKE at 350 degrees for 20 to 25 minutes, or until bubbly.
YIELD: 6 servings

# Cranberry Chicken

1/2 cup all-purpose flour
1/4 teaspoon pepper
6  boneless, skinless chicken breast halves
      (1 1/2 pounds)
3  tablespoons margarine
1  cup water
1  cup frozen or fresh cranberries
1/2 cup packed brown sugar
Dash of ground nutmeg
1  tablespoon red wine vinegar (optional)
Hot cooked rice (optional)

IN a shallow dish, combine flour and pepper; dredge chicken.

IN a skillet, melt margarine over medium heat. Brown the chicken on both sides. Remove and keep warm.

IN the same skillet, combine water, cranberries, brown sugar, nutmeg, and vinegar if desired. Cook and stir until berries burst, about 5 minutes.

RETURN chicken to skillet. Cover and simmer for 20 to 30 minutes, or until chicken is tender, basting occasionally with the sauce.

SERVE over rice if desired.

YIELD: 6 servings

PER serving:
CALORIES 284
(29% from fat)
FAT 9g
(saturated 1g)
PROTEIN 28g
CARBOHYDRATE 22g
CHOLESTEROL 73mg
SODIUM 122mg

# Dijon-Rosemary Lamb Chops

8   (4-ounce) lean lamb chops
2   tablespoons Dijon mustard
1   tablespoon dried rosemary, crushed
1/4 cup all-purpose flour
Vegetable cooking spray
1   tablespoon olive oil
1   cup dry white wine, divided
1/2 cup nonfat sour cream
1/8 teaspoon pepper

TRIM fat from chops; spread mustard over lamb chops, and sprinkle evenly with rosemary.
DREDGE chops in flour, shaking off excess flour.
COAT a large nonstick skillet with cooking spray; add oil and place skillet over medium-high heat until hot.
ADD chops and cook until browned, turning once.
REDUCE heat to medium; cover and cook 7 minutes.
TURN chops over; add 1/3 cup wine.
COOK 8 additional minutes or to desired degree of doneness.
REMOVE chops from skillet; keep warm.
ADD remaining 2/3 cup wine to pan drippings, stirring to loosen browned particles that cling to bottom.
COOK 10 minutes or until liquid is reduced to about 3/4 cup, stirring occasionally.
GRADUALLY stir in sour cream; cook until thoroughly heated (do not boil).
STIR in pepper; serve sauce with lamb chops.
Yield: 4 servings.

PER serving:
CALORIES 576
(72% from fat)
FAT 485g
(saturated 18.8g)
PROTEIN 28.4g
CARBOHYDRATE 9.4g
FIBER 0.4g
CHOLESTEROL 115mg
SODIUM 336mg

# Fish Bake

4    medium potatoes, sliced
1    teaspoon all-purpose flour
1    small onion, sliced into rings
1/4 teaspoon pepper
3/4 cup skim milk, divided
1 1/2 pounds whitefish or cod fillets
1    tablespoon grated Parmesan cheese
2    tablespoons minced fresh parsley
        or 2 tablespoons dried parsley flakes
1/4 teaspoon paprika

PLACE potatoes in a saucepan and cover with wa-
ter; bring to a boil. Cook until almost tender; drain.
Slice 1/8-inch-thick. Place in a shallow 2-quart bak-
ing dish coated with cooking spray. Sprinkle with
flour.
TOP with onion; sprinkle with pepper.
POUR half of the milk over potatoes. Place fish on
top; pour remaining milk over fish.
SPRINKLE with Parmesan cheese.
COVER and bake at 375 degrees for 20 to 30 min-
utes, or until fish flakes easily with a fork.
SPRINKLE with parsley and paprika.
YIELD: 4 servings

# Four-Cheese Manicotti

12 uncooked manicotti shells
Vegetable cooking spray
12 cups finely-chopped onion
3 garlic cloves, minced
1 cup (4 ounces) shredded part-skim
    Mozzarella cheese, divided
1/2 cup Parmesan cheese, divided
1 teaspoon dried Italian seasoning
1/2 teaspoon pepper
1 (15-ounce) carton nonfat ricotta cheese
1 (6-ounce) package garden vegetable-
    flavored light cream cheese, softened
    (f available); may use plain
4 ounce block nonfat cream cheese, softened
1/2 (10-ounce) package frozen chopped spinach,
    thawed, drained and squeezed dry
1 (27 1/2-ounce) jar reduced-fat, reduced-
    sodium tomato and herb pasta sauce
Oregano sprigs (optional)

PER serving:
CALORIES 386
(27% from fat)
FAT 11.7g
(saturated 6.9g)
PROTEIN 30g
CARBOHYDRATE 41.5g
FIBER 4.3g
CHOLESTEROL 49mg
SODIUM 1012mg

PREHEAT oven to 350 degrees.
COOK pasta according to package directions, omitting salt and fat; set aside.
COAT a small nonstick skillet with cooking spray and place skillet over medium-high heat until hot.
ADD onion and garlic; sauté 3 minutes, remove from heat and set aside.
COMBINE 1/2 cup Mozzarella cheese, 1/4 cup Parmesan cheese and next 5 ingredients in a bowl. Beat at medium speed of an electric mixer until smooth.
STIR in onion mixture and spinach.
SPOON Mozzarella cheese mixture into cooked manicotti (about 1/3 cup per shell).
DIVIDE 1 cup sauce evenly between 6 individual casserole dishes coated with cooking spray.
ARRANGE 2 stuffed manicotti in each dish; pour remaining sauce over each serving.
PLACE dishes on a baking sheet; cover each dish with foil, and bake at 350 degrees for 25 minutes.
SPRINKLE with remaining Mozzarella and Parmesan cheese. Bake, uncovered, an additional 5 minutes.
GARNISH with oregano, if desired.
YIELD: 6 servings

# Garlic Chicken

4 heads garlic
Olive oil-flavored cooking spray
1 (3-pound) broiler-fryer, skinned
1/2 cup dry white wine
1/2 cup + 2 tablespoons canned reduced-
    sodium chicken broth, divided
1/2 cup evaporated skim milk
1 tablespoon cornstarch
1/8 teaspoon pepper

PER serving:
CALORIES 235
(28% from fat)
FAT 7.4g
(saturated 2.0g)
PROTEIN 30.3g
CARBOHYDRATE 6.9g
FIBER 0.2g
CHOLESTEROL 87mg
SODIUM 168mg

PEEL outer skin from garlic heads, and discard.
CUT off top one-third of each garlic head.
SEPARATE garlic heads into 40 cloves. (Reserve any remaining cloves for another use.)
PLACE 35 cloves in center of a piece of heavy-duty aluminum foil; coat garlic with cooking spray.
FOLD foil over garlic, sealing tightly. Set aside garlic packet and remaining 5 cloves.
PLACE chicken, breast-side up, on a rack in shallow roasting pan.
PLACE 5 reserved garlic cloves in cavity.
PLACE garlic packet on rack in roasting pan.
BAKE, uncovered, at 375 degrees for 20 minutes.
POUR wine over chicken and bake 40 minutes, basting occasionally with pan juices.
REMOVE garlic from pan and let cool 10 minutes.
BAKE chicken 30 additional minutes or until done.
SQUEEZE pulp from garlic cloves into container of a mini food processor.
ADD 2 tablespoons broth; process until smooth, stopping once to scrape down sides. Set aside.
COMBINE remaining 1/2 cup broth, evaporated milk and cornstarch in a small saucepan, stirring until smooth.
COOK over medium-high heat 2 to 3 minutes, stirring occasionally.
STIR garlic mixture and pepper into broth mixture.
SERVE chicken with garlic sauce immediately.
Yield: 6 servings

# Grilled Chicken Caesar

1   tablespoon chili powder
2   tablespoons Worcestershire sauce
1   teaspoon ground cumin
1/4 teaspoon pepper
1   garlic clove, crushed
1   pound skinned, boned chicken breasts,
        cut into 1-inch-wide strips
Vegetable cooking spray
3/4 cup low-fat buttermilk
3   tablespoons grated Romano cheese
1   tablespoon lemon juice
1   teaspoon anchovy paste
1/2 teaspoon dry mustard
1/4 teaspoon pepper
1   garlic clove, minced
1   (10-ounce) package ready-to-eat romaine
        salad
2   c. halved cherry tomatoes
3/4 cup plain croutons

PER serving:
CALORIES 289
(26% from fat)
FAT 8.3g
(saturated 2.8g)
PROTEIN 33.8g
CARBOHYDRATE 19g
FIBER 3.2g
CHOLESTEROL 78mg
SODIUM 429mg

COMBINE first 6 ingredients in a medium bowl; stir well and set aside.

COAT grill rack with cooking spray; place grill rack on grill over medium-hot coals (350 to 400 degrees).

PLACE chicken strips on grill rack and grill, covered, 5 minutes on each side or until chicken strips are done.

COMBINE buttermilk and next 6 ingredients in large bowl; stir well.

ADD romaine salad, tomatoes and croutons; toss gently to coat.

SPOON salad mixture onto each of 4 plates, and top with chicken strips.

YIELD: 4 servings (serving size: 2 1/2 cups salad mixture and 3 ounces of chicken)

# Grilled Lamb with Mango Salsa

1   (4-pound) boneless leg of lamb
1   teaspoon cumin seeds
1   teaspoon coriander seeds
1/2 cup dry white wine
1/4 cup tequila
1/4 cup olive oil
2   tablespoons fresh lime juice
2   tablespoons minced fresh garlic
2   tablespoons chopped fresh cilantro
2   jalapeño peppers, seeded and finely
      chopped
1/4 teaspoon salt
1/2 teaspoon freshly-ground pepper
Mango Salsa (see below)

CUT large half of leg of lamb to, but not through, other side; slip cut piece over. Set aside.
COOK cumin and coriander seeds in a heavy skillet, stirring constantly, until browned; crush.
COMBINE crushed seeds, wine and next 8 ingredients in a large shallow dish.
ADD lamb, cover and chill 8 hours, turning occasionally.
PREPARE charcoal fire in one end of grill; let burn 15 to 20 minutes.
PLACE lamb on grill opposite medium-hot coals (350 to 400 degrees).
COOK lamb without grill lid, 1 hour or until meat thermometer inserted in thickest portion of meat registers 150 degrees (medium-rare), turning once.
CUT into thin slices; serve with Mango Salsa.
YIELD: 16 servings

Continued on following page.

Continued from preceding page.

MANGO SALSA:
4   medium mangoes, peeled and chopped
1/4 cup chopped celery
1/4 cup finely-chopped green onion
1/4 cup chopped yellow or red bell pepper
1/3 cup chopped fresh cilantro
1   jalapeño pepper, seeded and minced
1/4 cup honey
2   tablespoons olive oil
2   tablespoons fresh lime juice
1/4 teaspoon salt

COMBINE first 6 ingredients.
COMBINE honey and remaining 3 ingredients; pour
over mango mixture and toss.
CHILL 30 minutes.
YIELD: 4 cups

PER serving:
CALORIES 230
(41% from fat)
FAT 10.6g
(saturated 2.6g)
PROTEIN 20.0g
CARBOHYDRATE 10.6g
FIBER 0.7g
CHOLESTEROL 62mg
SODIUM 125mg

# Grilled Salmon Steak

2   tablespoons cracked pepper
6   (6-ounce) salmon steaks
2/3 cup rice vinegar
2   tablespoons fresh lemon juice
2   tablespoons Dijon mustard
1   tablespoon dark sesame oil
1/4 teaspoon salt
1/8 teaspoon pepper
4   cloves garlic, minced
Vegetable cooking spray
1/4 teaspoon cornstarch

SPRINKLE cracked pepper evenly over both sides of each salmon steak, and place steaks in an 11x9-inch baking dish.

COMBINE vinegar and next 6 ingredients in a small bowl; stir well.

POUR vinegar mixture over steaks; cover and marinate for 1 hour in refrigerator, turning steaks occasionally.

COAT grill rack with cooking spray; place on grill over medium-hot coals (350 to 400 degrees).

REMOVE steaks from dish, reserving marinade.

BRING marinade to a boil in a small saucepan.

PLACE steaks on rack and grill, covered, 5 minutes on each side, or until fish flakes easily when tested with a fork, basting often with half of reserved marinade.

COMBINE remaining half of marinade and cornstarch in a small saucepan; bring to a boil and cook 1 minute or until thickened, stirring constantly with a wire whisk.

SPOON about 1 tablespoon sauce over each steak.

YIELD: 6 servings

# Grilled Swordfish with Caper Sauce

1/2 cup dry white wine
5    cloves garlic, minced
2    teaspoons chopped fresh rosemary,
        divided
1/4 teaspoon salt
1/4 teaspoon pepper
4    (4-ounce) swordfish steaks
Vegetables cooking spray
1/3 cup lemon juice
3    tablespoons fine, dry bread crumbs
3    tablespoons extra-virgin olive oil
1    tablespoon capers
Garnish: fresh rosemary sprigs

COMBINE: wine, garlic and 1 teaspoon rosemary in
an 8-inch square baking dish.
SPRINKLE salt and pepper over fish; place fish in
baking dish, turning to coat.
COVER and chill at least 1 hour.
REMOVE fish from marinade, discarding marinade.
COAT food rack with cooking spray; place rack on
grill over hot coals (400 to 500 degrees).
COOK fish, covered with grill lid, 4 to 5 minutes on
each side, or until fish flakes easily when tested
with a fork.
COMBINE remaining 1 teaspoon rosemary, lemon
juice and next 3 ingredients.
SPOON over fish.
GARNISH, if desired, and serve immediately.
YIELD: 4 servings

PER serving:
CALORIES 271
(50% from fat)
FAT 15.1g
(saturated 2.7g)
PROTEIN 23.6g
CARBOHYDRATE 7.5g
FIBER 0.4g
CHOLESTEROL 44mg
SODIUM 461mg

# Grilled Trout

2   tablespoons herb-flavored vegetable oil
1/4 cup lemon juice
1/2 teaspoon salt
2   (2-pound) dressed trout
4   sprigs fresh tarragon
1   lemon, sliced
Vegetable cooking spray

COMBINE oil, lemon juice and salt in a small bowl, stirring well with a wire whisk. Brush half of mixture inside each trout. Place 2 sprigs tarragon and 2 lemon slices inside each trout.

PLACE trout in a large baking dish. Pour remaining oil mixture over trout. Cover and chill 2 hours.

PLACE trout in a grill basket coated with cooking spray. Cook, covered with grill lid, over hot coals (400 to 500 degrees), 5 to 7 minutes on each side or until fish flakes easily when tested with a fork.

YIELD: 6 servings

# Grilled Tuna with Herbed Mayonnaise

1./2 cup fat-free mayonnaise
1/4 cup fat-free yogurt
1   teaspoon chopped fresh oregano
1   teaspoon chopped tarragon
1   teaspoon lemon juice
1/4 teaspoon salt
1/4 teaspoon pepper
4   (6-ounce) tuna steaks (about 1-inch-thick)
Vegetable cooking spray

COMBINE first 5 ingredients in a small bowl; stir well, and set aside.
SPRINKLE salt and pepper over tuna; set aside.
PREPARE grill. Place tuna on a grill rack coated with cooking spray; grill 3 minutes on each side or until tuna is medium-rare, or to desired degree of doneness.
SERVE with mayonnaise mixture.
YIELD: 4 servings (serving size: 1 tuna steak and 2 tablespoons mayonnaise mixture)

PER serving:
CALORIES 267
(29% from fat)
FAT 8.5g
(saturated 2.2g)
PROTEIN 40.5g
CARBOHYDRATE 4.6g
FIBER 0.1g
CHOLESTEROL 65mg
SODIUM 41.4mg

# Ham Loaf

2   eggs
1   cup skim milk
1   cup dry bread crumbs
1/4 teaspoon pepper
1 1/2 pounds ground, fully-cooked low-fat ham
1/2 pound ground turkey breast

GLAZE:
1/3 cup packed brown sugar
1/4 cup vinegar
2   tablespoons water
1/2 teaspoon ground mustard

IN a large bowl, beat the eggs; add milk, bread crumbs and pepper. Add ham and turkey; mix well.
IN a shallow baking pan, shape meat mixture into a loaf, about 8 x 4 x 2 1/2-inches.
BAKE at 350 degrees for 30 minutes.
MEANWHILE, combine glaze ingredients; spoon over loaf.
CONTINUE baking about 40 minutes longer or until meat thermometer reads 165 to 170 degrees, basting occasionally with glaze.
YIELD: 8 servings

# Ham and Lima Bean Casserole

1 1/2 cups water
1 1/2 cups frozen baby lima beans, thawed
3/4 cup finely-chopped green bell pepper
1/3 cup chopped onion
1 1/4 cup chopped extra-lean ham (about
     6 ounces)
1   cup (4 ounces) shredded reduced-fat sharp
     Cheddar cheese
1   teaspoon Worcestershire sauce
1   (14 3/4-ounce) can no-salt-added cream-style corn
Vegetable cooking spray
1/4 cup plus 2 tablespoons skim milk
2   tablespoons chopped green onions
3/4 cup low-fat biscuit and baking mix

PREHEAT oven to 400 degrees.
BRING water to a boil in a medium saucepan. ADD lima beans, bell pepper and onion; cover and cook 5 minutes. Drain.
COMBINE lima bean mixture, ham, cheese, Worcestershire sauce and corn in a bowl; stir well.
SPOON into a 2-quart casserole coated with cooking spray.
COVER and bake at 400 degrees for 20 minutes.
COMBINE milk and green onions in a bowl, and stir in baking mix.
DROP batter by spoonfuls onto ham mixture to form 6 biscuits.
BAKE, uncovered, 20 minutes or until biscuits are golden.
YIELD: 6 servings (serving size: 3/4 cup casserole and 1 biscuit)

YOU can prepare this casserole ahead of time, except for biscuit topping; cover and chill overnight in the refrigerator or freeze up to 1 month. (Thaw frozen casserole in refrigerator overnight.) Let casserole stand at room temperature 30 minutes; add the biscuit topping. and bake as directed.

PER serving:
CALORIES 317
(18% from fat)
Fat 6.2g
(saturated 2.7g)
PROTEIN 19.8g
CARBOHYDRATE 70.7g
FIBER 2.2g
CHOLESTEROL 28mg
SODIUM 846mg

# Ham-Pineapple Nibbles

4 1/2 ounces lean cooked ham, coarsely
    chopped
1  (15 1/4-ounce) can crushed pineapple in
    juice, drained
1/2 cup (2 ounces) shredded part-skim
    Mozzarella cheese
1/3 cup soft bread crumbs
1/4 cup minced green bell pepper
1/4 cup egg substitute
4  green onions, chopped
1/4 teaspoon rubbed sage
1/4 cup all-purpose flour
3  (8-ounce) cans refrigerated crescent rolls

POSITION knife blade in food processor bowl; add ham.
PROCESS until ground, stopping once to scrape down sides.
COMBINE ham, pineapple and next 6 ingredients in a large bowl; set aside.
SPRINKLE flour evenly over work surface.
SEPARATE each package of rolls into 4 rectangles, pressing perforations to seal.
ROLL each rectangle into an 8x4-inch rectangle; cut each crosswise into thirds.
PLACE about 1 tablespoon ham mixture in center of each third of dough.
FOLD dough over ham mixture, pressing edges to seal; crimp with a fork.
PLACE on ungreased baking sheets.
BAKE at 375 degrees for 10 minutes, or until golden.
YIELD: 3 dozen

# Hash Brown-Ham Bake

3   cups frozen shredded potatoes
Vegetable cooking spray
1   tablespoon reduced-calorie margarine,
     melted
1   cup finely-chopped lean, cooked ham
1   cup (4 ounces) shredded reduced-fat sharp
     Cheddar cheese
1/4 cup finely-chopped green bell pepper
1/2 cup egg substitute
1/2 cup skim milk
1/4 teaspoon pepper

PER serving:
CALORIES 147
(39% from fat)
FAT 6.3g
(saturated 3.0g)
PROTEIN 13.9g
CARBOHYDRATE 9.0g
FIBER 0.6g
CHOLESTEROL 28mg
SODIUM 539mg

THAW potatoes between layers of paper towels to remove excess moisture.

PRESS potatoes in bottom and up sides of a 9-inch pie plate coated with cooking spray.

BRUSH potatoes with margarine, and coat lightly with cooking spray.

BAKE, uncovered, at 425 degrees for 20 minutes, or until lightly browned; cool potato shell on a wire rack 10 minutes.

COMBINE ham, cheese and bell pepper; spoon into potato shell.

COMBINE egg substitute, milk and pepper; pour over ham mixture.

BAKE, uncovered, at 350 degrees for 25 minutes, or until set; let stand 10 minutes before serving.

YIELD: 6 servings

# Ham Stroganoff on Cheesy Onion Biscuit

Vegetable cooking spray
1   teaspoon reduced-calorie margarine
1/4 cup finely-chopped onion
2   cups chopped, lean, cooked, reduced-
      sodium ham
1   (10 3/4-ounce) can low-sodium cream of
      chicken soup, undiluted
1/2 cup skim milk
1   (8-ounce) carton nonfat sour cream
1/8 teaspoon pepper
Cheesy Onion Biscuits (see recipe below)

COAT a large nonstick skillet with cooking spray;
add margarine.
PLACE skillet over medium-high heat until margarine melts; add ham and onion and cook, stirring
constantly until onion is tender.
STIR in soup and milk; cover and cook over medium heat, 3 to 4 minutes.
STIR in sour cream and pepper; cook over low heat
until mixture is thoroughly heated.
SERVE between Cheesy Onion Biscuits.
YIELD: 4 servings

CHEESY ONION BISCUITS:
2   cups all-purpose flour
3   tablespoons instant nonfat dry milk
      powder
4   teaspoons baking powder
1/2 teaspoon salt
1/3 cup reduced-calorie margarine
1/3 cup grated nonfat Parmesan cheese
2   tablespoons finely-chopped green onion
3/4 cup water
Vegetable cooking spray

Continued on following page.

Continued from preceding page.

COMBINE first 4 ingredients in a large bowl; cut in margarine with pastry blender or fork until mixture is crumbly.

STIR in Parmesan cheese and green onions.

ADD water, stirring with a fork until dry ingredients are moistened.

TURN biscuit dough out onto a lightly-floured surface, and knead lightly 5 or 6 times.

PAT dough to 1/2-inch thickness; cut with a 3-inch round cutter.

PLACE on a baking sheet coated with cooking spray.

BAKE at 400 degrees for 15 minutes, or until lightly browned.

YIELD: 8 biscuits

PER serving:
CALORIES 577
(28% from fat)
FAT 18.1g
(saturated 3.9g)
PROTEIN 28.0g
CARBOHYDRATE 73.3g
FIBER 1.9g
CHOLESTEROL 58mg
SODIUM 1773mg

# Herbed Meat Loaf with Sun-Dried Tomato Gravy

1   cup sun-dried tomatoes, packed without
      oil (about 24)
3   cups boiling water
Vegetable cooking spray
1   cup finely-chopped onion
1   cup finely-chopped green bell pepper
2   garlic cloves, crushed
1   (1-ounce) slice whole wheat bread, torn
      into small pieces
2   tablespoons 1% low-fat milk
1/2 cup (2 ounces) shredded sharp Provolone
      cheese
2   teaspoons dried basil
1   teaspoon dried oregano
1   teaspoon pepper
1/2 teaspoon salt
1/2 teaspoon dried thyme
2   egg whites
1 3/4-pound ultra-lean ground beef
Sun-Dried Tomato Gravy

COMBINE tomatoes and boiling water in a bowl;
cover and let stand 15 minutes or until softened.
DRAIN well, and finely chop; set aside.
PREHEAT oven to 350 degrees.
COAT a medium nonstick skillet with cooking
spray, and place over medium-high heat until hot.
ADD onion, bell pepper and garlic; sauté 5 minutes
or until tender. Set aside.
PLACE bread in a large bowl. Drizzle milk over
bread; toss well to moisten bread.
ADD tomatoes, onion mixture, cheese and next 6
ingredients, stirring well.
CRUMBLE beef mixture over tomato mixture, and
stir just until mixture is blended.

Continued on following page.

Continued from preceding page.

PACK meat mixture into a 9x5-inch loaf pan coated with cooking spray.
BAKE at 350 degrees for 55 minutes, or until meat loaf reaches 170 degrees.
LET meat loaf stand in pan for 10 minutes.
REMOVE meat loaf from pan, and reserve drippings for Sun-Dried Tomato Gravy.
YIELD: 8 servings (serving size: 2 slices meat loaf and 3 tablespoons gravy)

SUN-DRIED TOMATO GRAVY:
1/4 cup sun-dried tomatoes, packed without oil (about 6)
1   cup boiling water
2 1/2 tablespoons all-purpose flour
1 1/4 cups 1% low-fat milk
1/4 cup pan drippings
1 tablespoon finely-chopped green onion
1/4 teaspoon salt
1/4 teaspoon dried basil
1/8 teaspoon pepper

COMBINE tomatoes and boiling water in a bowl; cover and let stand 15 minutes. Drain well, and finely chop.
PLACE flour in small saucepan; gradually add milk, stirring with whisk until blended. Stir in tomatoes and remaining ingredients, and cook, stirring constantly, until thickened.
YIELD: 1 1/2 cups (serving size: 3 tablespoons)

PER serving:
CALORIES 230
(36% from fat)
FAT 9.3g
(saturated 4g)
PROTEIN 24.8g
CARBOHYDRATE 15.1g
FIBER 1.1g
CHOLESTEROL 71mg
SODIUM 752mg

excluding Sun-Dried Tomato Gravy

# Honey-Mustard
# Pork Tenderloin

PER serving:
CALORIES 183
(21% from fat)
FAT 4.3g
(saturated 1.4g)
PROTEIN 22.9g
CHOLESTEROL 12.0g
FIBER 0.0g
CHOLESTEROL 64mg
SODIUM 121mg

2   (3/4-pound) boneless pork tenderloins,
      trimmed
Vegetable cooking spray
1/4 cup honey
2   tablespoons apple cider vinegar
1   tablespoon Dijon mustard
1/2 teaspoon paprika

PLACE tenderloins on a rack coated with cooking spray; place rack in broiler pan. Set aside.
COMBINE honey and next 3 ingredients.
SPOON one-third of honey mixture over tenderloins; set remaining honey mixture aside.
BAKE, uncovered, at 350 degrees for 30 minutes, or until meat thermometer inserted in thickest portion registers 160 degrees, basting occasionally with honey mixture.
CUT tenderloin into thin slices.
YIELD: 6 servings

# Individual Barbecued Meat Loaves

1/2 cup reduced-calorie ketchup
1/3 cup cider vinegar
3 tablespoons brown sugar
1  teaspoon beef-flavored bouillon granules
1 1/2 pounds ground round
1  cup fine, dry bread crumbs
1  cup evaporated skinned milk
2  tablespoons finely-chopped onion
1/4 teaspoon salt
1/4 teaspoon pepper
Vegetable cooking spray

PER serving:
CALORIES 290
(21% from fat)
FAT 6.8g
(saturated 2.3g)
PROTEIN
CARBOHYDRATE 2.4.1g
FIBER 0.8g
CHOLESTEROL 67mg
SODIUM 588mg

COMBINE first 4 ingredients in a small saucepan; cook over medium heat, stirring until bouillon granules dissolve. Set barbecue sauce aside.
COMBINE ground round and next 5 ingredients, stirring until mixture is thoroughly blended.
SHAPE mixture into 6 loaves; place loaves on a rack of broiler pan coated with cooking spray.
BRUSH half of barbecue sauce over loaves.
BAKE, uncovered, at 350 degrees for 40 minutes.
BRUSH remaining half of barbecue sauce over loaves and bake 5 additional minutes.
SERVE immediately.
YIELD: 6 servings

# Italian Shrimp with Lemon and Garlic

2   teaspoons dried Italian seasonings
2   teaspoons Hungarian sweet paprika
2   teaspoons grated lemon rind
1/2 teaspoon salt
1/2 teaspoon freshly-ground pepper
3   garlic cloves, minced
1   pound large shrimp, peeled and deveined
Vegetable cooking spray
4   cups hot cooked angel hair (about 8 ounces
        uncooked pasta)
2   tablespoons fresh lemon juice
1   tablespoon chopped fresh parsley
Lemon zest (optional)

COMBINE first 6 ingredients in a medium bowl; stir well.
ADD shrimp; toss well to coat.
THREAD shrimp evenly onto each of 4 (8-inch) skewers.
PLACE kebabs on broiler pan coated with cooking spray; broil 2 minutes on each side.
REMOVE from skewers and arrange over pasta.
DRIZZLE with juice; sprinkle with parsley.
GARNISH with zest if desired.
YIELD: 4 servings (serving size: 3 ounces shrimp and 1 cup pasta)

# Lemon Grilled Chicken

2/3 cup lemon juice
1/4 cup canned low-sodium chicken broth
1/4 cup honey
2 tablespoons dried oregano
1 tablespoon rosemary
1/2 teaspoon salt
1/2 teaspoon pepper
3 tablespoons vegetable oil
4 cloves garlic
8 (4-ounce) skinned and boned chicken
   breast halves
Garnish: lemon slices

PER serving:
CALORIES 152
(23% from fat)
FAT 3.8g
(saturated 1.0g)
PROTEIN 25.8g
CARBOHYDRATE 2.0g
FIBER 0.0g
CHOLESTEROL 70mg
SODIUM 92mg

COMBINE first 9 ingredients in container of an electric blender, and process until smooth, stopping occasionally to scrape down sides.
PLACE chicken in a heavy-duty, zip-top plastic bag; pour lemon juice mixture over chicken.
SEAL bag, and marinate chicken in refrigerator 30 minutes.
DRAIN and discard marinade.
COOK chicken, covered with grill lid, over medium-hot coals (350 to 400 degrees), about 5 minutes on each side or until done, turning occasionally.
GARNISH, if desired.
YIELD: 8 servings

# Lemon-Roasted Chicken

PER serving:
CALORIES 225
(35% from fat)
FAT 8.6g
(saturated 2.3g)
PROTEIN 33.3g
CARBOHYDRATE 3.9g
FIBER 0.5g
CHOLESTEROL 101 mg
SODIUM 978mg

1 1/2 teaspoons salt
2   teaspoons freshly-ground pepper
2 to 3 teaspoons dried rosemary, crushed
1   (3-pound) broiler-fryer
1   medium lemon, cut in half

COMBINE first 3 ingredients; set aside.

LOOSEN skin from chicken breast by running fingers between the two; rub 1 teaspoon seasoning mixture under skin.

RUB remaining mixture over the outside of chicken.

PLACE chicken in a heavy-duty, zip-top plastic bag; seal and chill 8 hours.

REMOVE chicken from bag.

INSERT lemon halves in cavity; tie ends of legs together with string.

LIFT wing tips up and over back, and tuck under bird.

PLACE chicken, breast-side down, in a lightly-greased shallow pan.

BAKE, uncovered, at 450 degrees, turning over every 15 minutes, for 50 minutes, or until a meat thermometer inserted in thigh registers 180 degrees.

LET stand 10 minutes.

REMOVE skin before serving.

YIELD: 4 servings

# Marinated Flank Steak

1/2 cup low-sodium soy sauce
1/3 cup red wine vinegar
1/4 cup lemon juice
3   teaspoons low-sodium Worcestershire
     sauce
2   tablespoons vegetable oil
2   tablespoons Dijon mustard
1   teaspoon freshly-ground pepper
1   large onion, sliced
1   clove garlic, minced
2   (1-pound) flank steaks

COMBINE all ingredients, except steaks, in a shallow dish or large heavy-duty, zip-top plastic bag; add steaks.
COVER or seal, and chill 8 to 12 hours, turning occasionally.
REMOVE steaks and onion slices from marinade, discarding marinade; wrap onion in heavy-duty aluminum foil.
COOK steaks and onion slices, covered with grill lid, over medium-hot coals (350 to 400 degrees), about 15 minutes, or to desired degree of doneness, turning occasionally.
CUT steaks diagonally across the grain into thin strips, and serve with onion slices.
YIELD: 8 servings

PER serving:
CALORIES 290
(21% from fat)
FAT 6.8g
(saturated 2.3g)
PROTEIN 30.3g
CARBOHYDRATE 24.1g
FIBER 0.8g
CHOLESTEROL 67mg
SODIUM 909mg

# Meat Loaf

PER serving:
CALORIES 248
(42% from fat)
FAT 11g
(saturated 4g)
PROTEIN 27g
CARBOHYDRATE 8g
CHOLESTEROL 78mg
SODIUM 174mg

1 1/2 pounds ground round
1   cup skim milk
1   egg
3/4 cup soft bread crumbs
1   medium onion, chopped
1   tablespoon chopped green pepper
1   tablespoon ketchup
1   teaspoon prepared horseradish
1   teaspoon sugar
2   teaspoons ground thyme

IN a large bowl, combine all ingredients; mix well.
PRESS into an ungreased 8x4x2-inch loaf pan.
BAKE at 350 degrees for 1 hour and 15 minutes, or
until no pink remains. Drain.
YIELD: 6 servings

# Mexican Swiss Steak

1   tablespoon flour
1   tablespoon chili seasoning mix
4   (4-ounce) lean minute beef steaks
1 3/4 cups (one 15-ounce can) chunky tomato
       sauce
1/2 cup salsa

IN a flat dish, combine flour and chili seasoning
mix.
GENTLY coat steaks.
SPRAY a large skillet with olive-flavored cooking
spray.
BROWN steaks on both sides over medium heat.
IN a medium bowl, combine tomato sauce and
salsa.
POUR sauce mixture over steaks.
LOWER heat; cover, and simmer 20 to 30 minutes.
SERVE over rice, potatoes, or pasta.
YIELD: 4 servings

PER serving:
CALORIES 245
FAT 28g
PROTEIN 10g
SODIUM 764mg

# Oven-Fried Catfish

3/4 cup crushed corn flakes cereal
3/4 teaspoon celery salt
1/4 teaspoon onion powder
1/4 teaspoon paprika
Dash of pepper
4   (6-ounce) skinless farm-raised catfish fillets
Vegetable cooking spray

COMBINE first 5 ingredients; set aside.
CUT fillets in half; spray with cooking spray and coat with corn flake mixture.
ARRANGE in a single layer on a baking sheet coated with cooking spray.
SPRAY tops with cooking spray.
BAKE, uncovered, at 350 degrees for 30 minutes, or until fish flakes easily when tested with a fork.
YIELD: 4 servings

# Oven-Poached Halibut Provencale

Vegetable cooking spray
1   cup dry white wine
6   (6-ounce) halibut steaks
6   cups diced tomato
2   cups finely-chopped onion
1/4 cup chopped fresh parsley or 1 tablespoon
        plus 1 teaspoon dried parsley flakes
2   tablespoon pitted, minced olives
1   tablespoon olive oil
1/2 teaspoon salt
1/2 teaspoon anchovy paste
1/8 teaspoon pepper
2   garlic cloves, minced
1/4 cup fine, dry bread crumbs
1   tablespoon grated Parmesan cheese
1   teaspoon olive oil

PREHEAT oven to 350 degrees.
COAT a 13x9-inch baking dish with cooking spray.
ADD wine, and arrange halibut steaks in dish.
COMBINE tomato and next 8 ingredients in a bowl; stir well, and spoon over steaks.
BAKE at 350 degrees for 35 minutes, or until fish flakes easily when tested with a fork.
COMBINE bread crumbs, cheese and 1 teaspoon oil in a bowl; stir well.
SPRINKLE over tomato mixture and broil until crumbs are golden.
SERVE immediately.
YIELD: 6 servings (serving size: 5 ounces of fish and 1 cup tomato mixture)

PER serving:
CALORIES 305
(22% from fat)
FAT 8.6g
(saturated fat 1.3g)
PROTEIN 38.9g
CARBOHYDRATE 17.9g
FIBER 3.8g
CHOLESTEROL 81mg
SODIUM 446mg

# Oven-Fried Chicken

1   quart water
1   teaspoon salt
6   chicken drumsticks, skinned
4   (6-ounce) bone-in chicken breast halves, skinned
1/2 cup nonfat buttermilk
5   cups corn flakes cereal, coarsely crushed
2 to 3 teaspoons Creole seasoning
2   teaspoons dried Italian seasoning
1/2 teaspoon garlic powder
1/8 teaspoon freshly-ground black pepper
1/8 teaspoon ground red pepper
Vegetable cooking spray

COMBINE water and salt in a large bowl; add chicken pieces.

COVER and chill 8 hours.

DRAIN chicken; rinse with cold water and pat dry.

PLACE chicken in a shallow dish; pour buttermilk over chicken, turning pieces to coat.

COMBINE corn flake crumbs and next 5 ingredients in a large heavy-duty, zip-top plastic bag.

PLACE 2 pieces chicken in bag; seal.

SHAKE to coat completely; remove chicken and repeat procedure with remaining pieces.

PLACE coated chicken, bone-side down, in a 15x10x1-inch jellyroll pan coated with cooking spray.

PLACE pan on the lowest rack in oven.

BAKE, uncovered, at 400 degrees for 45 minutes (do not turn).

YIELD: 7 servings

# Oven Shrimp

1   cup dry white wine
1   pound reduced-calorie margarine
4   lemons, thinly sliced
3/4 cup low-sodium Worcestershire sauce
1/4 cup freshly-ground pepper
1   teaspoon salt
1   teaspoon dried rosemary
1   teaspoon hot sauce
10 pounds unpeeled, medium-size fresh
      shrimp
Garnish: fresh rosemary sprigs or parsley
      sprigs

PER serving:
CALORIES 250
(45% from fat)
FAT 12.4g
(saturated 2.5g)
PROTEIN 29.1g
CARBOHYDRATE 5.1g
FIBER 0.3g
CHOLESTEROL 215mg
SODIUM 487mg

COMBINE first 8 ingredients in large saucepan;
bring to a boil.
REMOVE from heat.
PLACE shrimp in two large roasting pans; pour
margarine mixture over shrimp, stirring to coat.
BAKE, uncovered, at 400 degrees for 20 to 25 min-
utes, stirring occasionally.
GARNISH, if desired.
YIELD: 24 servings

These shrimp make a really pretty platter with the
baked shrimp, lemon slices and freshly-ground
pepper. All you need with it are a big pile of nap-
kins, a good loaf of bread, and a chilled bottle of
wine.

# Peppery London Broil

1   flank steak (about 1 pound)
1   garlic love, minced
1/2 teaspoon salt-free seasoning blend
1/8 teaspoon crushed red pepper flakes
1/4 cup Worcestershire sauce

WITH meat fork, pierce holes in both sides of meat.
MAKE a paste with garlic, seasoning blend and red pepper; rub over both sides of meat.
PLACE the steak in a resealable gallon-size plastic bag. Add Worcestershire sauce and close the bag.
REFRIGERATE for at least 4 hours, turning once.
REMOVE meat; discard marinade.
BROIL or grill over hot coals until meat reaches desired doneness, 4 to 5 minutes per side.
TO SERVE, slice thinly across the grain.
YIELD: 4 servings

PER serving:
CALORIES 241
(41% from fat)
FAT 12g
(saturated 5g)
PROTEIN 31g
CARBOHYDRATE 2g
CHOLESTEROL 76mg
SODIUM 174mg

# Porcupine Meatballs

1/2 cup uncooked long-grain rice
1/2 cup water
1/3 cup chopped onion
1/2 teaspoon celery salt
1/8 teaspoon pepper
1/8 teaspoon garlic powder
1   pound ground round
1   (15-ounce) can tomato sauce
1   cup water
2   tablespoons brown sugar
2   teaspoons Worcestershire sauce

IN a bowl, combine the first 6 ingredients. Add beef
and mix well.
SHAPE into 1 1/2-inch balls.
IN a large skillet coated with cooking spray, brown
meatballs; drain.
COMBINE tomato sauce, water, brown sugar and
Worcestershire sauce; pour over meatballs.
REDUCE heat; cover and simmer for 1 hour.
YIELD: 6 servings

PER serving:
CALORIES 222
(29% from fat)
FAT 7g
(saturated 3g)
PROTEIN 18g
CARBOHYDRATE 22g
CHOLESTEROL 28mg
SODIUM 558mg

# Pork Medaillons with Port Wine and Dried Cranberry Sauce

1   large red bell pepper
1   teaspoon olive oil
1   medium-size purple onion, finely chopped
2   shallots, finely chopped
2   tablespoons minced fresh ginger
1/2 cup port wine
1/3 cup balsamic vinegar
2   tablespoons sugar
1   ripe pear, peeled, cored and chopped
2   teaspoons grated orange rind
1/2 cup dried cranberries
1   cup reduced-sodium chicken broth
2   tablespoons fresh thyme leaves
1/4 teaspoon ground red pepper
1   (1-pound) pork tenderloins, trimmed
1/2 teaspoon salt
1/2 teaspoon freshly-ground pepper

PLACE red bell pepper on an aluminum foil-lined baking sheet.
BAKE at 500 degrees for 20 minutes, or until skin looks blistered, turning once.
PLACE pepper immediately into a heavy-duty zip-top plastic bag; seal and let stand 10 minutes to loosen skin. Peel pepper, remove and discard seeds.
CUT pepper into strips; set aside.
POUR oil into a large skillet; place over medium heat until hot.
ADD onion and shallot, and cook 10 minutes, stirring often.
ADD minced ginger and next 3 ingredients; bring to a boil.
REDUCE heat and simmer 10 minutes or until

Continued on following page.

Continued from preceding page.

liquid is reduced by three-fourths, stirring often.
ADD pepper strips, pear, and next 5 ingredients;
simmer 10 minutes or until pear is tender, stirring
occasionally.
REMOVE from heat, and keep warm.
CUT each tenderloin into 8 slices.
PLACE each slice between two sheets of heavy-
duty plastic wrap; flatten slightly, using a meat
mallet or rolling pin.
SPRINKLE each side of slices with salt and pepper,
arrange in a single layer on a rack in broiler pan.
BROIL 5 1/2-inches from heat (with electric oven
door partially opened), 3 minutes on each side or
to desired degree of doneness.
SERVE with sauce.
YIELD: 8 servings

PER serving:
CALORIES 254
(32% from fat)
FAT 9.0g
(saturated 3.0g)
PROTEIN 25.0g
CARBOHYDRATE 18.3g
FIBER 1.7g
CHOLESTEROL 66mg
SODIUM 204mg

# Potato-Pork Chop Supper

2   loin pork chops (1-inch-thick), trimmed
2   cups shredded cabbage
2   tablespoons brown sugar
1   tablespoon chopped fresh parsley
2   medium potatoes, peeled & sliced 1/4-inch-
    thick
1   cup fresh or frozen green beans
1   teaspoon salt-free lemon-pepper seasoning
3/4 cup apple juice
1/4 cup seasoned bread crumbs
1   teaspoon margarine, melted

IN a large skillet, coated with vegetable cooking spray, brown chops on both sides over medium-high heat; remove and set aside.

TOSS cabbage with brown sugar and parsley; place in an 11x7x2-inch baking dish. Top with potatoes and beans. Arrange chops over vegetables. Sprinkle with lemon-pepper. Pour apple juice over all.

COVER and bake at 350 degrees for 45 minutes, or until the meat and vegetables are tender.

COMBINE the bread crumbs and margarine; sprinkle on top. Return to the oven for 15 minutes.

YIELD: 2 servings

# Reuben Casserole

1/4 cup fat-free mayonnaise
1/4 cup fat-free thousand island dressing
2 cups (one 16-ounce can) sauerkraut, well
    drained
1 (2 1/2-ounce) package sliced 90% lean
    corned beef
4 (3/4-ounce) slices (3/4 cup) reduced-fat
    Swiss cheese, shredded
1 cup sliced fresh tomato
2 slices reduced-calorie rye bread, cut into
    small pieces

PREHEAT oven to 350 degrees.
IN a small bowl, combine mayonnaise and thousand island dressing; layer in an 8x8-inch baking dish.
PLACE sauerkraut on bottom, then corned beef, dressing mixture, Swiss cheese, and tomatoes.
IN a nonstick pan, sprayed with butter-flavored cooking spray, lightly sauté bread; sprinkle on top of tomatoes.
BAKE for 20 minutes.
YIELD: 4 servings

PER serving:
CALORIES 189
FAT 7g
PROTEIN 11g
CALCIUM 21g
SODIUM 1663mg

# Rump Roast with Gravy

1   (5-pound) boneless rump roast, trimmed
1/2 cup cider vinegar
Pepper, to taste
1   cup water

GRAVY:
1/2 cup all-purpose flour
1   cup cold water
1   teaspoon browning sauce
Pepper, to taste

PLACE roast in a deep roasting pan. Puncture meat with tenderizing tool or meat fork; pour vinegar over. Let stand 15 minutes. Sprinkle with pepper. Add water to the pan.

COVER and bake at 400 degrees for 3 1/2 hours, or until meat is tender, adding additional water if needed.

ABOUT 15 minutes before roast is done, uncover to brown the top.

REMOVE roast from pan and keep warm; skim fat from pan juices. Measure the juices, adding water if needed, to equal 3 cups.

MIX flour and cold water until smooth; stir into pan juices. Cook and stir until thickened and bubbly. Cook and stir 1 minute more. Stir in browning sauce. Season with pepper.

SERVE gravy with roast.

YIELD: 20 servings

This roast is great used as leftovers. Many variations, such as: hot beef sandwiches, stew, with biscuit topping, cold sandwiches, or ground and made into a sandwich spread.

# Salisbury Steak

6 tablespoons (1 1/2 ounces) dried, fine bread
    crumbs
8 ounces 90% lean ground turkey or beef
1 egg, or equivalent in egg substitute
1/8 teaspoon black pepper
1/2 cup chopped onion
3 tablespoons lite ketchup
2 tablespoons Worcestershire sauce
1 (10 3/4 -ounce) can Healthy Request cream
    of mushroom soup

IN a medium bowl, combine bread crumbs, meat,
egg, black pepper and onion.
FORM into 4 patties; place in a hot skillet sprayed
with butter-flavored cooking spray.
BROWN patties on both sides; place in an 8x8-inch
baking dish.
IN a small bowl, combine Worcestershire sauce,
ketchup and mushroom soup; pour over patties.
BAKE at 350 degrees for 30 minutes.
YIELD: 4 servings

PER serving:
CALORIES 210
FAT 8g
PROTEIN 14g
SODIUM 697mg

# Sausage and Noodle Casserole

PER serving:
CALORIES 349
(30% from fat)
FAT 11.8g
(saturated 3.8g)
PROTEIN 21.7g
CARBOHYDRATE 38.3g
FIBER 1.1g
CHOLESTEROL 88mg
SODIUM 694mg

1   (8-ounce) package medium egg noodles
1   pound freshly-ground turkey breakfast
       sausage
1   (10 3/4-ounce) can low-fat, reduced-sodium
       cream of chicken soup, undiluted
1   (8-ounce) carton nonfat sour cream
1/3 cup crumbled blue cheese
1   (4 1/2-ounce) jar sliced mushrooms, drained
1   (2-ounce) jar diced pimiento, drained
2   tablespoons finely-ground green bell
       pepper
Vegetable cooking spray
1/2 cup soft bread crumbs
2   teaspoons reduced-calorie margarine,
       melted

COOK noodles according to package directions, omitting salt and fat; drain and set aside.
BROWN sausage in a large nonstick skillet, stirring until it crumbles; drain and set aside.
COMBINE soup, sour cream and blue cheese in a large saucepan; cook over medium heat, stirring constantly, until cheese melts.
ADD noodles, sausage, mushrooms, pimento and bell pepper; tossing to coat.
SPOON mixture into an 11 x 7 x 1 1/2-inch baking dish coated with cooking spray.
COMBINE bread crumbs and margarine; sprinkle over casserole.
BAKE, uncovered, at 350 degrees for 30 minutes.
YIELD: 6 servings

# Seafood Casserole

2   teaspoons margarine
1   medium onion, chopped
1   medium green pepper, chopped
1   celery rib, chopped
1   (10 3/4-ounce) can low-fat condensed cream
      of mushroom soup, undiluted
1   pound uncooked shrimp, peeled
      and deveined
1 1/2 cups cooked rice
4   slices day-old bread, cubed
2   (6-ounce) cans crabmeat, drained, flaked,
      and cartilage removed, or 1 1/2 pounds
      fresh crabmeat, cooked
3/4 cup skim milk
1/4 cup chopped green onions with tops
1/4 teaspoon pepper
Dash of cayenne pepper

TOPPING:
2   teaspoons margarine, melted
1/3 cup dry bread crumbs
2   tablespoons snipped fresh parsley

IN a skillet, melt margarine over medium heat.
Sauté onion, green pepper and celery until tender.
ADD soup and shrimp; cook and stir over medium
heat for 10 minutes or until shrimp turn pink.
STIR in rice, bread cubes, crab, milk, onion and
seasonings.
SPOON into a 2-quart baking dish coated with non-
stick cooking spray.
COMBINE topping ingredients; sprinkle over cas-
serole.
BAKE at 375 degrees for 30 minutes, or until heated
through.
YIELD: 8 servings

PER serving:
CALORIES 241
(19% from fat)
FAT 5g
(saturated 1g)
PROTEIN 21g
CARBOHYDRATE 28g
CHOLESTEROL 109mg
SODIUM 527mg

# Seafood Pizza

1   pound unpeeled large fresh shrimp
Vegetable cooking spray
1/2 cup chopped green bell pepper
1/2 cup chopped onion
1/2 cup celery
2   teaspoons salt-free Creole seasoning
2/3 cup Roasted Garlic Sauce (see below)
1   (12-inch) refrigerated pizza crust
1   cup (4 ounces) shredded part-skim Mozzarella cheese
1/4 cup freshly-grated Parmesan cheese

PEEL shrimp, and devein, if desired.
COAT a large nonstick skillet with cooking spray;
place over medium-high heat until hot.
ADD shrimp, bell pepper and next 3 ingredients to
skillet; cook 3 to 5 minutes or until shrimp turn pink.
SPREAD Roasted Garlic Sauce over pizza crust; top
with shrimp mixture.
SPRINKLE with cheeses.
BAKE, uncovered, at 425 degrees for 10 minutes, or
until bubbly. Serve immediately.
YIELD: 8 servings

ROASTED GARLIC SAUCE:
2   heads garlic, unpeeled
2   teaspoons canned reduced-sodium chicken broth
Olive oil-flavored vegetable cooking spray
1 1/2 tablespoons reduced-calorie margarine
1 1/2 tablespoons all-purpose flour
2/3 cup canned reduced-sodium chicken both

PLACE garlic on a piece of aluminum foil and drizzle
each head with 2 teaspoons chicken broth; coat with
cooking spray and fold edges of foil together to seal.
BAKE at 425 degrees for 45 minutes; let cool.
MELT margarine in a heavy saucepan over medium-
high heat. Cut top off each garlic head, and squeeze
cooked garlic into pan. (Garlic will be soft and sticky.)
ADD flour and cook, stirring constantly with a
wire whisk, 1 minute or until lightly browned.
ADD 2/3 cup chicken broth. Cook, stirring constantly, until mixture is thick and bubbly.
YIELD: 2/3 cup

PER serving:
CALORIES 223
(23% from fat)
FAT 5.6g
(saturated 2.6g)
PROTEIN 15.8g
CARBOHYDRATE 25.2g
FIBER 1.2g
CHOLESTEROL 59mg
SODIUM 396mg

# Sesame Ginger Chicken

2   tablespoons light soy sauce
2   tablespoons honey
1   tablespoon sesame seeds, toasted
1/2 teaspoon ground ginger
4   boneless chicken breast halves (1 pound)
2   green onion with tops, cut into thin strips

IN a small bowl, combine the first 4 ingredients; set aside.

FLATTEN the chicken breasts to 1/4-inch thickness.

GRILL over medium-hot coals, turning and basting frequently with soy sauce mixture, for 8 minutes or until juices run clear.

GARNISH with onions and cherry tomatoes.

YIELD: 4 servings

PER serving:
CALORIES 199
(18% from fat)
FAT 4g
(saturated 1g)
PROTEIN 28g
CARBOHYDRATE 11g
CHOLESTEROL 73mg
SODIUM 317mg

# Shrimp and Pasta

PER serving:
CALORIES 489
(25% from fat)
FAT 13.7g
(saturated 1.6g)
PROTEIN 32.5g
CARBOHYDRATE 61.4g
FIBER 3.5g
CHOLESTEROL 152mg
SODIUM 517mg

1   pound unpeeled medium-size fresh
       shrimp
8   ounces linguine, uncooked
Olive oil-flavored vegetable cooking spray
1   tablespoon olive oil
1/2 cup sliced green onions
3   cloves garlic, minced
1   (14-ounce) can quartered artichoke hearts,
       drained
6   Roma tomatoes, chopped
1   cup sliced fresh mushrooms
1/2 cup light olive oil vinaigrette
1/4 cup dry white wine
2   teaspoons dried Italian seasoning
1/4 teaspoon dried rosemary, crushed
1/4 teaspoon pepper
2   tablespoons freshly-grated Parmesan
       cheese

PEEL shrimp, and devein, if desired; set aside.
COOK linguine according to package directions,
omitting salt and fat.
DRAIN and keep warm.
COAT a large nonstick skillet with cooking spray;
add oil and place over medium-high heat until hot.
ADD green onions and garlic; and cook, stirring
constantly, until tender.
STIR in artichoke hearts and next 7 ingredients.
BRING to a boil; reduce heat, and simmer, uncov-
ered, 5 minutes.
ADD shrimp; cook 3 minutes or until shrimp turn
pink, stirring occasionally.
SERVE over pasta, and sprinkle with cheese.
YIELD: 4 servings

# Shrimp Scampi

1 pound unpeeled medium-size fresh
   shrimp
8 ounces angel hair pasta, uncooked
1/4 cup reduced-calorie margarine
4 cloves garlic, minced
1/2 cup dry white wine
1/4 teaspoon salt
1/4 teaspoon freshly-ground pepper
1/2 cup grated Romano cheese
1 tablespoon fresh parsley
Garnish: fresh leaf parsley sprigs

PEEL shrimp, and devein, if desired; set shrimp aside.

COOK pasta according to package directions, omitting salt and fat; drain pasta and keep warm.

MELT margarine in a large nonstick skillet over medium heat.

ADD garlic and shrimp and cook, stirring constantly, 3 to 5 minutes or until shrimp turn pink; add wine, salt and pepper.

BRING to a boil, and cook 30 seconds, stirring constantly.

PLACE pasta on a large serving platter; pour shrimp mixture over pasta, sprinkle with cheese and parsley and toss gently.

GARNISH, if desired.

SERVE immediately.

YIELD: 4 servings

PER serving:
CALORIES 440
(30% from fat)
FAT 14g
(saturated 2.7g)
PROTEIN 30.0g
CARBOHYDRATE 42.6g
FIBER 0.1g
CHOLESTEROL 144mg
SODIUM 595mg

# Southwestern Beef Burritos

PER serving:
CALORIES 314
(20% from fat)
FAT 7g
(saturated 2g)
PROTEIN 28g
CARBOHYDRATE 33g
CHOLESTEROL 70mg
SODIUM 686mg

2 pounds round steak, trimmed and cut into 1-inch cubes
2 large onions, chopped
2 garlic cloves, minced
1 (15-ounce) can enchilada sauce
1 (14 1/2-ounce) can diced tomatoes, undrained
1 (4-ounce) can green chilies, chopped
1/4 teaspoon pepper
2 tablespoons all-purpose flour
1/4 cup cold water
8 fat-free flour tortillas
Optional garnishes: diced tomatoes, sliced ripe olives, shredded fat-free Cheddar cheese, nonfat sour cream, chopped green onions and/or shredded lettuce

IN a large skillet coated with nonstick cooking spray, brown meat over medium heat; drain. Add onions and garlic; cook and stir for 2 minutes.

ADD the enchilada sauce, tomatoes, chilies and pepper; bring to a boil. Reduce heat; cover and simmer for 2 hours or until meat is tender.

COMBINE flour and water; add to beef mixture, stirring constantly. Bring to a boil; cook and stir 1 minute or until thickened.

WARM tortillas; spoon 1/2 cup filling, off-center, on each one. Fold sides and bottom of tortilla over filling, then roll up.

SPOON additional filling over top of burritos. Serve immediately. Garnish as desired.

YIELD: 8 servings.

# Spinach Linguine

4   ounces spinach linguine, uncooked
1/2 cup evaporated skimmed milk
1/2 cup canned reduced-sodium chicken broth
1   tablespoon cornstarch
2   slices turkey bacon, cooked and crumbled
1/2 cup frozen peas, thawed
1/2 cup freshly-grated Parmesan cheese

COOK linguine according to package directions, omitting salt and fat; drain and keep warm.
COMBINE evaporated milk, broth and cornstarch in a small saucepan, stirring until smooth.
COOK over medium heat, stirring constantly, until mixture is thickened and bubbly.
STIR in peas and bacon, and toss with linguine.
SPRINKLE with cheese and serve immediately.
YIELD: 2 servings.

PER serving:
CALORIES 406
(19% from fat)
(saturated 3.7g)
PROTEIN 24.4g
CARBOHYDRATE 55.8g
FIBER 3.6g
CHOLESTEROL 28mg
SODIUM 794mg

# Steak Fajitas

3/4 pound lean flank steak
2   teaspoons ground cumin
2   teaspoons chili powder
1/4 teaspoon salt
1/8 teaspoon garlic powder
1/8 teaspoon black pepper
1/8 teaspoon ground red pepper
4   (8-inch) flour tortillas
1   teaspoon vegetable oil
2   cups sliced onion
1/3 cup green bell pepper strips
1/3 cup red bell pepper strips
1/3 cup yellow bell pepper strips
1   tablespoon lime juice
1/4 cup nonfat sour cream
Commercial green salsa (optional)
Cilantro sprigs (optional)

TRIM fat from steak.
SLICE steak diagonally across grain into thin strips.
COMBINE steak, cumin, chili powder, salt, garlic
powder, black pepper and ground red pepper in a
heavy-duty, zip-top plastic bag; seal bag and shake
well to coat.
HEAT the tortillas according to package directions.
HEAT oil in a large nonstick skillet over medium-
high heat until hot.
ADD steak, onion and bell pepper; sauté 6 minutes
or until steak is done.
REMOVE from heat; stir in lime juice.
DIVIDE evenly among warm tortillas, and roll up.
SERVE with sour cream.
GARNISH with green salsa and cilantro sprigs, if
desired.
YIELD: 4 servings (serving size: 1 fajita and 1 table-
spoon sour cream)

# Steak and Pepper Stir-Fry

1 pound lean flank steak
1/4 cup low-sodium soy sauce
1 tablespoon cornstarch
1 tablespoon dry sherry
1 teaspoon sugar
2 tablespoons dark sesame oil, divided
1 cup julienne-cut green bell pepper
1 cup julienne-cut red bell pepper
1 cup vertically -sliced onion
1/4 teaspoon salt
1/4 teaspoon dried crushed red pepper
1 tablespoon peeled, grated gingeroot
1/4 cup water
6 cups hot, cooked lo mein noodles (about
    16 ounces uncooked)

PER serving:
CALORIES 394
(29% from fat)
FAT 12.8g
(saturated 3.9g)
PROTEIN 22.2g
CARBOHYDRATE 45.3g
FIBER 3.2g
CHOLESTEROL 38mg
SODIUM 416mg

TRIM fat from steak. Cut steak diagonally with the grain into 2-inch-thick slices.
CUT slices diagonally across the grain into thin strips.
COMBINE steak, soy sauce, cornstarch, sherry and sugar in a bowl; stir until well blended.
COVER and marinate in refrigerator 15 minutes.
HEAT 1 tablespoon oil in a wok or large nonstick skillet over high heat until hot.
ADD bell pepper, onion, salt and crushed red pepper; stir-fry 1 minute.
REMOVE bell pepper mixture from pan; set aside.
ADD remaining oil, steak mixture and gingeroot to pan; stir-fry 2 minutes.
RETURN bell pepper mixture to pan and stir in water; stir-fry 1 minute.
SERVE with lo mein noodles.
YIELD: 6 servings (serving size: 1 cup steak mixture and 1 cup noodles)

# Stuffed Artichokes

2   medium-size fresh artichokes
Lemon wedge
1 1/2 tablespoons fresh lemon juice
1   cup sliced fresh mushrooms
Olive oil-flavored vegetable cooking spray
3 ounces lean cooked ham, cut into strips
1   tablespoon dry vermouth or evaporated
      skim milk
1/4 cup evaporated skim milk
2   tablespoons fresh chives
1/2 cup (2 ounces) shredded reduced-fat Swiss
      cheese

WASH artichokes. Cut off stem end; trim about 1/2-inch from top of each artichoke.
REMOVE any loose bottom leaves.
TRIM one-fourth off top of each outer leaf; rub top and edges of leaves with lemon wedge.
PLACE artichokes in a large nonaluminum Dutch oven; cover with water and add lemon juice.
BRING to a boil; cover, reduce heat and simmer 35 minutes or until outer leaves pull out easily; drain.
SPREAD leaves apart gently to reach center; scrape out the fuzzy thistle center (choke) with a spoon.
PLACE artichokes in a pan; set aside.
COOK mushrooms in a large skillet coated with cooking spray, over medium-high heat, 3 minutes; stir.
ADD ham, and cook 3 minutes, stirring often.
ADD vermouth and milk; cook 3 minutes.
REMOVE from heat; stir in chives and cheese.
SPOON sauce over artichokes.
BROIL 5 1/2-inches from heat (with electric oven door partially opened), 3 minutes or until golden.
YIELD: 2 servings.

A lot of people feel artichokes to be too much work to prepare. Try them once, and you won't mind.

# Stuffing and Chicken

6   (4-ounce) skinned and boned chicken
      breast halves
Vegetable cooking spray
1/8 teaspoon garlic powder
1/8 teaspoon pepper
1   cup (4 ounces) shredded reduced-fat Swiss
      cheese
1   (10 3/4-ounce) can reduced-fat cream of
      chicken soup, undiluted
1/4 cup skim milk
3/4 cup reduced-sodium stuffing mix for
      chicken

PLACE chicken in a 13x9x2-inch baking dish coated
with cooking spray; sprinkle with garlic powder
and pepper.
TOP each chicken breast evenly with cheese; set
aside.
COMBINE soup and milk, stirring until smooth;
pour over chicken.
SPRINKLE with stuffing mix, and lightly coat with
cooking spray.
COVER and bake at 350 degrees for 50 minutes, or
until chicken is done.
YIELD: 6 servings

PER serving:
CALORIES 243
(25% from fat)
FAT 6.7g
(saturated 2.9g)
PROTEIN 35.0g
CARBOHYDRATE 9.1g
FIBER 0.4g
CHOLESTEROL 84mg
SODIUM 561mg

# Stuffed Shrimp with Hollandaise Sauce

24 unpeeled jumbo fresh shrimp
Vegetable cooking spray
1   medium onion, finely chopped
1/2 red bell pepper, finely chopped
1/2 green bell pepper, finely chopped
2   cloves garlic, minced
1/2 cup fine, dry bread crumbs
1   tablespoon Creole seasoning
1   egg white, lightly beaten
1/3 cup reduced-calorie mayonnaise
1   pound frozen crawfish tails, thawed
        and chopped
2   tablespoons lemon juice
2   tablespoons dry white wine
Hollandaise sauce

PEEL shrimp, leaving tails on; devein, if desired.
BUTTERFLY by making a deep slit down the back of each from the large end to the tail, cutting to, but not through, the inside curve. Set aside.
COAT a large saucepan with cooking spray; place over medium-high heat until hot.
ADD onion and next 3 ingredients; cook until tender, stirring often.
STIR in bread crumbs and seasoning.
COMBINE egg white, mayonnaise and crawfish; stir into onion mixture.
STUFF slit in each shrimp with crawfish mixture; arrange on an aluminum foil-lined 15x10x1-inch jellyroll pan.
COMBINE lemon juice and wine; drizzle over shrimp.
BAKE, uncovered, at 400 degrees for 20 minutes.
SERVE with Hollandaise Sauce.
YIELD: 8 servings

Continued on following page.

Continued from preceding page.

HOLLANDAISE SAUCE:
2/3 cup reduced-calorie mayonnaise
1/4 cup water
1/2 teaspoon grated lemon rind
1   tablespoon lemon juice
1/4 teaspoon salt

COMBINE all ingredients in a saucepan; stir with a wire whisk until mixture is smooth.
COOK over low heat, stirring constantly, 3 to 4 minutes or until thoroughly heated.
SERVE warm.
YIELD: 1 cup

PER serving:
CALORIES 260
(41% from fat)
FAT 11.8g
(saturated 2.1g)
PROTEIN 27.3g
CARBOHYDRATE 11.3g
FIBER 1.0g
CHOLESTEROL 261mg
SODIUM 982mg

# Sweet-Sour Shrimp

PER serving:
CALORIES 508
(11% from fat)
FAT 6.4g
(saturated 1g)
PROTEIN 23.5g
CARBOHYDRATE 87.2g
FIBER 2.2g
CHOLESTEROL 129mg
SODIUM 582mg

1   tablespoon cornstarch
1/4 teaspoon salt
1   egg white
1   pound large shrimp, peeled and
        deveined
1   (15 1/4-ounce) can unsweetened pineapple
chunks, undrained
1/3 cup water
3   tablespoons sugar
3   tablespoons ketchup
3   tablespoons cider vinegar
1   tablespoon dry sherry
2   teaspoons cornstarch
1   teaspoon dark sesame oil
1/4 teaspoon salt
1   tablespoon dark sesame oil
1/2 cup diced onion
1/3 cup diced fresh mushrooms
1/3 cup frozen green peas
4   cups hot, cooked rice (cooked without
        salt or fat)

COMBINE first 3 ingredients in a medium bowl; stir well with a wire whisk.
ADD shrimp; stir well.
COVER and marinate in refrigerator 15 minutes.
DRAIN pineapple, reserving 2 tablespoons juice.
COMBINE reserved pineapple juice, water and next 7 ingredients; stir until well-blended. Set aside.
REMOVE shrimp from marinade; discard marinade.
HEAT 1 tablespoon oil in wok or large nonstick skillet over medium-high heat until hot.
ADD shrimp; stir-fry 1 minute.
ADD onion and mushrooms; stir-fry 2 minutes.
ADD ketchup mixture and peas; stir-fry 1 minute or until thick and bubbly.
REMOVE from heat; stir in pineapple.
SERVE over rice.
YIELD: 4 servings (serving size: 1 cup shrimp mixture and 1 cup rice)

# Swiss Chicken Cutlets

2 thin-slices reduced-fat Swiss cheese
   (about 2 ounces)
4 chicken cutlets (4 ounces each),
   1/4-inch-thick
2 tablespoons all-purpose flour
1/2 teaspoon black pepper
1 tablespoon unsalted butter or margarine
1/2 cup reduced-sodium chicken broth
1/4 cup dry white wine or reduced-sodium
   chicken broth
1/4 teaspoon dried oregano
Chopped fresh parsley for garnish

CUT each cheese slice in half; place 1 half on top of each cutlet. Starting with a short end, tightly roll up cutlets, jellyroll-style. Tie securely with string.
ON waxed paper, combine flour and pepper; mix well. Add cutlets; toss gently to coat.
IN a large nonstick skillet, melt butter over medium heat. Add cutlets; cook, turning frequently, until golden, about 3 minutes.
ADD broth, wine and dried oregano to skillet, increase heat; bring to a boil.
REDUCE heat to medium-low; simmer until chicken is cooked through and sauce is slightly thickened, about 10 to 12 minutes.
PLACE on a serving plate; remove string.
GARNISH with parsley.
YIELD: 4 servings

PER serving:
CALORIES 223
(30% from fat)
FAT 7g
PROTEIN 32g
CARBOHYDRATE 4g
CHOLESTEROL 84mg
SODIUM 178mg

# Swiss Steak

PER serving:
CALORIES 258
(38% from fat)
FAT 11g
(saturated 3g)
PROTEIN 30g
CARBOHYDRATE 9g
CHOLESTEROL 82mg
SODIUM 313mg

1/4 cup all-purpose flour
1/4 teaspoon pepper
1 1/2 pounds round steak, trimmed
1 tablespoon cooking oil
1 cup chopped celery
1 cup chopped onion
1/2 pound fresh mushrooms, sliced
1 cup water
1 garlic clove, minced
1 tablespoon steak sauce

COMBINE flour and pepper. Cut steak into serving-size portions; dredge in flour mixture.
IN a skillet, brown steak in oil. Drain and place in a 2 1/2-quart casserole.
TOP with celery, onion and mushrooms.
COMBINE water, garlic and steak sauce; pour over vegetables.
COVER and bake at 350 degrees for 1 1/2 hours, or until meat is tender.
YIELD: 6 servings

# Turkey Casserole

8 ounces 90% lean turkey
1/2 cup chopped onion
3   full cups (10 ounces) frozen, shredded
        potatoes, thawed, or raw shredded
        potatoes
2   cups (one 16-ounce can) canned sliced
        carrots, rinsed and drained
1 3/4 cups (one 15-ounce can) chunky tomato
        sauce
1/8 teaspoon lemon pepper
1   teaspoon dried basil
1   cup frozen peas
3/4 cup (3 ounces) shredded reduced-fat
        Cheddar cheese

PER serving:
CALORIES 281
FAT 9g
PROTEIN 31g
SODIUM 1002mg

IN a skillet sprayed with butter-flavored cooking spray, sauté meat and onion until browned.
IN a large mixing bowl, combine potatoes, carrots, tomato sauce, lemon pepper and basil.
MIX in meat mixture, peas and Cheddar cheese; pour into an 8x8-inch baking dish, sprayed with butter-flavored cooking spray.
BAKE at 350 degrees for 20 to 30 minutes, or until cheese is melted and casserole is heated through.
YIELD: 4 servings

# Turkey Primavera

1/4 cup all-purpose flour
2   teaspoons minced fresh parsley
1 1/2 pounds turkey tenderloin, trimmed
       and cubed
1   tablespoon olive oil or vegetable oil
1/2 cup low-sodium chicken broth
1   cup sliced fresh mushrooms
1/2 cup chopped onion
4   garlic cloves, minced
1/2 medium green pepper, chopped
1 3/4 cups low-sodium beef broth
3/4 cup tomato purée
1/2 teaspoon dried thyme
1/2 teaspoon dried rosemary, crushed
1/2 teaspoon dried basil
1 bay leaf
1/8 teaspoon pepper
Hot cooked fettuccine or spaghetti
       (optional)

COMBINE flour and parsley; toss with turkey.

IN a skillet, brown turkey in oil; remove with a slotted spoon and set aside.

IN the same skillet, combine chicken broth, mushrooms, onion, garlic and green pepper; cook and stir for 3 to 4 minutes.

ADD beef broth, tomato purée and seasonings; cook and stir for 20 to 25 minutes, or until sauce is desired consistency.

ADD turkey, heat through. Remove bay leaf.

SERVE over pasta, if desired.

YIELD: 6 servings

# Vegetable Lasagna

9 lasagna noodles, uncooked
Olive oil-flavored vegetable cooking spray
1 (10-ounce) package frozen chopped
    spinach, thawed and well drained
2 cups sliced fresh mushrooms
1 cup grated carrot (about 1 large)
1/2 cup chopped onion
2 tablespoons water
1 (15-ounce) can tomato sauce
1 (12-ounce) can tomato paste
1 (4 1/2-ounce) can chopped green chilies,
    undrained
1 1/2 teaspoons dried oregano
2 cups nonfat cottage cheese
2 cups (8 ounces) shredded reduced-fat
    Monterey Jack cheese
1/4 cup grated Parmesan cheese

COOK noodles according to package directions,
omitting salt and fat.
DRAIN and set aside.
COAT a large nonstick skillet with cooking spray;
place over medium-high heat until hot.
ADD spinach and next 4 ingredients; cook, stirring
constantly, until tender.
STIR in tomato sauce and next 3 ingredients.
PLACE 5 noodles in a 13x9x2-inch baking dish coated
with vegetable spray.
LAYER with half each of cottage cheese, tomato
sauce mixture, Monterey Jack cheese and
Parmesan cheese.
REPEAT layers with remaining ingredients.
BAKE, uncovered, at 375 degrees for 30 minutes, or
until bubbly.
LET stand 10 minutes before serving.
YIELD: 8 servings

PER serving:
CALORIES 336
(20% from fat)
FAT 7.6g
(saturated 3.9g)
PROTEIN 26.3g
CARBOHYDRATE 44.0g
FIBER 5.7g
CHOLESTEROL 24mg
SODIUM 904mg

# Vegetable Skillet Supper with Turkey Meatballs

6 to 8 small red potatoes (about 1 pound), thinly sliced
Turkey Meatballs (see below)
2  medium sweet potatoes (about 1 pound), cut into thin wedges
1  medium onion, cut into wedges
1  medium red bell pepper, cut into 1-inch pieces
1  medium green bell pepper, cut into 1-inch pieces
2  tablespoons balsamic vinegar
1/2 teaspoon salt
1/4 teaspoon pepper
1  cucumber, halved lengthwise and sliced

PLACE potatoes in a large skillet; cover with water and bring to a boil.
COVER, reduce heat, and simmer 4 minutes or just until potatoes are tender.
DRAIN, place potatoes in a bowl; set aside.
ADD turkey meatballs, onion wedges and bell peppers to skillet; sauté 3 minutes.
ADD potatoes; cook 3 minutes, stirring gently.
REMOVE from heat; stir in vinegar, salt and pepper.
ADD cucumber; stir gently.
YIELD: 6 servings (serving size: 2 cups)

Continued on following page.

Continued from preceding page.

TURKEY MEATBALLS:
1   pound ground turkey or chicken
3   tablespoons fine, dry bread crumbs
1/2 teaspoon salt
1/4 teaspoon fennel seeds, crushed
1/4 teaspoon dried marjoram
1/4 teaspoon dried oregano
1/4 teaspoon thyme
1/4 teaspoon pepper
Dash of ground nutmeg
1   egg
1   garlic clove, crushed
Vegetable cooking spray

PREHEAT oven to 350 degrees.
COMBINE first 11 ingredients in a large bowl; stir well.
COAT hands with cooking spray and shape turkey mixture into 24 meatballs (mixture will be sticky).
PLACE meatballs on a baking sheet coated with cooking spray.
BAKE at 350 degrees for 8 minutes.
TURN meatballs over and bake an additional 8 minutes.
YIELD: 6 servings (serving size: 4 meatballs)

PER serving:
CALORIES 117
(24% from fat)
FAT 3.3g
(saturated 1g)
PROTEIN 18g
CARBOHYDRATE 2.7g
FIBER 0.2g
CHOLESTEROL 85mg
SODIUM 286mg

# Ziti with Sausage and Broccoli

PER serving:
CALORIES 420
(26% from fat)
FAT 12.3g
(saturated 1.0g)
PROTEIN 27.0g
CARBOHYDRATE 50.3g
FIBER 2.6g
CHOLESTEROL 62mg
SODIUM 776mg

3/4 pound turkey sausage links
Vegetable cooking spray
2  cloves garlic, crushed
1/2 teaspoon dried crushed red pepper
2  (14 1/2-ounce) cans diced tomatoes,
     undrained
8 ounces ziti pasta, uncooked
2  cups broccoli flowerets
3  tablespoons freshly-grated Parmesan
     cheese

CUT sausage diagonally into 1/2-inch-thick slices.
COOK sausage in a large nonstick skillet over medium-high heat until browned; remove sausage,
and set aside. Wipe skillet with paper towels.
COAT skillet with cooking spray; place over me-
dium heat until hot.
ADD garlic and pepper; cook, stirring constantly,
until lightly browned.
ADD sausage and tomatoes; cook until thoroughly
heated.
SET aside, and keep warm.
COOK pasta according to package directions, omit-
ting salt and fat, and adding broccoli during last 5
minutes of cooking time.
DRAIN and toss gently with sausage mixture and
cheese.
SERVE immediately.
YIELD: 4 servings

# Salads

# List Your Favorite Recipes

**Recipes**                               **Page**

_____   _____

_____   _____

_____   _____

_____   _____

_____   _____

_____   _____

_____   _____

_____   _____

_____   _____

_____   _____

_____   _____

_____   _____

_____   _____

_____   _____

_____   _____

_____   _____

_____   _____

_____   _____

# Apple Chicken Salad

1   medium apple, cored and chopped
1   cup diced cooked chicken breast
2   tablespoons fat-free mayonnaise
Lettuce leaf (optional)
2   tablespoons diced green pepper
1   teaspoon diced pimiento
Pinch crushed rosemary
Pinch lemon-pepper seasoning

IN a small bowl, combine the first seven ingredients. Chill until ready to serve.
PLACE lettuce on a serving plate and top with salad.
YIELD: 1 serving

PER serving:
CALORIES 238
(17% from fat)
FAT 5g
(saturated 1g)
PROTEIN 23g
CARBOHYDRATE 27g
CHOLESTEROL 85mg
SODIUM 228mg

# Black Bean and Corn Salad

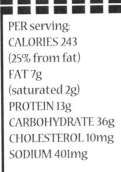

PER serving:
CALORIES 243
(25% from fat)
FAT 7g
(saturated 2g)
PROTEIN 13g
CARBOHYDRATE 36g
CHOLESTEROL 10mg
SODIUM 401mg

1 (15-ounce) can black beans, rinsed and
    drained
4 ounces reduced-fat Monterey Jack cheese,
    cut into 1/4-inch cubes
1 (8 3/4-ounce) can whole kernel corn,
    drained
1/4 cup sliced green onions with tops
3/4 cup thinly-sliced celery
1 small sweet red pepper, diced
3/4 cup picante sauce
2 tablespoons olive or vegetable oil
2 tablespoons lemon juice
1/2 teaspoon ground cumin
1 garlic clove, minced

COMBINE all ingredients in a large bowl; mix well.
COVER and chill several hours or overnight.
YIELD: 8 servings

# BLT Salad

DRESSING: Mix 24 hours before serving
1/2 cup nonfat sour cream
1/4 cup lite mayonnaise
1   tablespoon sugar
1/2 cup Parmesan cheese
1   teaspoon ranch dressing mix

SALAD:
1   head romaine lettuce
1   medium red onion, chopped
1   pint cherry tomatoes, halved
1   cup lean ham, diced
1   cup lite sharp Cheddar cheese, shredded

MIX dressing. Add skim milk to thin if desired.
Refrigerate
WASH and tear lettuce.
ADD chopped red onion, cherry tomatoes, ham
and cheese; toss.
TOP With dressing
YIELD: 8 servings

PER serving:
CALORIES 200
(41% from fat)
FAT 9g
SODIUM 273mg

# Broccoli Salad

PER serving:
CALORIES 145
(52% from fat)
FAT 8.4g
(saturated 1.2g)
PROTEIN 3.5g
CARBOHYDRATE 16.5g
CHOLESTEROL 11mg
SODIUM 250mg

1/2 cup raisins
2   pounds broccoli, cut into flowerets
1   cup purple seedless grapes, halved
3   green onions, thinly sliced
2/3 cup reduced-fat mayonnaise
2   tablespoons tarragon vinegar
2   tablespoons slivered almonds, toasted
4   slices turkey bacon, cooked and crumbled

SOAK raisins in hot water 5 minutes; drain.
COMBINE raisins and next 3 ingredients in a large
bowl. Combine mayonnaise and vinegar; stir into
broccoli mixture. Cover and chill.
STIR in almonds and bacon just before serving.
YIELD: 8 servings

# Caesar Salad with Bagel Croutons

4    cups (1/2-inch) cubed bagel (about 2 bagels)
Olive oil-flavored vegetable cooking spray
8    cups sliced romaine lettuce
2    tablespoons freshly-grated Parmesan
        cheese
Creamy Caesar Dressing

PREHEAT oven to 300 degrees.
PLACE bagel cubes on a baking sheet coated with cooking spray.
BAKE at 300 degrees for 15 minutes or until toasted.
COMBINE lettuce, cheese and croutons in a large bowl.
DRIZZLE Creamy Caesar Dressing over salad; toss well.
SERVE immediately.
YIELD: 8 servings (serving size: 1 cup)

PER serving:
CALORIES: 82
(30% from fat)
FAT 2.7g
(saturated 0.6g)
PROTEIN 3.8g
CARBOHYDRATE 10.6g
FIBER 1.3g
CHOLESTEROL 2mg
SODIUM 23.3g

# Creamy Caesar Dressing

1/3 cup plain fat-free yogurt
2   tablespoons fresh lemon juice
1   tablespoon olive oil
2   teaspoons Worcestershire sauce
1   teaspoon Dijon mustard
1   teaspoon anchovy paste
1/2 teaspoon freshly-ground black pepper
1   clove garlic, minced

COMBINE all ingredients in a small bowl and stir well with a whisk.
YIELD: 1/2 cup (serving size: 1 tablespoon)

# Chicken Cabbage Salad

6  ounces cooked chicken breast, cubed
2  tablespoons sesame seeds
2  tablespoons slivered almonds
1 1/2 cups red cabbage, shredded
1 1/2 cups green cabbage, shredded
1  medium onion, chopped

DRESSING:
3  packets artificial sweetener
2  tablespoons salad oil
1  teaspoon salt
1/2 teaspoon pepper
3  tablespoons vinegar
1/4 cup water
1  tablespoon caraway seed
1  package low-fat Ramen noodles, toasted
    (discard sauce)

COMBINE first 6 ingredients in a large bowl.
MIX together next 7 ingredients to make the dressing. Pour over vegetables and mix well.
ADD noodles just before serving.
YIELD: 6 servings

PER serving:
CALORIES 260
(9g from fat)
FAT 31g
SODIUM 863mg

# Chicken Noodle Salad

1   (3-ounce) package low-fat Oriental-flavored
        Ramen noodle soup mix
2   cups water
1   tablespoon reduced-calorie mayonnaise
2   teaspoons low-sodium soy sauce
1   teaspoon lemon juice
1/4 teaspoon ground red pepper
1   stalk celery, chopped
1   large carrot, scraped and chopped
3   green onions, chopped
1/2 cup chopped green bell pepper
1/2 cup chopped cooked chicken breast
        (skinned before cooking and cooked
        without salt)

REMOVE seasoning packet from soup mix.
BRING water to a boil; stir in noodles and cook 3
minutes; drain and set aside.
COMBINE mayonnaise and next 3 ingredients; add
to noodles, toss gently.
COMBINE 1/2 seasoning packet from soup mix, celery and remaining 4 ingredients in a medium bowl;
reserve remaining 1/2 seasoning packet for another
use. Add noodles and seasoned vegetables and toss.
Cover and chill.
YIELD: 2 servings

# Coleslaw

1/4 cup reduced-calorie mayonnaise
2  tablespoons cider vinegar
2  tablespoons grated onion
1/2 tsp. salt
1/4 teaspoon pepper
2  cups thinly-sliced green cabbage
2  cups thinly-sliced red cabbage
1/2 cup red bell pepper strips
1/2 cup yellow bell pepper strips
1/2 cup coarsely-shredded carrot
1/4 cup raisins

COMBINE first 5 ingredients in a medium bowl; stir well.
ADD green cabbage and remaining ingredients; toss mixture gently to coat.
COVER and chill 20 minutes.
YIELD: 5 servings (serving size: 1 cup)

PER serving:
CALORIES 80
(29% from fat)
FAT 2.6g
PROTEIN 1.3g
CARBOHYDRATE 14.2g
FIBER 2.5g
CHOLESTEROL 0mg
SODIUM 378mg

# Corn Salad

2   (11-ounce) cans white shoepeg corn, drained
1   green bell pepper, chopped
1/2 chopped purple onion
1/2 cup nonfat sour cream
1   tablespoon white vinegar
1/4 teaspoon celery salt
1/8 teaspoon pepper

COMBINE all ingredients, stirring well. Cover and chill at least 3 hours. Serve with a slotted spoon
YIELD: 8 servings

# Crab Salad

3 cups cooked rice
1 1/2 cups coarsely-chopped imitation crab
1 cup fat-free mayonnaise
1/2 cup finely-chopped green pepper
1/2 cup finely-chopped onion
1/2 cup finely-chopped celery
Leaf lettuce
Lemon slices or wedges (optional)

IN a bowl, combine rice, crab, mayonnaise, green pepper, onion and celery. Pack into a 6-cup mold coated with nonstick cooking spray.
CHILL 6 hours or overnight. Unmold onto a lettuce-lined platter.
GARNISH with lemon if desired.
YIELD: 6 servings

PER serving:
CALORIES 198
(3% from fat)
FAT 1g
(saturated trace)
PROTEIN 7g
CARBOHYDRATE 41g
CHOLESTEROL 7mg
SODIUM 791mg

# Cranberry Salad

PER serving:
CALORIES 80
(2% from fat)
FAT 0.2g
(saturated 0.0g)
PROTEIN 0.8g
CARBOHYDRATE 19.0g
CHOLESTEROL 0mg
SODIUM 43mg

2   cups fresh or frozen cranberries, thawed
1/2 cup sugar
1   (0.3-ounce) package sugar-free lemon-
       flavored gelatin
1   cup boiling water
1   cup chopped celery
1   cup chopped Granny Smith apple
Vegetable cooking spray
Green leaf lettuce (optional)
Garnishes: celery leaves, cranberries

POSITION knife blade in food processor bowl; add
cranberries. Process 30 seconds or until chopped.
COMBINE gelatin and boiling water in a large bowl;
stir 2 minutes or until gelatin dissolves. CHILL until
the consistency of unbeaten egg whites.
STIR cranberry mixture, celery and apple into gelatin mixture. Pour mixture into a 4-cup mold coated
with cooking spray; cover and chill until firm.
UNMOLD salad onto a lettuce-lined serving plate, if
desired.
GARNISH, if desired.
YIELD: 8 servings

# Fruit Salad with Poppy Seed Dressing

4   oranges
4   pink grapefruit
2   cups purple or red seedless grapes
1   purple onion
2   heads Bibb lettuce
1/4 cup sliced almonds, toasted
Poppy Seed Dressing

PEEL and section oranges and grapefruit; cut grapes in half. Cut onion into thin slices; separate into rings.
LINE individual serving plates with lettuce leaves. Arrange fruit, sliced onion and toasted almonds over lettuce. Drizzle with Poppy Seed Dressing; serve immediately.
YIELD: 8 servings

POPPY SEED DRESSING
1/2 cup sugar
1   teaspoon dry mustard
1/3 cup cider vinegar
2   tablespoons chopped onion
1/2 cup reduced-fat mayonnaise
1/2 cup nonfat sour cream
1 1/2 tablespoons poppy seeds

COMBINE all ingredients, stirring with a wire whisk. Serve immediately or cover and store in refrigerator. Allow to come to room temperature before serving.
YIELD: 1 2/3 cups

PER serving:
CALORIES 201
(31% from fat)
FAT 6.9g
(saturated 0.9)
PROTEIN 3.6g
CARBOHYDRATE 34.9g
CHOLESTEROL 5mg
SODIUM 121mg

# Garden Vegetable Salad

2   cups cooked rotini (corkscrew pasta)
1   cup broccoli florets
1   cup quartered cherry tomatoes
3/4 cup diced lean ham (3 ounces)
1/2 cup sliced carrot
1/2 cup vertically-sliced red onion
1/3 cup sliced ripe olives
1/4 cup grated Parmesan cheese
2   teaspoons dried basil
2   teaspoons dried parsley flakes
1/4 cup fat-free sour cream
1/4 cup low-fat buttermilk
1/4 cup light ranch dressing

COMBINE first 10 ingredients in a bowl.
COMBINE sour cream, buttermilk and dressing;
stir well.
POUR over salad; toss to coat.
YIELD: 7 servings (serving size: 1 cup)

# Ginger Melon Compote

1 1/2 cups water
3/4 cup sugar
2 tablespoons peeled, coarsely-chopped fresh
    ginger root
6 whole cloves
6 whole allspice
2 cups seeded, cubed watermelon
1 cup peeled, cubed cantaloupe
1 cup blueberries

COMBINE water, sugar, ginger root, cloves and all-
spice in a small saucepan; bring to a boil.
REDUCE heat, and simmer 15 minutes or until sugar
dissolves, stirring occasionally.
STRAIN sugar syrup through a sieve into a bowl;
discard solids.
COVER sugar syrup and chill.
DIVIDE watermelon, cantaloupe and blueberries
evenly among 6 dessert dishes.
SPOON 1/4 cup sugar syrup over each serving.
YIELD: 6 servings

PER serving:
CALORIES 137
(3% from fat)
FAT 0.4g
(saturated 0.2g)
PROTEIN 0.7g
CARBOHYDRATE 34.4g
FIBER 1.7g
CHOLESTEROL 0mg
SODIUM 5mg

# Greens and Grapefruit Salad

PER serving:
CALORIES 60
(23% from fat)
FAT 1.5g
(saturated 0.1g)
PROTEIN 2.2g
CARBOHYDRATE 9.7g
CHOLESTEROL 0mg
SODIUM 185mg

8  cups loosely-packed, torn mixed salad
    greens
2  heads radicchio, separated into leaves
1  medium-size purple onion, thinly sliced
2  tablespoons chopped fresh basil
2  pink grapefruit, peeled and sectioned
Dijon Vinaigrette
3  tablespoons sunflower kernels

COMBINE first 6 ingredients in a large bowl; drizzle with 3/4 cup Dijon Vinaigrette. Sprinkle with sunflower kernels. Serve with remaining vinaigrette.
YIELD: 12 servings

DIJON VINAIGRETTE:
1/2 cup red wine vinegar
1/4 cup Dijon mustard
2  tablespoons lime juice
1/4 teaspoon freshly ground pepper
1/4 cup water
1/2 cup canned no-salt-added chicken broth
2  tablespoons sugar

COMBINE all ingredients in container of an electric blender; process until smooth, stopping once to scrape down sides.
YIELD: 1 3/4 cups

# Ham and Potato Salad

1  pound small round red potatoes, cut into
     1/2-inch wedges (about 3 cups)
1  (16-ounce) package frozen mixed
     vegetables
1/3 cup reduced-fat mayonnaise
1/3 cup nonfat sour cream
1/2 cup sliced green onions
1/2 teaspoon pepper
1/2 teaspoon salt
1 1/2 cups diced, lean cooked ham

COVER and cook potato in boiling water to cover
for 10 minutes or until tender (do not overcook);
drain and set aside.

COOK frozen mixed vegetables according to package
directions, omitting salt and fat; drain and set
aside.

COMBINE mayonnaise and next 4 ingredients in a
large bowl. Gently stir in potato, vegetables and
ham. Cover and chill at least 8 hours.

YIELD: 6 servings

PER serving:
CALORIES 207
(27% from fat)
FAT 6.1g
(saturated 1.3g)
PROTEIN 13.1g
CARBOHYDRATE 25.2g
CHOLESTEROL 30 mg
SODIUM 924 mg

# Low-Fat Potato Salad

PER serving:
CALORIES 55
FAT trace
PROTEIN 2g
CARBOHYDRATE 11g
CHOLESTEROL 0mg
SODIUM 147mg

2 pounds red potatoes, cubed
1/2 cup Italian salad dressing
1 cup chopped celery
1/2 cup chopped green pepper
1/2 cup chopped red onion
1/2 cup thinly-sliced radishes (optional)
1/4 cup minced fresh parsley
1 teaspoon salt (optional)
12 teaspoon pepper
1/2 cup mayonnaise
1 1/2 teaspoons Dijon mustard
1/4 teaspoon sugar

COOK potatoes in boiling water until tender, about 15 to 20 minutes; drain thoroughly.
PLACE in a bowl; cool slightly.
POUR salad dressing over warm potatoes; toss to coat.
ADD celery, green pepper, onion, radishes, parsley, salt if desired, and pepper; mix well.
COMBINE mayonnaise, mustard and sugar; pour over potato mixture and toss to coat.
COVER and refrigerate for at least 2 hours.
YIELD: 14 servings (serving size: 1/2 cup)

# Marinated Mushroom Salad

2 1/2 quarts water
3   tablespoons lemon juice
3   pounds small fresh mushrooms
2   carrots, sliced
2   celery ribs, sliced
1/2 medium green pepper, chopped
1   small onion, chopped
1   tablespoon minced fresh parsley
1/2 cup sliced stuffed olives
1   (2 1/4 oz.) can sliced ripe olives, drained

DRESSING:
1/2 cup fat-free Italian salad dressing
1/2 cup red or white wine vinegar
1   garlic clove, minced
1/2 teaspoon dried oregano

IN a large saucepan, bring water and lemon juice
to a boil. Add mushrooms and cook for 3 minutes,
stirring occasionally. Drain; cool.
PLACE mushrooms in a large bowl with carrots,
celery, green pepper, onion, parsley and olives.
COMBINE all dressing ingredients in a small bowl
or a jar with tight-fitting lid; shake or mix well.
Pour over salad.
COVER and refrigerate overnight.
YIELD: 8 servings

PER serving:
CALORIES 87
(26% from fat)
FAT 3g
(saturated trace)
PROTEIN 4g
CARBOHYDRATE 14g
CHOLESTEROL 0mg
SODIUM 532mg

# Marinated Tomato and Brie Salad

PER serving:
CALORIES 143
(70% from fat)
FAT 11.1g
(saturated 5.1g)
PROTEIN 6.6g
CARBOHYDRATE 5.5g
CHOLESTEROL 27mg
SODIUM 249mg

1/2 (15-ounce) mini Brie
4   large tomatoes, seeded and cut into 1/2-inch
        cubes
1   cup fresh basil, cut into 1/8-inch-wide strips
4   cloves garlic, crushed
2   tablespoons olive oil
1/4 teaspoon salt
1/2 teaspoon freshly-ground ginger
1/2 teaspoon freshly-ground pepper
Garnish: fresh basil sprigs, if desired

REMOVE and discard ring from Brie; cut Brie into 3/4-inch cubes.
COMBINE Brie, tomato and next 6 ingredients; cover and let stand at room temperature 30 minutes.
GARNISH, if desired
YIELD: 8 servings.

NOTE: a vegetable peeler removes the rind from Brie easily.

# Mixed Green Salad with Parmesan Walnuts

3/4 cup walnut pieces
Butter-flavored vegetable cooking spray
2   tablespoons grated nonfat parmesan
        cheese
4   cups loosely packed torn iceberg lettuce
4   cups loosely packed torn leaf lettuce
3   cups loosely packed torn curly endive
3   cups loosely packed torn fresh spinach
2   cups loosely packed torn watercress
1/2 cup fat-free balsamic vinaigrette

PLACE walnuts in an 8-inch square pan. Coat walnuts with cooking spray.
BAKE at 350 degrees for 5 minutes. Sprinkle with cheese, tossing to coat. Bake 4 to 5 additional minutes or until cheese is lightly browned. Cool completely.
COMBINE iceberg lettuce and next 5 ingredients; toss gently to coat. Top with walnuts and serve immediately.
YIELD: 8 servings

PER serving:
CALORIES 101
(52% from fat)
FAT 5.8g
(saturated 0.4g)
PROTEIN 3.5g
CARBOHYDRATE 9.5g
CHOLESTEROL 0mg
SODIUM 270mg

# Orange-Carrot Salad

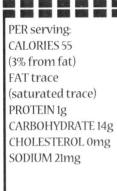

PER serving:
CALORIES 55
(3% from fat)
FAT trace
(saturated trace)
PROTEIN 1g
CARBOHYDRATE 14g
CHOLESTEROL 0mg
SODIUM 21mg

3 cups shredded carrots
2 medium oranges, peeled
3 tablespoons lemon juice
1 tablespoon sugar
1 teaspoon ground cinnamon

PLACE carrots in a medium bowl. Section oranges into the bowl to catch juices.
ADD remaining ingredients and mix well.
COVER and chill for several hours.
YIELD: 6 servings

# Orange-Buttermilk Salad

1   (20 ounce) can unsweetened crushed
      pineapple, undrained
1   (0.6-ounce) package sugar-free orange-
      flavored gelatin
2   cups nonfat buttermilk
1   (8-ounce) container frozen reduced-calorie
      whipped topping, thawed
1/3 cup finely-chopped pecans
Vegetable cooking spray
16  lettuce leaves

BRING pineapple and juice to a boil in a medium
saucepan. Remove from heat; add gelatin. Stir 2
minutes or until gelatin dissolves; cool.
ADD buttermilk to pineapple mixture; chill until
consistency of unbeaten egg white. Fold in whipped
topping and pecans.
SPOON mixture into a 9-cup mold coated with
cooking spray; cover and chill until firm. UNMOLD
onto a lettuce-lined serving plate.
YIELD: 16 servings

PER serving:
CALORIES 85
(39% from fat)
FAT 3.7g
(saturated 0.7g)
PROTEIN 2.7g
CARBOHYDRATE 11.1g
CHOLESTEROL 1mg
SODIUM 49mg

# Pasta-Vegetable Salad

PER serving:
CALORIES 124
(9% from fat)
FAT 1.2g
(saturated 0.4g)
PROTEIN 4.3g
CARBOHYDRATE 24.0g
CHOLESTEROL 2mg
SODIUM 343mg

6   ounces tricolor rotini pasta, uncooked
1   pound broccoli, cut into flowerets
3   stalks celery, sliced
1   (8-ounce) can sliced water chestnuts,
        drained
1   (1..05-ounce) package fat-free Italian
        dressing mix
3   tablespoons chopped fresh oregano
3/4 cup sliced radishes
1/3 cup crumbled reduced-fat Feta cheese

PREPARE pasta according to package directions, omitting salt and fat; drain. Rinse with cold water; drain.
COMBINE pasta, broccoli, celery and water chestnuts in a bowl; set aside.
PREPARE dressing mix according to package directions; stir in oregano. Pour over pasta mixture, stirring just to coat. Cover and chill at least 6 hours. Just before serving, stir in radishes and sprinkle with cheese.
YIELD: 9 servings

# Potato Salmon Salad

8   small red potatoes (about 1 pound),
        quartered
1/2 teaspoon salt
1/2 teaspoon pepper
1 1/2 pound salmon fillet (1-inch thick)
Vegetable cooking spray
1   cup (1/2-inch-thick) slices onion
1   cup julienne-cut red bell pepper
1/4 cup chopped fresh cilantro
2   teaspoons seeded, minced jalapeño pepper
1/4 cup white wine vinegar
1/2 teaspoon grated lime rind
2   tablespoons fresh lime juice
1   teaspoon dried oregano
1/2 teaspoon pepper
4   cups mixed salad greens

PLACE potatoes in a saucepan; cover with water
and bring to a boil. Reduce heat; simmer 15 min-
utes or until potatoes are tender. Drain set aside.
SPRINKLE salt and 1/2 teaspoon pepper over salmon
fillet.
COAT a large nonstick skillet with cooking spray;
place over medium-high heat until hot.
ADD fillet; cook 5 minutes.
TURN fillet over; add onion and cook 5 minutes.
REMOVE fillet from skillet; set aside.
COOK onion an additional 3 minutes or until golden;
remove and set aside.
ADD potatoes to skillet; sauté over high heat 3
minutes or until browned.
REMOVE from heat; set aside.
FLAKE salmon into bite-size pieces.
COMBINE salmon, onion, potatoes, bell pepper,
cilantro and jalapeño pepper in a bowl.
COMBINE vinegar and next 4 ingredients in a small
bowl; stir well.
DRIZZLE vinegar mixture over salmon mixture;
toss gently to coat.
SERVE on a bed of mixed greens.
YIELD: 4 servings (serving size: 2 cups)

PER serving:
CALORIES 404
(34% from fat)
FAT 15.2g
(saturated 2.6g)
PROTEIN 40.2g
CARBOHYDRATE 25.6g
FIBER 3.7g
CHOLESTEROL 115mg
SODIUM 397mg

# Raspberry-Applesauce Salad

PER serving:
CALORIES 155
(13% from fat)
FAT 2g
(saturated trace)
PROTEIN 2g
CARBOHYDRATE 34g
CHOLESTEROL 0mg
SODIUM 38mg

1  (8-ounce) can unsweetened crushed
      pineapple
1  (10-ounce) package frozen unsweetened
      raspberries, thawed
1  (3-ounce) package raspberry gelatin
1  cup applesauce
3  tablespoons coarsely-chopped pecans
Fat-free mayonnaise (optional)

DRAIN pineapple and raspberries, reserving juices.
Place fruit in a large bowl; set aside.
ADD enough water to the juice to measure 1 cup.
Pour into a saucepan; bring to a boil. Remove from
heat; stir in gelatin until dissolved. Pour over fruit
mixture.
ADD the applesauce and pecans.
POUR into a 1-quart bowl. Chill until set.
SPOON into individual dessert dishes; top with a
dollop of mayonnaise, if desired.
YIELD: 6 servings

# Roasted Onion Salad

5 medium onions, unpeeled and cut into
    1/2-inch-thick slices
Olive oil-flavored vegetable cooking spray
8 cups loosely packed mixed baby lettuces
1/4 cup chopped walnuts, toasted
1/2 cup crumbled blue cheese
Garlic Vinaigrette

ARRANGE onion slices in a roasting pan coated
with cooking spray. Coat slices lightly with cooking spray.
BAKE, uncovered, at 500 degrees for 20 minutes or
until onion slices are lightly charred; cool. Remove
and discard outer skin of onion slices. Set slices
aside.
COMBINE lettuces, walnuts and blue cheese; toss
gently. Top with roasted onion slices; drizzle with
Garlic Vinaigrette.
YIELD: 8 servings

GARLIC VINAIGRETTE:
2 cloves garlic
1 tablespoon chopped shallot
1/4 cup chopped fresh parsley
1/4 teaspoon dried crushed red pepper
1/4 teaspoon salt
1/2 teaspoon freshly ground black pepper
2 tablespoons white wine vinegar
1/2 cup plus 1 tablespoon canned vegetable
    broth
2 1/2 tablespoons olive oil

POSITION knife blade in food processor bowl; add
garlic and shallot and pulse 3 or 4 times.
ADD parsley and next 5 ingredients; process 20
seconds, stopping once to scrape down sides.
POUR olive oil through food chute in a slow steady
stream with processor running; process until
blended.
YIELD: 1 cup

PER serving:
CALORIES 121
(64% from fat)
FAT 8.6g
(saturated 2.0g)
PROTEIN 4.2g
CARBOHYDRATE 7.0g
CHOLESTEROL 5mg
SODIUM 259mg

# Strawberry and Stilton Salad

PER serving:
CALORIES 158
(23% from fat)
FAT 4g
(saturated 1.5g)
PROTEIN 5.3g
CARBOHYDRATE 25.1 g
FIBER 3.1g
CHOLESTEROL 7mg
SODIUM 275mg

2   cups sliced strawberries
2   tablespoons chopped fresh basil
2   tablespoons raspberry vinegar
1   teaspoon olive oil
1   teaspoon water
4   cups gourmet salad greens
1/4 cup crumbled Stilton or Feta cheese
4   (1-ounce) slices French bread

COMBINE first 3 ingredients in a medium bowl;
toss well to coat.
COVER and refrigerate for 1 hour.
STRAIN mixture through a sieve into a jar, reserving liquid.
SET strawberries aside.
ADD oil and water to jar; cover tightly and shake vigorously.
ARRANGE 1 cup greens on each of 4 salad plates.
TOP with 1/2 cup berries, 2 teaspoons dressing and 1 tablespoon cheese.
SERVE with French bread.
YIELD: 4 servings

# Taffy Apple Salad

1 tablespoon cornstarch
2 egg whites
2 tablespoons apple cider vinegar
1 (8-ounce) can crushed pineapple in its own juice, drained, and juices reserved
4 cups unpeeled apples, diced
1/2 cup raisins
6 packets artificial sweetener
1 cup lite Cool Whip
3 tablespoons sesame seeds, toasted
1 teaspoon cinnamon

COMBINE first 3 ingredients and pineapple juice in saucepan.
COOK over low heat, stirring constantly until thick. Set aside to cool.
IN a large bowl, combine apples, pineapple and raisins.
ADD artificial sweetener to the cooled fruit sauce, pour over fruit and add Cool Whip. Mix thoroughly.
SPRINKLE with sesame seeds and cinnamon.
YIELD: 8 servings

PER serving:
CALORIES 120
(23% from fat)
FAT 3g
SODIUM 28mg

# Three-Bean Salad with Balsamic Dressing

2 1/2 cups (2-inch) sliced green beans (about 1/2 pound)
1/3 cup balsamic vinegar
1   tablespoon dried parsley flakes
1   teaspoon dried basil
2   tablespoons grated Parmesan cheese
1   teaspoon dried dillweed
1   tablespoon olive oil
1/2 teaspoon garlic powder
1/4 teaspoon salt
1/4 teaspoon pepper
1 1/2 cups sliced carrots
1/2 cup vertically sliced red onion
1   (15 1/2-ounce) can garbanzo beans, drained
1   (15-ounce) can kidney beans, drained
1   (14-ounce) can artichoke hearts, drained and coarsely chopped
1   large tomato, cut into 16 wedges
Dillweed sprigs (optional)

ARRANGE green beans in a steamer basket over boiling water.
COVER and steam 2 minutes.
RINSE under cold water; drain well.
COMBINE vinegar and next 8 ingredients in a large bowl; stir well.
ADD green beans, carrot and next 4 ingredients; toss gently to coat.
SERVE with tomato wedges; garnish with dillweed sprigs, if desired.
YIELD: 8 servings (serving size: 1 cup)

# Tossed Bacon
# and Pea Salad

16  cups torn salad greens
1   (16-ounce) package frozen peas, thawed
1   large red onion, thinly sliced into rings
4   celery ribs, thinly sliced
1   (12-ounce) block reduced-fat Cheddar
       cheese, julienned
12  turkey bacon strips, cooked and crumbled
1/2 cup fat-free sour cream
1/2 cup fat-free mayonnaise
1   tablespoon Dijon mustard
2   teaspoons sugar
1/2 teaspoon ground nutmeg
1/4 teaspoon pepper

IN a large salad bowl, toss the greens, peas, onions,
celery, cheese and bacon.
IN a small bowl, combine remaining ingredients;
pour over salad and toss to coat.
SERVE immediately.
YIELD: 16 servings

PER serving:
CALORIES 111
(19% from fat)
FAT 2g
(saturated 1g)
PROTEIN 13g
CARBOHYDRATE 11g
CHOLESTEROL 12mg
SODIUM 436 mg

# Turkey-Peanut Salad

PER serving:
CALORIES 236
(20% from fat)
FAT 6g
(saturated 1g)
PROTEIN 26g
CARBOHYDRATE 23g
CHOLESTEROL 63mg
SODIUM 361mg

2   cups diced, cooked turkey breast
1   cup unsweetened pineapple chunks, well
        drained
1   cup diced celery
1   cup seedless green grapes
1/2 cup sliced green onions
1/4 cup reduced-fat honey-roasted peanuts
2/3 cup fat-free mayonnaise
2   tablespoons prepared chutney
1   tablespoon lime juice
1/2 teaspoon curry powder

IN a bowl, toss the first 6 ingredients.
IN a small bowl, combine mayonnaise, chutney, lime juice and curry; pour over turkey mixture and mix gently. Chill.
YIELD: 4 servings

# Tuna Salad with Wild Rice

1   (6-ounce) package long-grain and wild rice
      mix
1   (12-ounce) can solid white tuna in spring
      water, drained and flaked
1/2 cup reduced-fat mayonnaise
1/2 cup finely-chopped celery
1/4 cup nonfat sour cream
1/4 cup unsalted roasted cashews, chopped
2   tablespoons finely-chopped onion
2   teaspoons Mrs. Dash table blend seasoning
1/2 teaspoon salt
6 lettuce leaves
3/4 cup alfalfa sprouts (optional)
YIELD: 6 servings

COOK rice according to package directions, omitting seasoning packet; cover rice and chill completely.
ADD tuna and next 7 ingredients, stirring well.
Serve on lettuce leaves; top with alfalfa sprouts, if
desired.
YIELD: 6 servings

PER serving:
CALORIES 254
(32% from fat)
FAT 9.1g
(saturated 0.7g)
PROTEIN 17.4g
CARBOHYDRATE 26.2g
CHOLESTEROL 26mg
SODIUM 542mg

# Vegetable Salad with Creamy Feta Dressing

PER serving:
CALORIES 79
(41% from fat)
FAT 3.6g
(saturated 2.2g)
PROTEIN 3.9g
CARBOHYDRATE 9.1g
FIBER 2.3g
CHOLESTEROL 13 mg
SODIUM 180mg

1 1/4 cups seeded, diced tomato
1    cup peeled, seeded and diced cucumber
1    cup diced green bell pepper
1/2 cup diced red bell pepper
1/2 cup diced radishes
1/3 cup finely-chopped fresh parsley
1/4 cup finely-chopped green onions
Dash of ground red pepper
1/2 cup crumbled Feta cheese
2    tablespoons boiling water
3/4 teaspoon white wine vinegar
2 tablespoons plain fat-free yogurt

COMBINE first 8 ingredients in a large bowl; set aside.
PLACE cheese, boiling water and vinegar in a food processor; process until smooth.
ADD yogurt; process until blended.
POUR cheese mixture over vegetable mixture; toss well.
SERVE immediately.
YIELD: 4 servings (serving size: 1 cup)

# Warm Salmon Salad

3   cups cubed red potatoes
4   cups (1-inch) diagonally sliced asparagus
1/4 teaspoon salt
1/4 teaspoon pepper
1 1/2 pounds salmon fillet
2   teaspoons vegetable oil
8   cups gourmet salad greens
4   tablespoons sliced green onions
8   cherry tomatoes, quartered
2   tablespoons balsamic vinegar
2   tablespoons pesto basil sauce (such as
     Pesto Sanremo)

PER serving:
CALORIES 506
(39% from fat)
FAT 21.8g
(saturated 3.9g)
PROTEIN 46.1g
CARBOHYDRATE 33.9g
CHOLESTEROL 117mg
SODIUM 356 mg

PLACE potatoes in a large saucepan; cover with water and bring to a boil. Reduce heat; simmer 12 minutes. Add asparagus; cook 3 minutes or until potatoes are tender. Drain and set aside.

SPRINKLE salt and pepper over salmon. Heat oil in a medium nonstick skillet over medium-high heat until hot. Add salmon; cook 4 minutes on each side or until fish flakes easily when tested with a fork. Discard skin from salmon; flake salmon into chunks.

COMBINE salmon, potato mixture, salad greens, green onions and tomatoes in a bowl. Combine vinegar and pesto; drizzle over salad and toss gently.

YIELD: 4 servings

# Wild Rice Fruit Salad

DRESSING:
3  tablespoons olive or vegetable oil
1/2 cup orange juice
2  tablespoons honey

SALAD:
1  cup uncooked wild rice
2  Golden Delicious apples, chopped
Juice of 1 lemon
1  cup golden raisins
1  cup seedless red grapes, halved
2  tablespoons each minced fresh mint,
     parsley and chives
Pepper, to taste
1/3 cup chopped pecans

COMBINE dressing ingredients; set aside.
COOK rice according to package instructions; drain
if needed, and allow to cool.
IN a large bowl, toss apples with lemon juice. ADD
raisins, grapes, mint, parsley, chives and rice.
ADD dressing and toss. Season with pepper.
COVER and chill several hours or overnight. JUST
before serving, top with pecans.
YIELD: 10 servings

# Side Dishes
# and Vegetables

# List Your Favorite Recipes

**Recipes**                                      **Page**

_____      _____

_____      _____

_____      _____

_____      _____

_____      _____

_____      _____

_____      _____

_____      _____

_____      _____

_____      _____

_____      _____

_____      _____

_____      _____

_____      _____

_____      _____

_____      _____

_____      _____

_____      _____

# Asparagus with Garlic Cream

1   (8-ounce) carton reduced-fat sour cream
3   tablespoons skim milk
1   tablespoon white wine vinegar
2   cloves garlic, minced
1/8 teaspoon salt
1/8 teaspoon freshly-ground pepper
2   pounds fresh asparagus
2   teaspoons chopped fresh chives

STIR together first 6 ingredients. Cover and chill at least 2 hours.
SNAP off tough ends of asparagus; remove scales from stalks with a vegetable peeler, if desired.
COVER and cook asparagus in a small amount of boiling water 4 minutes, or until crisp-tender; drain. Plunge into ice water to stop the cooking process; drain. Cover and chill.
SERVE chilled asparagus on a serving platter. TOP with sauce, and sprinkle with chives.
YIELD: 8 servings

PER serving:
CALORIES 58
(56% from fat)
FAT 3.6g
(saturated 2.2g)
PROTEIN 2.7g
CARBOHYDRATE 5.0g
CHOLESTEROL 11mg
SODIUM 51mg

# Basil Green Beans

2   cups fresh green beans, cut into 2-inch
        pieces
2   tablespoons chopped onion
2   tablespoons chopped celery
1/4 cup water
1   tablespoon reduced-fat margarine
1 1/2 teaspoons minced fresh basil, or
        1/2 teaspoon dried basil
Pepper, to taste

IN a saucepan, combine beans, onion, celery and water. Cover and cook for 5 minutes, or until beans are tender.
DRAIN and add the margarine, basil and pepper; stir to coat. Serve immediately.
YIELD: 2 servings

# Broccoli-Cauliflower Gratin

1/3 cup dry bread crumbs
2   tablespoons (1/2-ounce) finely-shredded
      extra-sharp Cheddar cheese
2   cups each, small broccoli and cauliflower
      flowerets
Vegetable cooking spray
1   tablespoon reduced-calorie margarine,
      melted
1   tablespoon coarse-grained mustard
1/4 teaspoon white pepper

PREHEAT oven to 425 degrees.
COMBINE bread crumbs and Cheddar cheese; stir
bread crumb mixture well, and set aside.
ARRANGE broccoli and cauliflower in a steamer
basket over boiling water. Cover and steam for 4
minutes, or until vegetables are crisp-tender. Drain
vegetables, and place in a 1 1/2-quart casserole dish
coated with cooking spray.
COMBINE margarine, mustard and white pepper
in a small bowl; drizzle over broccoli and cauliflower, and toss well. Sprinkle bread crumb mixture over vegetables, and bake at 425 degrees for 8
minutes, or until thoroughly heated.
YIELD: 4 servings

PER serving:
CALORIES 90
(36% from fat)
FAT 3.6g
(saturated 1.1g)
PROTEIN 4.5g
CARBOHYDRATE 11.3g
CHOLESTEROL 4mg
SODIUM 174mg

# Broccoli with Stuffing

■ ■ ■ ■ ■ ■ ■

PER serving:
CALORIES 134
(28% from fat)
FAT 4.1g
(saturated 1.9g)
PROTEIN 8.9g
CARBOHYDRATE 16.1g
CHOLESTEROL 13mg
SODIUM 537mg

2  (10-ounce) packages frozen broccoli spears
Butter-flavored vegetable cooking spray
1  cup (4-ounce) shredded reduced-fat sharp
      Cheddar cheese
1/2 cup egg substitute
1  (10 3/4-ounce) can reduced-fat, reduced-
      sodium cream of mushroom soup,
      undiluted
1/2 cup nonfat mayonnaise
1/2 cup finely-choped onion
1  (16-ounce) can box reduce-sodium stuffing
      mix for chicken

COOK broccoli according to package directions;
drain.
ARRANGE broccoli in an 11 x 7 x 1 1/2-inch baking dish
coated with cooking spray. Sprinkle with cheese.
COMBINE egg substitute and next 3 ingredients;
spread over cheese.
COMBINE 3/4 cup stuffing mix and 2 1/2 teaspoons
of the mix's seasoning packet, tossing well. Reserve remaining stuffing mix and seasoning packet
for another use. Sprinkle over casserole; coat with
cooking spray.
BAKE at 350 degrees for 30 minutes, or until thoroughly heated.
YIELD: 8 serving

# Brussels Sprouts

1 small onion, sliced
1 tablespoon margarine
1 cup tomato juice
2 tablespoons all-purpose flour
1 teaspoon sugar
1/8 tsp. pepper
1 (10-ounce) package frozen Brussels sprouts,
    or 1 1/4 pounds fresh Brussels sprouts,
    cooked and drained
1/4 cup shredded reduced-fat Cheddar cheese

PER serving:
CALORIES 87
(37% from fat)
FAT 4g
(saturated 1g)
PROTEIN 2g
CARBOHYDRATE 15g
CHOLESTEROL 0mg
SODIUM 110mg

IN skillet, sauté onion in margarine until tender.
Remove onion and set aside.
COMBINE tomato juice and flour; add to skillet.
Cook and stir over low heat until thickened and
smooth. Stir in sugar, pepper and onion.
ARRANGE Brussels sprouts in a 1-quart baking dish
coated with nonstick cooking spray; top with the
tomato sauce.
BAKE, uncovered, at 350 degrees for 15 minutes.
Sprinkle with cheese. Let stand 5 minutes before
serving.
YIELD: 6 servings

# Cheese Fries

1 1/2 pounds baking potatoes, peeled and cut
    into thin strips
1   tablespoon grated Parmesan cheese
1   tablespoon vegetable oil
1/4 teaspoon salt
1/4 teaspoon garlic powder
1/4 teaspoon paprika
1/4 teaspoon pepper

PREHEAT oven to 450 degrees.
COMBINE all ingredients in a bowl, and toss well.
ARRANGE potatoes in a single layer on a baking sheet.
BAKE at 450 degrees for 35 minutes, or until golden.
YIELD: 4 servings

BY baking fries instead of deep-frying them, you practically eliminate the oil.
TO get really crispy fries without the fat, you need to slice them very thin.
BY slicing the potatoes thinly, you also create more surface area for the seasoning to cover.

PER serving:
CALORIES 200
(18% from fat)
FAT 4g
(saturated 0.9g)
PROTEIN 3.9g
CARBOHYDRATE 37g
FIBER 3.6g
CHOLESTEROL 1mg
SODIUM 178mg

McDONALD'S
   Small fries
CALORIES 210
(43% from fat)
FAT 10g
   Large fries
CALORIES 450
(44% from fat)
FAT 22g

OVEN FRIES
CALORIES 193
(17% from fat)
FAT 3.6g

# Corn Casserole

1/4 cup egg substitute
1/4 cup reduced-calorie stick margarine,
    melted
1   (8 3/4-ounce) can no-salt-added whole-
    kernel corn, drained
1   (8 3/4-ounce) can no-salt-added cream-style
    corn
1   (8 1/2-ounce) package corn muffin mix
1   (8-ounce) carton plain fat-free yogurt
Vegetable cooking spray

PREHEAT oven to 350 degrees.
COMBINE first 6 ingredients in a medium bowl; stir
well.
POUR into an 8-inch square baking dish coated
with cooking spray.
BAKE at 350 degrees for 45 minutes, or until set.
YIELD: 8 servings

PER serving:
CALORIES 220
(31% from fat)
FAT 7.5g
(saturated 2.5g)
PROTEIN 5.4g
CARBOHYDRATE 34.6g
FIBER 0.6g
CHOLESTEROL 1mg
SODIUM 287mg

# Country Green Beans

1 pound fresh green beans, trimmed
1/4 cup chopped onion
1/4 cup chopped, fully-cooked, low-fat ham
1/4 cup water
2 teaspoons margarine
1 garlic clove, minced
1/4 teaspoon pepper

IN a saucepan, combine all ingredients.
COVER and simmer for 15 to 20 minutes, or until beans are tender.
YIELD: 4 servings

# Creamed Peas and Potatoes

4   medium red potatoes, cubed
1   (10-ounce) package frozen peas
1   teaspoon sugar
1   tablespoon margarine
2   tablespoons all-purpose flour
1/4 teaspoon white pepper
1 1/2 cups skim milk
2   tablespoons minced fresh dill

PLACE potatoes in saucepan; cover with water and cook until tender.
COOK peas according to package directions, adding the sugar.
MEANWHILE, melt margarine in a saucepan; add flour and pepper to form a paste. Gradually stir in milk. Bring to a boil; boil for 1 minute. Add dill; cook until thickened and bubbly.
DRAIN potatoes and peas; place in a serving bowl. Pour sauce over and stir to coat.
SERVE immediately.
YIELD: 8 servings

PER serving:
CALORIES 126
(14% from fat)
FAT 2g
(saturated trace)
PROTEIN 5g
CARBOHYDRATE 19g
CHOLESTEROL 1mg
SODIUM 86mg

# French Onion Casserole

3   medium-size sweet onions
Vegetable cooking spray
1   tablespoon reduced-calorie margarine
1   (8-ounce) package fresh mushrooms, sliced
2   cups (8 ounces) shredded, reduced-fat
       Swiss cheese, divided
1   (10 3/4-ounce) can reduced-fat, reduced-
       sodium cream of mushroom soup,
       undiluted
2/3 cup evaporated skim milk
2   teaspoons reduced-sodium soy sauce
6   (1/2-inch-thick) slices French bread
1/4 cup finely-chopped fresh parsley

CUT onions crosswise into 1/4-inch slices; cut each slice in half.

COAT a large nonstick skillet with cooking spray; add margarine, and place over medium-high heat until hot. Add onions and mushrooms, and cook, stirring constantly, until tender.

SPOON mixture into a 2-quart baking dish coated with cooking spray. Sprinkle with 1 cup cheese.

COMBINE soup, evaporated milk and soy sauce, stirring well. Pour over cheese. Top with bread slices, and sprinkle with remaining 1 cup cheese and parsley.

COVER and chill 4 to 8 hours. Remove baking dish from refrigerator and let stand at room temperature 30 minutes.

COVER and bake at 375 degrees for 30 minutes. Uncover and bake 15 additional minutes, or until thoroughly heated. Let stand 5 minutes before serving.

YIELD: 6 servings

# Grilled Shiitakes

1   pound large, fresh shiitake mushrooms
1/4 cup chopped fresh parsley
1/4 cup canned, reduced-sodium chicken broth
3   tablespoons reduced-calorie margarine,
     melted
4   cloves garlic, minced
1/2 teaspoon freshly-ground pepper
1/4 teaspoon salt

REMOVE stems from mushrooms; discard. Combine parsley and remaining 5 ingredients; brush evenly on both sides of mushroom caps.
COOK mushrooms without grill lid, over medium-hot coals (350 to 400 degrees) 8 minutes, turning once.
YIELD: 4 servings

PER serving:
CALORIES 95
(54% from fat)
FAT 5.7g
(saturated 0.1g)
PROTEIN 1.7g
CARBOHYDRATE 12.4g
CHOLESTEROL 0mg
SODIUM 268mg

# Grilled Stuffed Onions

PER serving:
CALORIES 222
(28% from fat)
FAT 7.0g
(saturated 2.2g)
PROTEIN 10.5g
CARBOHYDRATE 31.4g
CHOLESTEROL 13mg
SODIUM 362mg

1   (6-ounce) box reduced-sodium stuffing mix
      for chicken
1   cup (4 ounces) shredded sharp reduced-fat
      Cheddar cheese
1/2 cup canned, reduced-sodium chicken broth
2   tablespoons reduced-calorie margarine,
      melted
1   teaspoon poultry seasoning
6   medium-size sweet onions
Vegetable cooking spray
Fresh oregano sprigs, for garnish

COMBINE 1 1/2 cups stuffing mix and 1 1/2 tablespoons of the stuffing mix packet in a medium
bowl, tossing well. Reserve remaining stuffing mix
and seasoning packet for another use. Add cheese
and next 3 ingredients, stirring well; set aside.
CUT each onion horizontally into 3 slices. SPREAD 2
tablespoons stuffing mixture between slices, and
reassemble onions. Place each onion on a 12-inch-
square piece of heavy-duty aluminum foil coated
with cooking spray; bring opposite corners together and twist foil to seal.
COOK, covered with grill lid, over medium-hot coats
(350 to 400 degrees) 25 minutes, or until tender.
Garnish, if desired.
YIELD: 6 servings

# Homemade Noodles

2 to 2 1/2 cups all-purpose flour, divided
1/2 teaspoon salt
3   eggs
1   tablespoon cold water
1   teaspoon cooking oil

PLACE 2 cups flour and salt on a pastry board or in a deep mixing bowl. Make a well in the center of the flour; add eggs and water. GRADUALLY mix with hands or a wooden spoon until well blended. Gather into a ball and knead on a floured surface until smooth, about 10 minutes. If necessary, add remaining flour to keep dough from sticking to surface or hands.

DIVIDE the dough into thirds. On a floured surface, roll each section into a paper-thin rectangle. Dust top of dough with flour to prevent sticking while rolling. Trim the edges and flour both sides of dough.

ROLL dough, jellyroll style. Cut dough into 1/2-inch slices, using a sharp knife.

UNROLL noodles and allow to dry on a lightly-floured surface or on paper towels before cooking.

COOK: bring 8 cups of water to a rapid boil; add 1 teaspoon of oil to water, and drop noodles into water. Cook until tender, but not too soft.

YIELD: 12 servings

PER serving:
CALORIES 98
(18% from fat)
FAT 2g
(saturated trace)
PROTEIN 4g
CARBOHYDRATE 16g
CHOLESTEROL 53mg
SODIUM 114mg

# Lemon Mashed Potatoes

PER serving:
CALORIES 175
(3% from fat)
FAT 0.6g
(saturated 0.3g)
PROTEIN 5.4g
CARBOHYDRATE 38.2g
FIBER 3g
CHOLESTEROL 2mg
SODIUM 324mg

5   cups peeled, cubed baking potato
1/2 cup plain low-fat yogurt
1   tablespoon fresh lemon juice
2   teaspoons sugar
1/2 teaspoon salt
1/4 teaspoon pepper

PLACE potato in a large saucepan; cover with water and bring to a boil.
REDUCE heat; simmer 15 minutes, or until tender.
DRAIN potato, and return to pan.
ADD yogurt, lemon juice, sugar, salt and pepper; beat at medium speed of an electric mixer until smooth.
YIELD: 4 servings (serving size: 1 cup)

# Macaroni and Cheese

2   teaspoons butter
1   cup sliced mushrooms
3/4 cup diced red bell pepper
1/2 cup finely-chopped celery
1/4 cup chopped shallots
3/4 cup part-skim ricotta cheese
1/2 teaspoon tarragon
1   teaspoon salt
1   teaspoon granulated tapioca (optional)
1/4 teaspoon white pepper
1/4 teaspoon ground nutmeg
1   (12-ounce) can evaporated skim milk
1   large egg, lightly beaten
4   cups hot, cooked elbow macaroni (about 7
     ounces uncooked)
Vegetable cooking spray
1   medium tomato, cut into 1/4-inch-thick slices
1/4 cup fine, dry bread crumbs
1/4 cup grated Parmesan cheese
1   teaspoon grated lemon rind

PREHEAT oven to 350 degrees.
MELT butter over medium-high heat in a medium,
nonstick skillet.
ADD mushrooms, bell pepper, celery and shallots;
sauté 4 minutes, or until tender. Set aside.
COMBINE ricotta cheese and next 7 ingredients in
a large bowl. Stir until well blended.
ADD mushroom mixture and macaroni; stir well.
SPOON mixture into a 2-quart casserole coated
with cooking spray.
PRESS tomato slices gently between paper towels
until barely moist.
ARRANGE tomatoes in a circular pattern over top
of macaroni mixture.
COMBINE bread crumbs, Parmesan cheese and
lemon rind in a small bowl; stir well.
SPRINKLE bread crumb mixture over tomatoes.
BAKE at 350 degrees for 35 minutes, or until lightly
browned.
YIELD: 8 servings

PER serving:
CALORIES 218
(21% from fat)
FAT 5.2g
(saturated 2.6g)
PROTEIN 12g
CARBOHYDRATE 30.0g
FIBER 1.9g
CHOLESTEROL 41mg
SODIUM 474mg

# Mashed Potatoes with Horseradish

PER serving:
CALORIES 168
(21% from fat)
FAT 4g
(saturated 1g)
PROTEIN 5g
CARBOHYDRATE 29g
CHOLESTEROL 0mg
SODIUM 170mg

6   medium potatoes, peeled and cubed
2   tablespoons margarine, melted
1/2 teaspoon salt
1/8 teaspoon pepper
1/2 cup light sour cream
2   tablespoons prepared horseradish

COOK the potatoes in boiling water until tender, about 8 to 10 minutes; drain.
ADD margarine, salt and pepper. Whip with an electric mixer on low speed, or mash with a potato masher.
ADD sour cream and horseradish; mix well.
SERVE immediately.
YIELD: 6 servings

# Molasses Baked Beans

2 1/2 cups dry Great Northern beans (1 pound)
12 turkey bacon strips, cooked and crumbled
1   cup packed brown sugar
2   tablespoons molasses
3   small onions, chopped

PLACE beans in a saucepan; add water to cover by 2 inches. Bring to a boil; boil for 2 minutes. Remove from heat; cover and let stand for 1 hour.

DRAIN, discarding liquid, and return beans to pan. Cover with fresh water; bring to a boil. Reduce heat; cover and simmer for 1 hour, or until beans are tender. Drain, reserving liquid.

COMBINE beans, 1 cup liquid, and the remaining ingredients in a 2 1/2-quart baking dish coated with nonstick cooking spray.

COVER and bake at 350 degrees for 1 1/4 hours, or until beans are tender, stirring occasionally (add reserved liquid as needed).

YIELD: 10 servings

PER serving:
CALORIES 189
(5% from fat)
FAT 1g
(saturated trace)
PROTEIN 9g
CARBOHYDRATE 51g
CHOLESTEROL 6mg
SODIUM 148mg

# Mushroom Casserole

1   tablespoon reduced-calorie stick
        margarine
3   (8-ounce) packages sliced fresh mushrooms
1 1/3 cups chopped onion
1/2 cup chopped celery
1/2 cup chopped green bell pepper
1/2 cup reduced-fat mayonnaise
8   (1-ounce) slices white bread, cut into 1-inch
        pieces
Vegetable cooking spray
1/2 cup egg substitute
1 1/2 cups skim milk
1   (10 3/4-ounce) can reduced-fat cream of
        mushroom soup, undiluted
1   cup freshly-ground Romano cheese

MELT margarine in a large Dutch oven. Add mushrooms and next 3 ingredients; cook over medium-high heat, stirring constantly, until tender. Drain well. Stir in mayonnaise.

PLACE half of bread evenly into a 9x13x2-inch baking dish coated with cooking spray. Spoon mushroom mixture evenly over bread. Top with remaining bread.

COMBINE egg substitute and milk; pour over bread. Cover and chill at least 8 hours.

POUR soup over casserole; top with cheese.

BAKE, uncovered, at 350 degrees for 1 hour, or until hot and bubbly.

YIELD: 8 servings

# Mustard and Herb Marinated Vegetables

2   small red potatoes (about 6 ounces)
1 1/2 cups small broccoli flowerets
1 1/2 cups cherry tomatoes, halved
1 1/2 cups small mushrooms, halved
1 1/2 cups cubed zucchini
2/3 cup white wine vinegar
1/2 cup water
1/4 cup minced shallots
2   tablespoons Dijon mustard
1 1/2 tablespoons olive oil
1   teaspoon dried basil
1   teaspoon dried oregano
1   teaspoon dried rosemary, crushed
1/2 teaspoon salt
1/4 teaspoon dried, crushed red pepper

ARRANGE potatoes in a steamer basket over boiling water. Cover and steam 15 minutes, or until tender. Let cool. Cut each potato into 4 wedges, and cut each wedge in half crosswise.

COMBINE potatoes and next 4 ingredients in a large glass dish; set aside. Combine vinegar and remaining 9 ingredients in a jar; cover tightly and shake vigorously. Pour over vegetables; toss gently to coat. Cover and marinate in refrigerator 8 hours, stirring occasionally.

YIELD: 8 servings

PER serving:
CALORIES 77
(37% from fat)
FAT 3.2g
(saturated 0.4g)
PROTEIN 2.3g
CARBOHYDRATE 10.4g
CHOLESTEROL 0mg
SODIUM 273mg

# Oven-Roasted Potatoes

2   pounds small, unpeeled red potatoes, cut
       into wedges
2   garlic cloves, minced
1   tablespoon minced, fresh rosemary, or
       1 teaspoon  dried rosemary, crushed
1/4 teaspoon pepper

PLACE potatoes in a 9x13x2-inch baking pan coated with nonstick cooking spray. Mix potatoes with cooking spray.
SPRINKLE with garlic, rosemary and pepper; toss gently to coat.
BAKE, uncovered, at 450 degrees for 20 to 30 minutes, or until potatoes are golden and tender when pierced with a fork.
YIELD: 8 servings

# Parsley Carrots

2   cups fresh or frozen sliced carrots
2   tablespoons sliced green onion
1   tablespoon water
2   teaspoons margarine
Chopped fresh parsley

IN a saucepan, combine the first 4 ingredients;
cover and simmer for 8 to 10 minutes, or until the
carrots are crisp-tender.
SPRINKLE with parsley.
YIELD: 4 servings

PER serving:
CALORIES 47
(38% from fat)
FAT 2g
(saturated 2g)
PROTEIN 1g
CARBOHYDRATE 7g
CHOLESTEROL 0mg
SODIUM 46mg

# Pasta with Asparagus

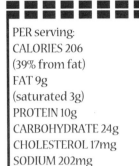

PER serving:
CALORIES 206
(39% from fat)
FAT 9g
(saturated 3g)
PROTEIN 10g
CARBOHYDRATE 24g
CHOLESTEROL 17mg
SODIUM 202mg

2   pounds fresh asparagus, sliced diagonally
        into 1-inch pieces
1   pound thin spaghetti
6   turkey bacon strips, cut into 1-inch pieces
1/2 cup sliced green onions
1/2 teaspoon pepper
3   tablespoons reduced-fat margarine
1/2 cup light sour cream
1/3 cup grated Parmesan cheese

COOK asparagus in boiling water for 3 to 4 minutes, or until crisp-tender; drain and set aside.
COOK spaghetti according to package directions.
MEANWHILE, in a skillet, cook bacon until crisp. Drain and remove to paper towel.
IN the same skillet, sauté the onions until soft. Add asparagus and pepper; heat through.
DRAIN spaghetti; toss with asparagus mixture, bacon, margarine, sour cream and cheese.
SERVE immediately.
YIELD: 8 servings.

# Potato Dumplings

6   medium potatoes
5   tablespoons all-purpose flour
1   egg, beaten
1   teaspoon salt
1/4 teaspoon ground nutmeg
2   slices white bread, toasted
1/3 cup mashed potato flakes (optional)

COOK potatoes in water just until tender; drain.
Refrigerate for 2 hours, or overnight.
PEEL and grate potatoes.
IN a bowl, combine the flour, egg, salt and nutmeg.
ADD potatoes and mix until a stiff batter is formed,
adding additional flour, if necessary.
SLICE toasted bread into 24 squares, 1/2-inch each;
shape 2 tablespoons of the potato mixture around
2 bread squares, forming a 2-inch ball.
IN a large skillet, bring water to a boil; add the test
dumpling. Reduce heat; cover and simmer for 15 to
20 minutes, or until the dumpling is no longer
sticky in the center.
IF test dumpling falls apart during cooking, add
the mashed potato flakes to the mixture. Let potato mixture stand for 45 minutes; form remaining dumplings. Add to boiling water; return to a
boil and follow the same cooking procedure.
REMOVE dumplings with a slotted spoon to a serving bowl.
YIELD: 8 servings

PER serving:
CALORIES 134
(7% from fat)
FAT 1g
(saturated trace)
PROTEIN 4g
CARBOHYDRATE 27g
CHOLESTEROL 27mg
SODIUM 337mg

# Roasted Garlic Mashed Potatoes

4   heads garlic
1   tablespoon olive oil
4   pounds baking potatoes, peeled and cut
        into 8-inch pieces
3   tablespoons reduced-calorie margarine
1   cup skim milk
1   teaspoon salt
1/2 teaspoon pepper

PLACE garlic on a square of aluminum foil; drizzle with oil and wrap in foil.
BAKE at 425 degrees for 30 minutes; set aside.
COOK potatoes in boiling water to cover, for 15 to 20 minutes, or until tender. Drain. Transfer to large mixing bowl of a heavy-duty electric mixer. Add margarine and remaining 3 ingredients; beat at medium speed 2 minutes, or until fluffy.
CUT off ends of garlic; squeeze pulp from cloves. Stir into potato mixture.
YIELD: 11 servings

# Sausage-Cornbread Dressing

2 (7 1/2-ounce) packages complete yellow corn
    muffin mix
Vegetable cooking spray
1   pound freshly-ground turkey breakfast
    sausage
2   cups chopped onion
1 3/4 cups chopped celery
3   cups white bread cubes, toasted
2   teaspoons rubbed sage
1   teaspoon pepper
4   cups canned, reduced-sodium chicken
    broth
1/2 cup egg substitute

PER serving:
CALORIES 143
(33% from fat)
FAT 5.3g
(saturated 3.8g)
PROTEIN 9.6g
CARBOHYDRATE 13.8g
CHOLESTEROL 24mg
SODIUM 501mg

PREPARE muffin mix according to package directions for cornbread, using skim milk. Let cool, and crumble. Set aside.

COAT a large nonstick skillet with cooking spray. Place over medium heat until hot. Add sausage, onion and celery. Cook, stirring constantly, until sausage crumbles and vegetables are tender. Drain and pat dry with paper towels.

COMBINE cornbread, bread cubes, sage and pepper in a large bowl; stir in sausage mixture. Add chicken broth and egg substitute, stirring well. Spoon mixture into a 12x9x2-inch baking dish coated with cooking spray.

BAKE, uncovered at 350 degrees for 1 hour, or until browned.

YIELD: 12 servings

# Spinach Noodles

1   (10-ounce) package frozen, chopped
       spinach, thawed and well drained
2   eggs
1/2 teaspoon salt
2   cups all-purpose flour

IN a blender or food processor, combine the spinach, eggs and salt; process until smooth. Pour into a bowl. Gradually add enough flour to make a firm, but not sticky, dough.

ON a floured surface, knead about 20 times. Wrap in plastic wrap and let rest 30 minutes.

DIVIDE dough in half. On a floured surface, roll each half to 1/16-inch thickness. Roll up, jellyroll-style, and cut into 1/4-inch slices.

SEPARATE the slices and let rest on a clean towel for at least 1 hour.

COOK noodles in boiling water until tender, about 15 to 20 minutes; drain.

YIELD: 6 servings.

# Squash Soufflé

3 cups chopped, unpeeled eggplant
2 cups chopped yellow squash
2 cups chopped zucchini
1 red bell pepper, chopped
1 yellow bell pepper, chopped
Vegetable cooking spray
1 medium onion, chopped
4 cloves garlic, minced
1 1/2 cups spaghetti sauce
1/4 cup coarsely-chopped, fresh flat-leaf
     parsley
1 teaspoon dried oregano
1 teaspoon dried thyme
1 tablespoon finely-chopped fresh basil

PER serving:
CALORIES 97
(36% from fat)
FAT 3.9g
(saturated 0.1g)
PROTEIN 2.9g
CARBOHYDRATE 15.4g
CHOLESTEROL 0mg
SODIUM 272mg

PLACE eggplant in a 9-inch pie plate; cover with a paper towel and microwave at HIGH 4 minutes. Transfer to a large bowl. Repeat procedure with squash, zucchini and peppers. Set vegetable mixture aside.
COAT a very large skillet or Dutch oven with cooking spray; place over medium heat until hot. Add onion and garlic; cook, stirring constantly, until tender.
STIR in vegetable mixture, spaghetti sauce, and next 3 ingredients. Cook 4 minutes, stirring occasionally. Stir in basil.
YIELD: 6 servings

# Stove-Top Baked Beans

1   tablespoon margarine
1 1/4 cups chopped onion
3/4 cup chopped green bell pepper
2   garlic cloves, minced
1   cup reduced-calorie ketchup
1/4 cup firmly-packed brown sugar
1/4 cup maple syrup
2   tablespoons Worcestershire sauce
2   teaspoons barbecue smoke seasoning
2   teaspoons prepared mustard
1 (16-ounce) can red beans, drained
1 (15.8-ounce) can Great Northern beans,
       drained

MELT margarine in a medium saucepan over medium-high heat.
ADD onion, bell pepper and garlic; sauté 4 minutes.
STIR in ketchup and remaining ingredients; bring to a boil.
REDUCE heat; simmer 15 minutes, stirring occasionally.
YIELD: 8 (1/2-cup) servings

# Stuffed Sweet Potatoes

6   medium sweet potatoes
1   (8-ounce) can crushed, unsweetened
       pineapple, drained
1/2 cup orange juice
1   tablespoon margarine, melted

PIERCE sweet potatoes with a fork.
BAKE at 400 degrees for 55 to 65 minutes, or until tender. Cool slightly.
CUT a thin slice off the top of each potato and discard.
CAREFULLY scoop out pulp while leaving shell intact.
IN a bowl, mash pulp with pineapple, orange juice and margarine.
REFILL potato shells; place in a 13x9x2-inch baking dish coated with cooking spray.
BAKE at 400 degrees for 20 minutes, or until heated through.
YIELD: 6 servings

PER serving:
CALORIES 238
(8% from fat)
FAT 2g
(saturated trace)
PROTEIN 3g
CARBOHYDRATE 53g
CHOLESTEROL 0mg

# Sweet Potatoes

8  medium sweet potatoes
1 1/4 cups packed brown sugar
1/2 cup apple juice
1/2 cup water
1/2 cup raisins (optional)
1  tablespoon margarine

COOK and peel sweet potatoes; allow to cool. Slice and place in a 2 1/2-quart baking dish coated with cooking spray.

IN a small saucepan, combine remaining ingredients; bring to a boil, stirring frequently. Pour over the potatoes.

BAKE, uncovered, at 350 degrees for 45 minutes, basting occasionally.

YIELD: 10 servings

PER serving:
CALORIES 294
(5% from fat)
FAT 2g
(saturated trace)
PROTEIN 3g
CARBOHYDRATE 70g
CHOLESTEROL 0mg
SODIUM 38mg

# Vegetarian Sauté

Vegetable cooking spray
1  tablespoon olive oil
1  medium onion, chopped
1  medium-size green bell pepper, chopped
1  medium zucchini, chopped
2  cloves garlic, minced
1  stalk celery, chopped
1  (14.5-ounce) can no-salt-added stewed
    tomatoes
1  (15-ounce) can dark red kidney beans,
    drained
1  tablespoon sugar
1/2 teaspoon dried oregano
1/4 teaspoon salt
1/4 teaspoon pepper
1/2 cup (2 ounces) shredded, reduced-fat extra-
    sharp Cheddar cheese

COAT a large nonstick skillet with cooking spray.
Add oil. Place over medium-high heat until hot.
Add onion and next 4 ingredients; cook, stirring
constantly, until tender.
STIR in tomatoes and next 5 ingredients. Bring to a
boil; reduce heat to medium. Cook uncovered, 5
minutes, or until liquid is almost absorbed, stirring often. Sprinkle with cheese. Serve immediately.
YIELD: 4 servings

PER serving:
CALORIES 198
(32% from fat)
FAT 7.1g
(saturated 2.5g)
PROTEIN 9.2g
CARBOHYDRATE 25.9g
CHOLESTEROL 10mg
SODIUM 505mg

# Notes & Recipes

# Soups, Stews
# and Sandwiches

# List Your Favorite Recipes

**Recipes**                                    **Page**

_____    _____

_____    _____

_____    _____

_____    _____

_____    _____

_____    _____

_____    _____

_____    _____

_____    _____

_____    _____

_____    _____

_____    _____

_____    _____

_____    _____

_____    _____

_____    _____

# Bean and Barley Soup

1   tablespoon olive oil
1   cup chopped onion
1   cup chopped carrot
1/2 cup chopped celery
2   garlic cloves, minced
1/2 cup uncooked pearl barley
1/4 pound smoked turkey sausage, cut into
      1/2-inch cubes
2   cups frozen lima beans
1 3/4 cups water
1/8 teaspoon pepper
2   (14 1/4-ounce) cans fat-free chicken broth
1   (14.5-ounce) can diced tomatoes, undrained
1/2 teaspoon hot sauce

PER serving:
CALORIES 228
(26% from fat)
FAT 6.6g
(saturated 1.6g)
PROTEIN 13.4g
CARBOHYDRATE 29.5g
CHOLESTEROL 16mg
SODIUM 423mg

HEAT oil in a large Dutch oven over medium-high heat until hot. Add chopped onion, carrot, celery and garlic; sauté 5 minutes.

ADD barley and sausage; sauté 4 minutes. Add beans, water, pepper, broth and tomatoes; bring to a boil. Reduce heat; simmer, uncovered, 45 minutes.

REMOVE from heat; stir in hot sauce.

YIELD: 6 (1 1/2-cup) servings

# Beef Minestrone Soup

1   (4-pound) beef chuck roast, trimmed
1   gallon water
2   bay leaves
2   medium onions, diced
2   cups sliced carrots
2   cups sliced celery
1   (28-ounce) can diced tomatoes, undrained
1   (15-ounce) can tomato sauce
1/4 cup chopped fresh parsley
Pepper, to taste
4   teaspoons dried basil
1   teaspoon garlic powder
1   (16-ounce) package frozen peas
2 (16-ounce) cans kidney beans, rinsed and
      drained
2   (9-ounce) packages frozen, cut green beans
2   (7-ounce) packages shell macaroni, cooked
      and drained

PLACE beef roast, water and bay leaves in a large
kettle or Dutch oven; bring to a boil. Reduce heat;
cover and simmer until meat is tender, about 3
hours. Remove meat from broth; cool.
ADD onions, carrots and celery to broth; cook for
20 minutes, or until vegetables are tender.
CUT meat into bite-size pieces; add to broth. Add
tomatoes, tomato sauce, parsley, seasoning, peas
and beans. Cook until vegetables are done, about
10 minutes. Add macaroni and heat through. Remove bay leaves.
YIELD: 40 servings

THIS recipe may be divided to make a smaller
amount, and will also freeze well.

# Beef Stew

2 pounds lean beef stew meat
6 medium potatoes, peeled and cut into
  1 1/2-inch pieces
2 medium onions, cut into wedges
8 medium carrots, cut into 1-inch pieces
4 celery ribs, cut into 1-inch pieces
1 (4-ounce) can sliced mushrooms, drained
1/3 cup quick-cooking tapioca
1 low-sodium beef bouillon cube
1 teaspoon sugar
2 bay leaves
1 1/2 teaspoons dried thyme
3 cups tomato juice

IN a large Dutch oven or baking dish, layer the first
11 ingredients; pour tomato juice over all.
COVER and bake at 300 degrees for 3 hours, stirring
occasionally, or until the meat and vegetables are
tender.
REMOVE bay leaves before serving.
YIELD: 8 servings

PER serving:
CALORIES 338
(22% from fat)
FAT 8g
(saturated 3g)
PROTEIN 25g
CARBOHYDRATE 42g
CHOLESTEROL 70mg
SODIUM 646mg

# Black Bean Soup

2   cups dry black beans, rinsed
2   quarts water
1   medium onion, chopped
1/2 pound lean pork, cubed
3   garlic cloves, minced
1   teaspoon dried oregano
1   (6-ounce) can tomato paste
Optional toppings: finely-shredded cabbage,
    minced fresh chili peppers, and nonfat
    sour cream

IN a Dutch oven, combine beans and water; bring
to a boil. Reduce heat; cover and simmer until
beans wrinkle and crack, about 1 1/2 hours.
ADD onion, pork, garlic and oregano. Simmer, covered, 1 1/2 to 2 hours, or until beans and pork are
tender.
STIR in tomato paste; heat through. Garnish, if
desired.
YIELD: 8 servings

# Broccoli-Cheddar Soup

Vegetable cooking spray
1   cup chopped onion
4   cups chopped fresh broccoli (about 3/4
       pound), divided
2   cups peeled, diced red potato (about 3/4
       pound)
1/2 teaspoon garlic powder
2   (10 1/2-ounce) cans low-salt chicken broth
1   bay leaf
3/4 cup (3-ounces) shredded reduced-fat sharp
       Cheddar cheese
1   (12-ounce) can evaporated skim milk
Dash of pepper

COAT a large Dutch oven with cooking spray; place over medium heat until hot.
ADD onion; sauté 5 minutes.
ADD 2 cups broccoli and next 4 ingredients; bring to a boil.
COVER; reduce heat and simmer 20 minutes, or until vegetables are tender.
DISCARD bay leaf.
PLACE half of broccoli mixture in container of a blender; cover and process until smooth.
SPOON into a bowl.
REPEAT procedure with remaining broccoli mixture.
RETURN broccoli purée to pan; add cheese, milk, pepper and remaining 2 cups broccoli.
COOK over medium heat 4 minutes, or until chopped broccoli is just tender, stirring until cheese melts.
YIELD: 7 (1-cup) servings

PER serving:
CALORIES 143
(21% from fat)
FAT 3.3g
PROTEIN 10.6g
CARBOHYDRATE 191.g
FIBER 3.5g
CHOLESTEROL 10mg
SODIUM 187mg

# Chunky Vegetable Soup

PER serving:
CALORIES 224
(12% from fat)
FAT 2.9g
(saturated 1g)
PROTEIN 10.6g
CARBOHYDRATE 40.4g
CHOLESTEROL 4mg
SODIUM 574mg

2   teaspoons vegetable oil
1   cup chopped onion
2   garlic cloves, minced
7   cups water
1   tablespoon dried basil
3/4 teaspoon salt
1/2 teaspoon dried marjoram
1/2 teaspoon pepper
1   pound red potatoes, cut into 1-inch cubes
1/2 pound small carrots, cut into 1-inch pieces
1   (15 1/2-ounce) can cannellini beans, or other
      white beans, drained
1   (14.5-ounce) can whole tomatoes, undrained
      and chopped
1   (10-ounce) package frozen lima beans
1/2 cup uncooked orzo (rice-shaped pasta)
1/2 cup shredded part-skim Mozzarella cheese

COAT a large Dutch oven with cooking spray; add oil, and place over medium-high heat until hot. Add chopped onion and garlic; sauté until onion is tender. Add water and next 9 ingredients; bring to a boil. Cover; reduce heat and simmer 20 minutes. ADD orzo; cook, uncovered, over medium heat an additional 10 minutes. Ladle soup into individual bowls and sprinkle with cheese.

YIELD: 8 servings (1 1/2 cups soup and 1 teaspoon cheese)

SOUP may be refrigerated up to 1 week, or frozen for up to 3 months.

# Corn Chowder

3/4 cup chopped onion
1   cup diced, cooked, peeled potatoes
1   cup diced, fully-cooked ham
2   cups fresh or frozen sweet corn
1   cup cream-style corn
1   (10 3/4-ounce) can low-fat condensed cream
      of mushroom soup, undiluted
1 1/2 cups skim milk
Pepper, to taste
1   tablespoon chopped fresh parsley

IN a heavy saucepan, coated with nonstick cooking spray, sauté the onion until tender. Add remaining ingredients; bring to a boil. Reduce heat;
simmer, uncovered, for 20 to 30 minutes.
YIELD: 8 servings

PER serving:
CALORIES 152
(12% from fat)
FAT 2g
(saturated 1g)
PROTEIN 9g
CARBOHYDRATE 26g
CHOLESTEROL 13mg
SODIUM 546mg

# Clam Chowder

2   (15 1/2-ounce) cans minced clams
1 1/2 cups water
6   potatoes, peeled and diced
6   carrots, diced
1/2 cup chopped onion
1/4 cup margarine
2   (10 3/4-ounce) cans low-fat condensed
        mushroom soup, undiluted
2   (12-ounce) cans evaporated skim milk
1/2 teaspoon pepper

DRAIN clams, reserving liquid. Set the clams aside.
IN a large kettle, combine clam juice, water, potatoes, carrots, onion and margarine; cook over medium heat for 15 minutes, or until the vegetables
are tender.
STIR in soup, milk and pepper; simmer until heated
through. Stir in clams.
YIELD: 12 servings.

# Creamy Corn and Zucchini Soup

6   cups low-salt chicken broth
2   cups diced zucchini
1/2 c. chopped onion
6   cups fresh corn kernels (about 12 ears)
1/2 teaspoon salt
1/4 teaspoon pepper
3/4 cup plain fat-free yogurt
Jalapeño hot sauce (optional)

BRING broth to a simmer in a large saucepan.
ADD zucchini and onion; cover and simmer 2 minutes.
STIR in corn, salt and pepper; cover and simmer 2 minutes.
PLACE one-third of corn mixture in a blender; cover and process until mixture is smooth.
REPEAT procedure with remaining corn mixture.
LADLE soup into bowls; top with yogurt.
SERVE with jalapeño sauce, if desired.
YIELD: 12 servings (1 cup soup and 1 tablespoon yogurt)

PER serving:
CALORIES 96
(46% from fat)
FAT 1.7g
(saturated 0.4g)
PROTEIN 4.8g
CARBOHYDRATE 18.2g
FIBER 2.7g
CHOLESTEROL 0mg
SODIUM 160mg

# German Potato Soup

6 cups cubed, peeled potatoes
1 1/4 cups sliced celery
1/2 cup chopped onion
5 cups water
1/8 teaspoon pepper

DROP DUMPLINGS:
1 egg
1/3 cup water
1/2 teaspoon salt
3/4 cup flour
Chopped fresh parsley

IN a kettle, combine the first 5 ingredients; bring to a boil. Reduce heat and simmer until vegetables are tender, about 1 hour. With a potato masher, mash most of the vegetables (you may leave vegetables, without mashing, if you prefer).
DUMPLINGS: Combine egg, water, salt and flour. Stir until smooth and stiff. Drop by the teaspoonful into the boiling soup. Cover and simmer until dumplings are cooked through, about 10 to 15 minutes. Sprinkle with parsley.
YIELD: 6 servings

# Golden Squash Soup

3 cups coarsely-ground, chopped onion
1/4 teaspoon ground nutmeg
1/4 teaspoon ground cinnamon
1/4 teaspoon dried thyme
2 bay leaves
1 1/2 cups water
2 celery ribs, chopped
1 medium carrot, chopped
2 cups mashed, cooked butternut squash,
    divided
1 1/2 cups tomato juice, divided
1 cup apple juice, divided
1 cup orange juice, divided
Pepper, to taste

IN a large saucepan or Dutch oven, coated with nonstick cooking spray, sauté onion with nutmeg, cinnamon, thyme and bay leaves until onion is tender. Add water, celery and carrot; cover and simmer until carrot is tender. Discard bay leaves. IN a blender container, place half of the squash and half of the tomato, apple and orange juices; add half of the vegetable mixture. Purée; return to pan. Repeat with the remaining squash, juices and vegetable mixture. Return to pan. Add pepper; heat through.
YIELD: 8 servings

PER serving:
CALORIES 80
(0% from fat)
FAT trace
(saturated trace)
PROTEIN 2g
CARBOHYDRATE 21g
CHOLESTEROL 0mg
SODIUM 190mg

# Macaroni and Cheese Soup

1   cup elbow macaroni, uncooked
2   tablespoons margarine
Butter-flavored vegetable cooking spray
1/2 cup finely-chopped carrot
1/2 cup finely-chopped celery
1   small onion, finely chopped
4   cups 1% low-fat milk
1   tablespoon chicken-flavored bouillon
      granules
1/2 teaspoon ground white pepper
2   tablespoons cornstarch
2   tablespoons water
6   ounces reduced-fat loaf of process cheese
      spread, cubed
1   cup frozen whole kernel corn,  thawed
1/2 cup frozen peas, thawed

COOK macaroni according to package directions, omitting salt and fat. Drain. Rinse with cold water; drain and set aside.

COAT a large skillet with cooking spray; add margarine. Place over medium-high heat until margarine melts. Add carrot, celery and onion; cook, stirring constantly, until tender. Remove vegetable mixture from heat; set aside.

COMBINE milk, bouillon granules and white pepper in a large saucepan. Combine cornstarch and water, stirring until smooth; stir into milk mixture. Stir in vegetable mixture, and cook over medium heat, stirring constantly, until mixture thickens and comes to a boil. Boil 1 minute, stirring constantly.

ADD cheese and cook over medium heat until cheese melts, stirring often.

ADD macaroni, corn and peas; cook over low heat, stirring constantly, just until thoroughly heated.

YIELD: 7 cups

# Old-Fashioned Chicken-Noodle Soup

3   boneless, skinless chicken breast halves
2   quarts water
1   medium onion, chopped
2   low-sodium chicken bouillon cubes
2   celery ribs, diced
2   carrots, diced
2   medium potatoes, peeled and cubed
1 1/2 cups fresh or frozen cut green beans
1/4 teaspoon pepper

NOODLES:
1   cup all-purpose flour
1   egg
1/2 teaspoon salt
1   teaspoon margarine, softened
1/4 teaspoon baking powder
2   tablespoons skim milk

PER serving:
CALORIES 237
(13% from fat
FAT 3g
(saturated 1g)
PROTEIN 19g
CARBOHYDRATE 32g
CHOLESTEROL 72mg
SODIUM 94mg

PLACE chicken and water in a soup kettle; bring to a boil. Reduce heat; cover and simmer until chicken is tender. Cool broth and skim off fat. Cut chicken into bite-size pieces; return to broth. Add the next 7 ingredients; bring to a boil. Reduce heat; simmer, uncovered, for 50 to 60 minutes, or until vegetables are tender.
MEANWHILE, for noodles, place flour on a pastry board or countertop and make a well in the center. Stir together remaining ingredients; pour into well. Gradually fold flour into wet ingredients with hands until dough can be rolled into a ball. Knead for 5 to 6 minutes. Cover and let rest for 10 minutes. ON a floured surface, roll dough out to a square (1/16- to 1/8-inch thick), and cut into 1/4-inch-wide strips. Cook noodles in boiling water for 2 to 3 minutes, or until done. Drain and add to soup just before serving.
YIELD: 6 servings

# Pasta Meatball Stew

1    pound ground turkey breast
1    egg
1/4 cup dry bread crumbs
1/4 cup skim milk
1/2 teaspoon ground mustard
1/2 teaspoon pepper
1    cup chopped onion
2    garlic cloves, minced
2    tablespoons all-purpose flour
1 1/2 cups low-sodium beef broth
2    tablespoons no-salt-added tomato paste
1    (14 1/2-ounce) can no-salt-added tomatoes,
        diced and undrained
1    bay leaf
3/4 teaspoon dried thyme
1 1/2 cups sliced carrots
1 1/2 cups chopped zucchini
1    cup chopped green pepper
1    cup chopped sweet red pepper
1    tablespoon minced fresh parsley
2    cups cooked pasta

COMBINE the first 6 ingredients; mix well. Shape into 1-inch balls. In a Dutch oven, coated with cooking spray, brown meatballs over medium heat; drain and set aside.

IN the same pan, cook onion and garlic until onion is tender. Stir in flour. Gradually add broth, stirring constantly. Bring to a boil. Cook and stir 1 to 2 minutes, or until thickened.

ADD tomato paste, tomatoes, bay leaf and thyme; mix well. Add meatballs and carrots; bring to a boil. Reduce heat; cover and simmer 30 minutes.

ADD zucchini and peppers; bring to a boil. Reduce heat; cover and simmer 10 to 15 minutes, or until vegetables are tender.

ADD parsley and pasta; heat through. Remove bay leaf.

YIELD: 8 servings

# Pork Stew with Sweet Potatoes andCorn

1 1/2 pounds lean boned pork loin
1   tablespoon olive oil
2   cups quartered mushrooms
1 1/2 cups thinly-sliced leek
2   cups julienne-cut carrot
1   cup low-salt chicken broth
2   teaspoons poultry seasoning
2   bay leaves
1/2 teaspoon salt
1/2 teaspoon coarsely-ground pepper
2   (14.5-ounce) cans no-salt-added whole
     tomatoes, undrained and chopped
3 1/2 cups peeled, chopped sweet potato (about
     1 pound)
1   (10-ounce) package frozen whole-kernel
     corn
2   cups coarsely-chopped spinach

PER serving:
CALORIES 394
(27% from fat)
FAT 12g
(saturated 3.4g)
PROTEIN 29.4g
CARBOHYDRATE 44.7g
CHOLESTEROL 68mg
SODIUM 344mg

TRIM fat from pork; cut pork into 1-inch cubes.
HEAT olive oil in a large Dutch oven over medium-high heat until hot.
ADD pork cubes, mushrooms and leek; sauté 10 minutes, or until browned.
STIR in carrot and next 6 ingredients; bring to a boil.
COVER; reduce heat and simmer 1 hour, or until pork is tender.
ADD sweet potatoes and corn; cover and simmer 20 minutes, or until sweet potato is tender.
ADD spinach; cover and simmer 2 minutes.
DISCARD bay leaves.
YIELD: 6 (1 3/4-cups) servings

# Roasted Chicken-Noodle Soup

2   teaspoons olive oil
1   cup chopped onion
1   cup diced carrots
1   cup sliced celery
1   garlic clove, minced
1/4 cup all-purpose flour
1/2 teaspoon dried oregano
1/4 teaspoon dried thyme
1/4 teaspoon poultry seasoning
6   cups low-fat chicken broth
4   cups peeled, diced baking potato
1   teaspoon salt
2   cups diced, roasted chicken
1   cup evaporated skim milk
4   ounces (2 cups) uncooked wide egg noodles
Fresh thyme sprigs (optional)

HEAT olive oil in a Dutch oven over medium heat. Add onion and next 3 ingredients; sauté 5 minutes.
SPRINKLE flour and next 3 ingredients over vegetables; cook 1 minute. Stir in broth, potato and salt. Bring to a boil; reduce heat and simmer, partially covered, for 25 minutes, or until potato is tender.
ADD roasted chicken, milk and noodles; cook 10 minutes, or until noodles are tender.
GARNISH with fresh thyme, if desired.
YIELD: 2 1/2 quarts (serving size: 1 cup)

# Round Steak Chili

1   pound beef round steak, trimmed and cut
      into 1/2-inch cubes
1   large onion, chopped
2   garlic cloves, minced
1   (46-ounce) can V8 juice
1   (28-ounce) can crushed tomatoes
2   cups sliced celery
1   medium green pepper, chopped
1   bay leaf
2   tablespoons chili powder
1   teaspoon dried oregano
1   teaspoon brown sugar
1/2 teaspoon each: celery seed, paprika, ground
      mustard and cumin
1/4 teaspoon cayenne pepper
1/4 teaspoon dried basil
1   (16-ounce) can kidney beans, rinsed and
      drained

IN a large kettle or Dutch oven, coated with non-stick cooking spray, brown meat, onion and garlic. Add V8 juice, tomatoes, celery, green pepper and seasonings; bring to a boil. Reduce heat; simmer, uncovered, for 3 hours.
ADD kidney beans; heat through. Remove bay leaf before serving.
YIELD: 10 servings

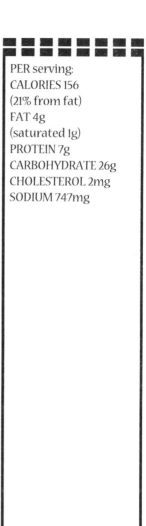

PER serving:
CALORIES 156
(21% from fat)
FAT 4g
(saturated 1g)
PROTEIN 7g
CARBOHYDRATE 26g
CHOLESTEROL 2mg
SODIUM 747mg

# Spinach Garlic Soup

1   (10-ounce) package fresh spinach, trimmed
      and coarsely chopped
4   cups low-sodium chicken broth, divided
1/2 cup shredded carrots
1/2 cup chopped onion
8   garlic cloves, minced
1/4 cup all-purpose flour
3/4 cup evaporated skim milk
1/4 cup skim milk
1/2 teaspoon pepper
1/8 teaspoon ground nutmeg

IN a 5-quart Dutch oven, bring spinach, 3 1/2 cups broth and carrot to a boil. Reduce heat; simmer for 5 minutes, stirring occasionally. Remove from heat; cool to lukewarm.

MEANWHILE, in a skillet coated with cooking spray, sauté onion and garlic until onion is soft, about 5 minutes.

COMBINE flour and remaining broth until smooth. Add to skillet; cook and stir over low heat for 3 to 5 minutes. Add to spinach mixture.

PURÉE in small batches in a blender or food processor until finely chopped.

PLACE in a large saucepan. Add evaporated milk, milk, pepper and nutmeg. Heat through, but do not boil.

YIELD: 6 servings

# Southwestern Bean Soup

4   turkey bacon strips
3/4 cup chopped onion
3/4 cup chopped celery
1/8 teaspoon garlic powder
1   (16-ounce) can fat-free refried beans
1/4 cup picante sauce
1   (14 1/2-ounce) can low-sodium chicken broth
1   tablespoon chopped fresh parsley

IN a medium saucepan coated with nonstick cooking spray, cook bacon until crisp; remove to paper towel to drain. Crumble and set aside.
IN the same pan, sauté onion and celery; sprinkle with garlic powder. Cover and simmer for 10 minutes, or until vegetables are tender.
ADD beans, picante sauce, broth, parsley and bacon; bring to a boil. Reduce heat and simmer, uncovered, for 5 to 10 minutes.
YIELD: 4 servings.

PER serving:
CALORIES 167
(20% from fat)
FAT 4g
(saturated 1g)
PROTEIN 10g
CARBOHYDRATE 24g
CHOLESTEROL 14mg
SODIUM 770mg

# Split Pea Vegetable Soup

1 1/2 cups dry split peas, rinsed
2 1/2 quarts water
7   whole allspice, tied in a cheesecloth bag
1/2 teaspoon pepper
1/2 medium head cabbage, shredded
6   large potatoes, peeled and cut into 1/2-inch
       cubes
6   carrots, chopped
2   medium onions, chopped
2   cups cubed, fully-cooked low-fat ham

IN a large kettle, combine peas, water, allspice and pepper; bring to a boil. Reduce heat; cover and simmer for 1 hour.

STIR in cabbage, potatoes, carrots, onions and ham. Bring to a boil. Reduce heat; cover and simmer for 30 minutes, or until vegetables are tender, stirring occasionally.

DISCARD allspice.

YIELD: 20 servings

RECIPE may be cut in half for less servings.

# Sweet Potato Minestrone with Turkey Sausage

1/2 pound smoked turkey sausage, cut into
    1/4-inch-thick slices
1   cup dried onion
1   cup sliced carrot
3/4 cup thinly-sliced celery
3   cups water
2   cups peeled, diced sweet potato (about
    9 ounces)
1   teaspoon dried oregano
1/4 teaspoon salt
1/2 teaspoon coarsely-ground pepper
2   (14.5-ounce) cans no-salt-added whole
    tomatoes, undrained and coarsely
    chopped
1   (15-ounce) can Great Northern beans, rinsed
    and drained
8   cups coarsely-chopped spinach

COMBINE first 4 ingredients in a Dutch oven; sauté over medium-high heat 7 minutes, or until sausage is browned.
ADD water and next 6 ingredients.
BRING to a boil; cover. Reduce heat and simmer 30 minutes, or until vegetables are tender.
STIR in spinach; cook an additional 2 minutes.
YIELD: 7 (1 1/2-cup) servings

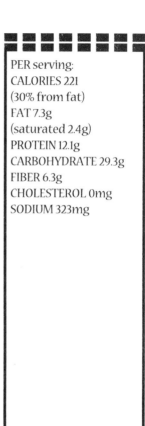

PER serving:
CALORIES 221
(30% from fat)
FAT 7.3g
(saturated 2.4g)
PROTEIN 12.1g
CARBOHYDRATE 29.3g
FIBER 6.3g
CHOLESTEROL 0mg
SODIUM 323mg

# Veal Stew with Cilantro-Chile Sauce

1   (2-pound) boneless veal leg roast
3 1/2 cups low-salt chicken broth
1   cup sliced carrots
3/4 cup sliced celery
1/2 cup thinly-sliced green onions
1/3 cup seeded, thinly-sliced jalapeño pepper
1/3 cup fresh cilantro leaves
6   garlic cloves
1   bay leaf
1/2 cup orange juice
1/4 cup fresh lemon juice
1/2 teaspoon salt
1/4 cup thinly-sliced green onions
2   tablespoons minced fresh cilantro

PREHEAT oven to 325 degrees.
TRIM fat from roast. Combine roast, broth and next 7 ingredients in a large Dutch oven; bring to a boil. Remove from heat; cover and bake at 325 degrees for 1 hour and 15 minutes, or until roast is tender. Remove roast from pan, reserving cooking liquid and vegetables. Let roast stand for 10 minutes. Separate roast into bite-size pieces and shred with 2 forks; set aside.
REMOVE bay leaf from cooking liquid and discard. Place cooking liquid and vegetables in a blender. Cover and process until smooth. Return vegetable purée to pan. Add fruit juices; bring to a boil and cook 18 minutes, or until vegetable purée is reduced to 2 cups.
RETURN shredded roast to pan; stir in salt. Cook over medium heat until thoroughly heated. Ladle stew into individual bowls; top with 1/4 cup chopped green onion and minced cilantro.
SERVE with flour tortillas.
YIELD: 4 (1-cup) servings.

# Vegetarian Minestrone

2   teaspoons olive oil
3/4 cup chopped onion
3   cups water
2   cups diced zucchini
1   cup diced carrot
1   cup drained, canned cannellini beans, or
      other white beans
3/4 cup diced celery
1/2 teaspoon dried basil
1/4 teaspoon each salt, dried oregano
1/8 teaspoon coarsely-ground pepper
1   (14.5-ounce) can diced tomatoes, undrained
1   garlic clove, minced
1/4 cup uncooked elbow, or very short ditalini
      macaroni
1   tablespoon plus 1 teaspoon grated
      Parmesan cheese

HEAT oil in a large saucepan over medium-high
heat until hot. Add onion; sauté 4 minutes, or until
lightly browned.
ADD water and next 9 ingredients to saucepan;
bring to a boil. Cover; reduce heat to medium-low
and cook 25 minutes.
ADD pasta; cover and cook an additional 10 minutes. Ladle into individual bowls; sprinkle with
cheese.
YIELD: 4 servings (1 1/2 cups soup and 1 teaspoon
cheese)

PER serving:
CALORIES 176
(17% from fat)
FAT 3.3g
(saturated 0.7g)
PROTEIN 8.8g
CARBOHYDRATE 30.2g
CHOLESTEROL 1mg
SODIUM 699mg

# Bacon-Cheese-Mushroom Burgers

PER serving:
CALORIES 317
(40% from fat)
FAT 14g
(saturated 4g)
PROTEIN 24g
CARBOHYDRATE 26g
CHOLESTEROL 83mg
SODIUM 417mg

1 1/2 pounds ground round
3   tablespoons onion, finely chopped
Dash of garlic powder
1/2 teaspoon pepper
6   turkey bacon strips, cooked and crumbled
1/3 can sliced mushrooms
1   cup (4 ounces) shredded, reduced-fat
        Cheddar cheese
1/4 cup reduced-fat mayonnaise
Pearl onion, 8 thinly-sliced pieces (optional)
8   hamburger buns, split
Lettuce leaves and tomato slice (optional)

IN a medium bowl, combine beef, onion, garlic powder and pepper; mix well.

SHAPE into 8 patties, 3/4-inch thick.

IN a small bowl, combine the bacon, mushrooms, cheese and mayonnaise; refrigerate.

GRILL over medium-hot coals for 8 to 10 minutes, or until no longer pink, turning once. (You may use an indoor grill.)

DURING the last 3 minutes of cooking, spoon a scant 1/4 cup of the cheese mixture onto each burger.

SERVE on buns with lettuce and tomato, and onion if desired.

YIELD: 8 sandwiches

# Barbequed Beef Sandwiches

2 pounds boneless round steak, trimmed and
   cubed
2 cups water
4 cups shredded cabbage
1/2 cup barbeque sauce
1/2 cup ketchup
1/3 cup Worcestershire sauce
1 tablespoon prepared horseradish
1 tablespoon prepared mustard
10 hamburger buns, split

IN a covered Dutch oven or saucepan, simmer beef
in water for 1 1/2 hours, or until tender.
DRAIN cooking liquid, reserving 3/4 cup.
COOL beef; shred and return to Dutch oven. Add
cabbage, barbeque sauce, ketchup, Worcestershire
sauce, horseradish, mustard and the reserved cook-
ing liquid.
COVER and simmer for 1 hour.
SERVE warm on buns.
YIELD: 10 sandwiches

PER serving:
CALORIES 279
(22% from fat)
FAT 7g
(saturated 2g)
CHOLESTEROL 51mg
SODIUM 716mg
CARBOHYDRATE 32g
PROTEIN 21g

# Barbequed Pork Sandwiches

PER serving:
CALORIES 258
(25% from fat)
FAT 7g
(saturated 2g)
CHOLESTEROL 40mg
SODIUM 560mg
CARBOHYDRATE 30g
PROTEIN 18g

2   boneless pork loin roasts (2 1/2 pounds
        each)
1   cup water
2   cups ketchup
2   cups diced celery
1/3 cup steak sauce
1/4 cup packed brown sugar
1/4 cup vinegar
2   teaspoons lemon juice
25 hamburger buns, split

PLACE roasts in an 8-quart Dutch oven; add water.
Cover and cook on medium-low heat for 2 1/2 hours,
or until meat is tender. Remove roasts and shred
with a fork; set aside.
SKIM fat from cooking liquid and discard.
DRAIN all but 1 cup of cooking liquid; add meat,
ketchup, celery, steak sauce, brown sugar, vinegar
and lemon juice.
COVER and cook on medium-low heat for 1 1/2 hours.
SERVE on buns.
YIELD: 25 sandwiches

YOU may use only 1 roast and half of the remaining
ingredients in the recipe; however, I found it freezes
very well.

# Beef Fajitas

1 pound top sirloin steak, trimmed and cut
   across the grain into 1/4-inch strips
2 tablespoons water
2 tablespoons lemon juice
1 tablespoon vegetable oil
1 teaspoon dried oregano
1 garlic clove, minced
1/4 teaspoon salt
1/4 teaspoon pepper
1/2 medium onion, sliced
1 medium sweet red pepper, sliced into thin
   strips
6 fat-free flour tortilla shells, warmed
Salsa and nonfat sour cream (optional)

IN a bowl or resealable plastic bag, combine the
first 7 ingredients. Add beef and toss. Cover and
refrigerate 3 to 6 hours, or overnight, stirring several times. Drain meat, discarding marinade.
IN a skillet coated with nonstick cooking spray,
sauté onion and red pepper until crisp-tender; remove.
IN same skillet, sauté meat until no longer pink,
about 4 minutes.
RETURN vegetables to the pan and heat through.
SPOON onto tortillas; top with salsa and sour cream
if desired. Roll tortilla around filling.
YIELD: 6 servings

PER serving:
CALORIES (without salsa
   and sour cream) 237
(20% from fat)
FAT 2g
(saturated 2g)
CHOLESTEROL 50mg
SODIUM 422mg
CARBOHYDRATE 26g
PROTEIN 20g

# Cajun Burgers

CAJUN SEASONING:
3   tablespoons ground cumin
3   tablespoons dried oregano
1   tablespoon garlic powder
1   tablespoon paprika
1   teaspoon cayenne pepper

BURGERS:
1   pound ground round
1/4 cup finely-chopped onion
1   teaspoon Cajun seasoning blend (above)
1/2 teaspoon hot pepper sauce
1/2 teaspoon dried thyme
1/4 teaspoon dried basil
1   garlic clove, minced
4   hamburger buns, split
Sautéed onions (optional)

COMBINE all seasoning blend ingredients in a small bowl or resealable plastic bag; mix well.
IN a bowl, combine the first 7 burger ingredients; shape into 4 patties.
COOK in a skillet, or on grill over medium-hot coals, for 4 to 5 minutes per side, or until burgers reach desired doneness.
SERVE on buns; top with sautéed onions, if desired.
YOU may store leftover seasoning blend in an air-tight container.
YIELD: 4 sandwiches

# Grilled Vegetable Sandwich

1/4 cup balsamic vinegar
2   tablespoons olive oil
1   tablespoon fresh, or 1 teaspoon dried basil
2   teaspoons molasses
1 1/2 teaspoons fresh, or 1/2 teaspoon dried thyme
1/4 teaspoon salt
1/4 teaspoon pepper
3   medium zucchini, cut lengthwise into
       1/4-inch-thick oblong slices
1   medium yellow bell pepper, cut into 6 wedges
2   medium red bell peppers, each cut into 6 wedges
1   large onion, cut into 1/2-inch slices
1   (16-ounce) loaf French bread
Vegetable cooking spray
3/4 cup crumbled Feta cheese
2   tablespoons fat-free mayonnaise
1/4 cup (1 ounce) freshly-grated Parmesan cheese

PER serving:
CALORIES 294
(27% from fat)
FAT 8.8g
(saturated 3.1g)
PROTEIN 9.8g
CARBOHYDRATE 44g
FIBER 2.1g
CHOLESTEROL 14mg
SODIUM 692mg

COMBINE first 7 ingredients in a large, heavy-duty, zip-top plastic bag.
ADD zucchini, bell peppers and onion; seal bag. Marinate in refrigerate 2 hours, turning bag occasionally.
REMOVE vegetables from bag, reserving marinade.
SET vegetables aside.
CUT French bread loaf in half horizontally, and brush 3 tablespoons reserved marinade over cut-sides of bread. Set bread halves and remaining marinade aside.
PLACE vegetables in a wire grilling basket coated with cooking spray.
PLACE grilling basket on grill rack over medium-hot coals (350 to 400 degrees); grill 5 minutes, basting occasionally with remaining marinade.
TURN basket over; grill 2 minutes, basting occasionally.
PLACE bread, cut-sides down, on grill rack; grill an additional 3 minutes, or until vegetables are tender and bread is toasted.
COMBINE Feta cheese and mayonnaise in a bowl; stir well. Spread mixture evenly over cut-sides of toasted bread; place grilled vegetables on bottom half of bread.
SPRINKLE Parmesan cheese over the vegetables; top with half of bread.
CUT loaf into 8 pieces.
YIELD: 8 servings

# Ham Sandwiches

2   cups (8 ounces) shredded reduced-fat
       Cheddar cheese
1 1/2 cups ground, fully-cooked low-fat ham
1/2 cup finely-chopped onion
1/3 cup fat-free French salad dressing
2   tablespoons prepared mustard
4   teaspoons caraway seeds
5   hamburger buns, split

COMBINE the first 6 ingredients; mix well.
SPREAD over cut-side of buns.
PLACE on a baking sheet coated with nonstick cooking spray.
BAKE at 350 degrees for 15 to 20 minutes, or until cheese is melted.
YIELD: 10 sandwiches

# Italian Beef Sandwiches

1   (4-pound) beef sirloin tip roast
3   onions, thinly sliced
1/2 teaspoon onion powder
1/4 teaspoon garlic powder
1   teaspoon dried oregano
2   teaspoons Italian seasoning
1   teaspoon salt-free seasoning salt blend
1   teaspoon dried basil
3   low-sodium beef bouillon cubes
7   hot banana peppers, seeded and sliced
24 hard rolls, split

PER serving:
CALORIES 286
(19% from fat)
FAT 6g
(saturated 2g)
CHOLESTEROL 50mg
PROTEIN 27g
CARBOHYDRATE 29g
SODIUM 400mg

IN a baking pan, place roast and 1-inch of water; cover with onions. Bake, covered, at 350 degrees for 1 1/2 hours, or until meat is tender.
REMOVE meat from baking pan; reserve and chill broth.
REFRIGERATE meat until firm; skim fat from broth.
IN a medium saucepan, combine broth and remaining ingredients, except rolls.
BRING to a boil; reduce heat and simmer 10 minutes.
MEANWHILE, cut meat into thin slices; place in a 13x9x2-inch baking pan.
POUR broth mixture over meat; cover and refrigerate for 24 hours.
REHEAT, covered, at 325 degrees for 1 hour.
SERVE on hard rolls.
YIELD: 24 sandwiches

# Italian Chicken-Mozzarella Melt

PER serving:
CALORIES 509
(26% from fat)
FAT 14.6g
(saturated 3.2g)
PROTEIN 41.7g
CARBOHYDRATE 50.9g
FIBER 2.1g
CHOLESTEROL 78mg
SODIUM 1062mg

4   (4-ounce) skinned and boned chicken
        breast halves
1   tablespoon olive oil
1/4 teaspoon salt
1/2 teaspoon dried oregano, divided
1   cup pizza pasta sauce
1/2 teaspoon dried basil
4   (2.8-ounce) hoagie buns, halved and
        toasted
1   small zucchini, shredded
1/4 cup (2 ounces) shredded part-skim
        Mozzarella cheese
1/4 cup grated Parmesan cheese
Basil leaves, for garnish (optional)

BRUSH each piece of chicken with olive oil; sprinkle with salt and 1/4 teaspoon oregano.

COOK chicken in a large nonstick skillet over medium-high heat about 4 minutes on each side, or until done. Set chicken aside.

COMBINE pizza pasta sauce, basil and remaining 1/4 teaspoon oregano in skillet; cook over medium-high heat until thoroughly heated.

REMOVE sauce from heat; add chicken and keep warm.

PLACE rolls on a baking sheet; spread sauce mixture evenly on bottom half of each roll. Top evenly with chicken, zucchini and cheeses.

BROIL 3 inches from heat; (with electric oven door partly opened) 2 to 3 minutes, or until cheeses melt. Cover each bottom half with tops of rolls. Garnish, if desired.

YIELD: 5 servings

# Mexican Beef Tortillas

2   eggs
2   (4-ounce) cans chopped green chilies
1/4 cup minced onion
1/3 cup salsa
1/2 teaspoon pepper
1   garlic clove, minced
3/4 cup finely-crushed baked tortilla chips
2   pounds ground round
10  (10-inch) fat-free tortillas, warmed

TOPPINGS:
Chopped tomatoes
Chopped ripe olives
Shredded fat-free Cheddar cheese
Shredded lettuce
Extra salsa (optional)

IN a bowl, combine the first 6 ingredients.
ADD chips and beef; mix well.
SHAPE into 10 patties.
PAN-fry or grill, or broil until no longer pink.
WRAP burgers and desired toppings into the tortillas.
YIELD: 10 servings

PER wrap:
CALORIES 213
(29% from fat)
FAT 10g
(saturated 4g)
CHOLESTEROL 76mg
SODIUM 623mg
CARBOHYDRATE 30g
PROTEIN 23g

# Open-Faced Turkey Sandwiches

4   teaspoons light cream cheese, softened
2   slices whole wheat bread, toasted
2   (1-ounce) slices reduced-fat Cheddar cheese
4 ounces thinly-sliced cooked turkey breast
6 fresh spinach leaves, shredded

SPREAD cream cheese on toast; layer cheese, turkey and spinach over cream cheese.
BROIL until cheese is melted.
SERVE immediately.
YIELD: 2 sandwiches

# Philly Cheese Sandwich

1   teaspoon olive oil
1 1/2 cups sliced onion
1 1/2 cups sliced green bell pepper
1/4 teaspoon black pepper
4   (1-ounce) slices of French bread
Olive oil-flavored vegetable cooking spray
8   ounces thinly-sliced deli roast beef
4   (1-ounce) slices reduced-fat Swiss cheese

HEAT oil in a nonstick skillet over medium heat until hot. Add onion; cook 10 minutes, stirring frequently. Add bell pepper, and black pepper; cook 3 minutes, or until bell pepper is crisp-tender.
COAT top-sides of bread with cooking spray. Top each slice with 2 ounces of beef, 1/4 cup onion mixture, and a cheese slice.
PLACE sandwiches on a baking sheet coated with cooking spray; broil 2 minutes, or until cheese melts.
YIELD: 4 servings

PER slice:
CALORIES 291
(27% from fat)
FAT 8.6g
(saturated 3.7g)
CHOLESTEROL 39mg
SODIUM 819mg
PROTEIN 24.8g
CARBOHYDRATE 28.4g

# Roast Beef and Blue Cheese Sandwich

2   tablespoons nonfat mayonnaise
1   tablespoon Dijon mustard
1/4 teaspoon pepper
2 (2-ounce) onion sandwich buns, sliced
2   romaine lettuce leaves
4   tomato slices
4   green bell pepper rings
4   red onion slices
4 ounces thinly-sliced lean deli roast beef
2   tablespoons crumbled blue cheese

COMBINE mayonnaise, mustard and pepper; stir
well. Spread on cut-sides of sandwich buns.
LINE the bottom half of each sandwich bun with
lettuce leaf; top with tomato, bell pepper, onion,
roast beef, cheese, and top halves of buns.
YIELD; 2 servings

# Reuben Loaf

3 1/4 to 3 3/4 cups all-purpose flour
1 (1/4-ounce) package quick-rise yeast
1   tablespoon sugar
1   tablespoon margarine, softened
1   teaspoon salt
1   cup warm water (120 to 130 degrees)
1/4 cup reduced-fat thousand island salad
      dressing
6 ounces thinly-sliced reduced-fat corned beef
4 ounces sliced reduced-fat Swiss cheese
1   (8-ounce) can sauerkraut, drained
1   egg white, beaten
Caraway seeds (optional)

IN a mixing bowl, combine 2 1/4 cups flour, yeast,
sugar, margarine and salt.
STIR in warm water; mix until a soft dough forms.
Add remaining flour, if necessary.
TURN onto a lightly-floured surface; knead until
smooth, about 4 minutes.
ON a baking sheet coated with nonstick cooking
spray, roll dough to a 14x10-inch rectangle.
SPREAD dressing down center third of dough. Top
with layers of beef, cheese and sauerkraut.
MAKE cuts from filling to edges of dough, 1 inch
apart, on both sides of the filling.
ALTERNATING sides, fold the strips at an angle
across filling.
COVER dough and let rise in a warm place for 15
minutes. Brush with egg white and sprinkle with
caraway seeds, if desired.
BAKE at 400 degrees for 25 minutes, or until lightly
browned.
SERVE immediately; refrigerate leftovers.
YIELD: 8 servings.

PER 1/8 loaf:
CALORIES 298
(18% from fat)
FAT 6g
(saturated 2g)
CHOLESTEROL 32mg
SODIUM 835mg
CARBOHYDRATE 45g
PROTEIN 16g

# Salmon Salad Sandwiches

3 ounces fat-free cream cheese, softened
1   tablespoon fat-free mayonnaise
1   tablespoon lemon juice
1   teaspoon dill weed
1/8 teaspoon pepper
1   (6-ounce) can pink salmon, drained, skin
        and bones removed
1/2 cup shredded carrot
1/2 cup shredded celery
Lettuce leaves (optional)
2   whole wheat buns, split

IN a mixing bowl, beat cream cheese, mayonnaise,
lemon juice, dill and pepper until smooth; add the
salmon, carrot and celery. Mix well.
PLACE a lettuce leaf, if desired, and about 1/2 cup
salmon salad on each bun.
YIELD: 2 sandwiches

# Shredded Chicken Coleslaw Sandwich

1 (12-ounce) bag coleslaw
1/3 cup light coleslaw dressing
1/4 teaspoon celery seeds
1 cup no-salt-added ketchup
1/2 cup water
1/4 cup cider vinegar
2 tablespoons instant diced or finely-diced
    onions
2 tablespoons dark brown sugar
1 tablespoon prepared mustard
1 teaspoon pepper
1 teaspoon hot sauce
1/2 teaspoon garlic powder
1 1/2 cups (3/4-pound) skinned, shredded
    roasted chicken breast
4 (2-ounce) slices Texas toast, lightly toasted

COMBINE first 3 ingredients in a bowl; toss well to coat.
COMBINE ketchup and next 8 ingredients in a medium saucepan; bring to a boil. Reduce heat and simmer 5 minutes, or until mixture begins to thicken. Stir in chicken, and cook 4 minutes, or until chicken is thoroughly heated.
TOP each bread slice with 1/2 cup chicken mixture and 1/2 cup coleslaw mixture.
YIELD: 4 servings.

PER slice:
CALORIES 421
(19% from fat)
FAT 8.9g
(saturated 1.9g)
CHOLESTEROL 76mg
PROTEIN 26.5g
CARBOHYDRATE 64.4g

# Southwestern Chicken Heros

PER sandwich:
CALORIES 309
(23% from fat)
FAT 8g
(saturated 1g)
CHOLESTEROL 83mg
PROTEIN 38g
CARBOHYDRATE 21g
SODIUM 476mg

6 boneless, skinless chicken breast halves
1/4 teaspoon pepper
1/4 teaspoon crushed red pepper flakes
1/4 teaspoon chili powder
6 slices part-skim Mozzarella cheese
6 French or Italian rolls, split
2 tablespoons fat-free margarine
Lettuce leaves and tomato slices
Salsa or picante sauce (optional)

POUND chicken breasts slightly to flatten evenly. Spray both sides with nonstick cooking spray. Combine seasonings; sprinkle on both sides of chicken.
GRILL or broil for 6 to 8 minutes; turn and cook 4 to 6 minutes more, or until chicken is tender and no longer pink.
TOP with cheese; allow to melt, about 2 minutes.
HEAT or grill rolls just until toasted; spread with margarine.
PLACE chicken on rolls; top with lettuce, tomato, and salsa or picante sauce if desired.
YIELD: 6 sandwiches

# Stuffed French Bread

2  turkey Italian sausages
1/2 pound ground round
1/2 cup chopped onion
1/4 cup chopped green pepper
1  medium tomato, chopped
1  (15-ounce) can tomato sauce
1/2 teaspoon dried basil
1/2 teaspoon dried oregano
1/2 teaspoon sugar
1/4 teaspoon aniseed
1/8 teaspoon garlic powder
1  (1-pound) loaf French bread
1/4 c. grated Parmesan cheese
Coarsely-ground pepper

PER serving:
CALORIES 375
(28% from fat)
FAT 12g
(saturated 4g)
CHOLESTEROL 42mg
SODIUM 1062mg
CARBOHYDRATE 48g
PROTEIN 20g

IN a skillet, cook sausages until no longer pink; remove and set aside.

IN the same skillet, cook the beef, onion and green pepper and tomato until beef is no longer pink; drain, and stir in tomato sauce and seasonings.

CUT sausages in half lengthwise and slice; add to meat sauce

CUT a wedge out of the top of the bread about 2 inches wide and 3/4 of the way through the loaf.

FILL the loaf with meat sauce. Sprinkle with Parmesan cheese and pepper.

BAKE at 400 degrees for 15 to 20 minutes, or until heated through.

YIELD: 6 servings

# Stuffed Italian Meatball Sub

1  pound ground chuck
1/4 cup fine, dry Italian seasoned bread crumbs
1/4 cup minced fresh onion
1/4 teaspoon salt
1/4 teaspoon pepper
1  egg white
1  tablespoon olive oil
1  cup chopped onion
3  garlic cloves, minced
2  tablespoons tomato paste
1  teaspoon sugar
1  teaspoon dried rosemary
1/4 teaspoon salt
1  (14.5-ounce) can no-salt-added whole
    tomatoes, undrained and chopped
1/4 cup coarsely-chopped fresh basil, or
    4 teaspoons dried basil
1  (16-ounce) loaf French bread
1/2 cup (2 ounces) shredded part-skim
    Mozzarella cheese

PREHEAT oven to 375 degrees.
COMBINE the first 6 ingredients in a bowl; stir well.
SHAPE mixture into 30 (1-inch)meatballs; place on
a broiler pan.
BAKE meatballs at 375 degrees for 20 minutes, or
until done.
HEAT oil in a large saucepan over medium-high
heat until hot; add 1 cup onion and garlic; sauté 3
minutes, or until tender.
ADD tomato paste, sugar, rosemary, 1/4 teaspoon
salt, and tomatoes; bring to a boil.
REDUCE heat; simmer 15 minutes.
REMOVE from heat; stir in meatballs and basil.
CUT bread loaf in half horizontally.
SCOOP out bread from bottom half of loaf, leaving a 1-
inch-thick bread shell; reserve bread for another use.
SPOON meatballs and sauce into bread shell;
sprinkle with cheese.
TOP with top half of bread. Cut loaf into 8 pieces.
YIELD: 8 sandwiches

# Tuna Burgers

3 (6-ounce) cans solid white tuna, in spring
    water, drained and flaked
1 teaspoon cracked black pepper
1/2 cup soft bread crumbs
1/2 cup egg substitute
1 teaspoon low-sodium Worcestershire
    sauce
1 small onion, finely chopped
2 tablespoons dried parsley flakes
2 drops hot sauce
1 teaspoon lemon juice
1 teaspoon salt-free lemon-pepper seasoning
1/2 teaspoon onion powder
1/2 teaspoon garlic powder
1 teaspoon cracked black pepper
1/2 teaspoon thyme
Vegetable cooking spray
6 kaiser rolls, split
6 lettuce leaves
6 slices tomato
1/4 cup plus 2 tablespoons reduced-calorie
    mayonnaise
2 tablespoons sweet pickle relish

PER serving:
CALORIES 453
(22% from fat)
FAT 11.1g
(saturated 1.2g)
PROTEIN 30.9g
CARBOHYDRATE 56.4g
FIBER 1.7g
CHOLESTEROL 35mg
SODIUM 1042mg

COMBINE first 10 ingredients; shape tuna mixture
into 6 patties.
COMBINE onion powder and next 3 ingredients;
sprinkle evenly on both sides of patties.
COOK patties in a large nonstick skillet coated with
cooking spray, 4 minutes on each side, or until
done.
PLACE each patty on a roll with lettuce and tomato
slices; serve with mayonnaise and pickle relish.
YIELD: 6 servings

# Turkey Burritos

1   pound ground turkey breast
1/2 cup chopped onion
1   (14 1/2-ounce) can diced tomatoes,
       undrained
1   (16-ounce) can fat-free refried beans and
       green chilies
1   (4-ounce) can chopped green chilies
1   (2 1/4-ounce) can sliced ripe olives, drained
1   envelope taco seasoning mix
1/4 cup frozen corn
1/4 cup uncooked instant rice
12  fat-free flour tortillas

IN a large nonstick saucepan, brown turkey and onion; drain.
ADD the next 6 ingredients; bring to a boil. Reduce heat; cover and simmer for 15 minutes.
RETURN to a boil; stir in rice. Remove from the heat.
COVER; let stand for 5 minutes.
SPOON about 1/2 cup down the center of each tortilla; fold in sides.
YIELD: 12 servings

# Turkey-Vegetable Sloppy Joes

1 pound ground turkey
1 cup chopped onion
1 garlic clove, minced
1/2 cup chopped green bell pepper
1 (14 1/2-ounce) can diced tomatoes
1/4 cup tomato paste
1 tablespoon mustard
1 teaspoon chili powder
3/4 teaspoon ground cumin
1/2 teaspoon salt
1/2 teaspoon ground black pepper
4 (2-ounce) kaiser rolls or hamburger buns, split
1 cup (4 ounces) shredded Cheddar cheese

COOK turkey, onion and garlic in a large nonstick skillet over medium-high heat until turkey is browned, stirring to crumble. Stir in bell pepper and next 7 ingredients.
BRING to a boil; cove,, reduce heat and simmer 10 minutes.
SPOON 1/2 cup turkey mixture onto each roll half; top each with 2 tablespoons cheese.
YIELD: 8 servings

PER serving:
CALORIES 232
(25% from fat)
FAT 6.4g
(saturated 2.5g)
CHOLESTEROL 46mg
SODIUM 576mg
CARBOHYDRATE 22.8g
PROTEIN 20.8g

# Notes & Recipes

# Breads

# List Your Favorite Recipes

**Recipes**                                                    **Page**

_____     _____

_____     _____

_____     _____

_____     _____

_____     _____

_____     _____

_____     _____

_____     _____

_____     _____

_____     _____

_____     _____

_____     _____

_____     _____

_____     _____

_____     _____

_____     _____

_____     _____

# Baked Hush Puppies

1　cup yellow cornmeal
1　cup all-purpose flour
1　tablespoon baking powder
1　teaspoon sugar
1　teaspoon salt
1/8 teaspoon ground red pepper
2　large eggs, lightly beaten
3/4 cup skim milk
1/4 cup vegetable oil
1/2 cup finely-chopped onion
Vegetable cooking spray

COMBINE first 6 ingredients in a large bowl; make a well in center of mixture; set aside.
COMBINE eggs and next 3 ingredients, stirring well; add to dry mixture, stirring just until dry ingredients are moistened.
COAT miniature (1 3/4-inch) muffin pans with cooking spray.
SPOON about 1 tablespoon batter into each muffin cup (cups will be about three-fourths full).
BAKE at 425 degrees for 15 minutes, or until done.
REMOVE from pans immediately.
YIELD: 3 dozen

PER 2-hush puppies serving:
CALORIES: 55
(39% from fat)
FAT 2.4g
(saturated 0.2g)
PROTEIN 1.3g
CARBOHYDRATE 6.9g
FIBER 0.4g
CHOLESTEROL 13mg
SODIUM 71mg

# Beer-Cheese Bread

3/4 cup beer
1/4 cup margarine
3 1/2 cups bread flour, divided
1   tablespoon sugar
1/2 teaspoon salt
1/2 teaspoon dry mustard
1/4 teaspoon ground red pepper
1   package active dry yeast
1   egg, lightly beaten
1   cup shredded reduced-fat sharp Cheddar
        cheese
Vegetable cooking spray

COMBINE beer and margarine in a small saucepan; place over medium-low heat until very warm (120 degrees to 130 degrees).

COMBINE 1 1/2 cups flour and next five ingredients in a large bowl; add beer mixture and egg; beat at medium speed of electric mixer 2 minutes, or until smooth.

STIR in cheese and 1 1/2 cups flour to form a soft dough.

TURN dough out onto a lightly floured surface; knead dough until smooth and elastic (about 8 minutes); add enough of remaining 1/2 cup flour, 1 tablespoon at a time, to prevent dough from sticking to hands.

PLACE dough in a large bowl coated with cooking spray, turning to coat top; cover and let rise in a warm place (85 degrees), free from drafts, for 1 hour, or until doubled in bulk.

PUNCH dough down; cover and let rest 10 minutes.

PLACE dough in a 1-quart soufflé dish coated with cooking spray; cover and let rise 40 minutes, or until doubled in bulk.

PREHEAT oven to 375 degrees.

BAKE loaf at 375 degrees for 20 minutes; cover loosely with foil and bake an additional 20 minutes, or until loaf sounds hollow when tapped.

REMOVE loaf from dish; let cool on a wire rack.

YIELD: 16 servings; serving size, 1 slice

# Butter Crescent Rolls

1 package active dry yeast
1/4 cup warm water (105 to 115 degrees)
1/4 cup sugar
1/2 cup plain nonfat yogurt
3 tablespoons margarine, melted
2 egg whites, lightly beaten
3/4 teaspoon salt
3 1/4 cup all-purpose flour
Butter-flavored vegetable cooking spray

COMBINE yeast and warm water in a 1-cup liquid measuring cup; let stand 5 minutes.

COMBINE yeast mixture, sugar and next 4 ingredients in a large bowl, stirring until blended.

GRADUALLY stir in enough flour to make a soft dough.

TURN dough out into a lightly-floured surface, and knead 3 or 4 times.

PLACE in a bowl coated with cooking spray, turning to coat top.

COVER and let rise in a warm place (85 degrees), free from drafts, one hour or until doubled in bulk.

PUNCH dough down, and divide into thirds; shape each portion into a ball; roll each ball into a 12-inch circle on a lightly-floured surface and coat lightly with cooking spray.

CUT each circle into 12 wedges; roll up each wedge, starting with wide end; place rolls, point-side down, on baking sheets coated with spray.

COVER and let rise in a warm place (85 degrees), free from drafts, 30 minutes or until doubled in bulk.

BAKE at 375 degrees for 12 minutes or until golden; serve immediately.

YIELD: 3 dozen

PER 1-roll serving:
CALORIES 59
(17% from fat)
FAT 1.1g
(saturated 0.2g)
PROTEIN 1.6g
CARBOHYDRATE 10.3g
FIBER 0.4g
CHOLESTEROL 0mg
SODIUM 65mg

# Cheese-French Bread

1 1/2 cups (6 ounces) shredded reduced-
    fat Monterey Jack cheese
1/2 cup reduced-fat mayonnaise
1 1/2 teaspoons dried parsley flakes
1   clove garlic, pressed
1   (16-ounce) loaf French bread, cut in
    half horizontally

COMBINE first 4 ingredients; spread on cut sides of
bread; place on a baking sheet.
BAKE at 350 degrees for 15 minutes, or until cheese
is melted; serve immediately.
YIELD: 1 loaf

PER slice:
CALORIES 71
(30% from fat)
FAT 2.4g
(saturated 0.7g)
PROTEIN 3.1g
FIBER 0.4g
CARBOHYDRATE 8.7g
CHOLESTEROL 6mg
SODIUM 154mg

# Dilly Cheese Muffins

3 cups reduced-fat biscuit and baking mix
1 cup (4 ounces) shredded reduced-fat
 Swiss cheese
1 tablespoon sugar
1 1/4 cups nonfat buttermilk
1/4 cup egg substitute
1 1/2 tablespoons chopped fresh dill
1/2 teaspoon dry mustard
1 1/2 teaspoons vegetable oil
Vegetable cooking spray

COMBINE first 3 ingredients in a large bowl, and make a well in center of mixture.

COMBINE buttermilk and next 4 ingredients in bowl, stirring well; add to dry ingredients, stirring just until moistened.

PLACE paper baking cups in muffin pans, and coat with cooking spray; spoon batter into cups, filling two-thirds full.

BAKE at 350 degrees for 25 to 28 minutes or until lightly browned; remove muffins from pans immediately.

YIELD: 1 1/2 dozen

PER muffin:
CALORIES 135
(14% from fat)
FAT 2.1g
(saturated 0.2)
PROTEIN 5.1g
CARBOHYDRATE 28g
FIBER 0.0g
CHOLESTEROL 4mg
SODIUM 374mg

# Dilly Garlic Bread

1/4 cup reduced-calorie margarine
3   cloves garlic, pressed
1/4 cup finely-chopped fresh dill
1   (16-ounce) loaf French bread, cut in
        half horizontally
1/4 cup grated nonfat Parmesan cheese

COMBINE first 3 ingredients; spread mixture evenly on cut sides of bread; sprinkle with Parmesan cheese, and place on a baking sheet.
BROIL 5 1/2 inches from heat (with electric oven door partially opened) 2 to 4 minutes or until golden.
SLICE bread crosswise into 1-inch slices, and serve immediately.
YIELD: 1 loaf

PER 2 slices:
CALORIES 70
(21% from fat)
FAT 1.6g
(saturated 0.3g)
PROTEIN 1.8g
CARBOHYDRATE 12g
FIBER 0.5g
CHOLESTEROL 1mg
SODIUM 147mg

# Easy Yeast Rolls

2   pkg. active dry yeast
1/2 cup warm water (105 to 115 degrees)
1 cup skim milk
1/4 cup egg substitute
2   tablespoons sugar
1   tablespoon vegetable oil
1 1/2 teaspoons salt
4   cups all-purpose flour, divided
Butter-flavored vegetable cooking spray

COMBINE yeast and warm water in a 2-cup liquid measuring cup; let stand 5 minutes.

COMBINE yeast mixture, milk, and next 4 ingredients in a large bowl.

GRADUALLY stir in enough remaining flour to make a soft dough.

PLACE in a bowl coated with cooking spray, turning to coat top.

COVER and let stand in a warm place (85 degrees), free from drafts, 15 minutes.

PUNCH dough down; cover and let stand in a warm place (85 degrees), free from drafts, 15 additional minutes.

TURN dough out onto a lightly-floured surface; knead 3 or 4 times.

DIVIDE dough into 24 pieces; shape into balls.

PLACE into two 9-inch square pans or round pans coated with spray.

COVER and let stand in a warm place (85 degrees), free from drafts, 15 minutes.

BAKE at 400 degrees for 15 minutes, or until golden.
YIELD: 2 dozen

PER 1 roll:
CALORIES: 92
(8% from fat)
FAT 0.8g
(saturated 0.2g)
FIBER 0.7g
PROTEIN 3.0g
CARBOHYDRATE 17.7g
CHOLESTEROL 0mg
SODIUM 156mg

# English Muffin Bread

3 1/2 to 3 3/4 cups all-purpose flour, divided
1   cup whole wheat flour
1/2 cup oat bran
2   teaspoons salt
1   package rapid-rise yeast
1   cup skim milk
1   cup water
3   tablespoons reduced-calorie margarine
Vegetable cooking spray
2   tablespoons cornmeal

COMBINE 1 1/2 cups all-purpose flour, wheat flour, and next 3 ingredients in a large mixing bowl; set aside.

COMBINE skim milk, water and margarine in a 4-cup liquid measuring cup; microwave at HIGH 2 minutes; pour over flour mixture.

BEAT at medium speed with an electric mixer 2 minutes.

GRADUALLY stir in 2 cups all-purpose flour.

TURN dough out onto a lightly-floured surface; if dough is sticky, knead in remaining 1/4 cup flour.

COVER dough with a large mixing bowl; let stand 10 minutes.

COAT two 8 1/2 x 4 1/2 x 3-inch loaf pans with cooking spray; sprinkle evenly with cornmeal.

DIVIDE dough in half and shape each portion into a loaf and place in pan.

COVER and let dough rise in a warm place (85 degrees), free from drafts, 1 hour or until dough is doubled in bulk.

BAKE at 400 degrees for 25 minutes; remove loaves from pans and cool on a wire rack.

YIELD: 2 loaves

# Herb-Cheese Bread

1/4 cup reduced-calorie margarine
1/4 cup minced green onion
2   garlic cloves, crushed
1/4 teaspoon dried oregano
1/4 teaspoon ground cumin
1/8 teaspoon dried crushed red pepper
1/8 teaspoon salt
1   (1-pound) loaf Italian bread, split
1/2 cup (2 ounces) shredded reduced-
     fat Monterey Jack cheese

PREHEAT oven to 400 degrees.
MELT margarine in a small skillet over medium-high heat; add minced green onions and garlic; sauté 2 minutes.
STIR in oregano, cumin, red pepper and salt.
BRUSH margarine mixture evenly on cut sides of bread.
SPRINKLE cheese over bottom half of loaf; top with top half of loaf.
WRAP in aluminum foil; bake at 400 degrees for 20 minutes.
SERVE warm.
YIELD: 12 servings

PER 1 slice:
CALORIES 140
(23% from fat)
PROTEIN 4.9g
FAT 3.6g
(saturated 1g,
    mono 1.4g, poly 0.8g)
CARBOHYDRATE 21.8g
FIBER 1.1g
CHOLESTEROL 3mg
IRON 0.9mg
SODIUM 313mg
CALCIUM 48mg

# Honey Biscuits

1   package active dry yeast
1/4 cup warm water (105 to 115 degrees)
3   cups all-purpose flour
1   teaspoon baking powder
1   teaspoon baking soda
1/2 teaspoon salt
1   cup nonfat buttermilk
1/2 cup vegetable oil
3   tablespoons honey

COMBINE yeast and warm water in a 1-cup liquid measuring cup; let stand 5 minutes.

COMBINE flour and next 3 ingredients in a large bowl.

COMBINE yeast mixture, buttermilk, oil and honey; add to dry ingredients, stirring just until dry ingredients are moistened.

TURN dough out onto a lightly-floured surface and knead 4 or 5 tunes,

PAT dough to 1/2-inch thickness; cut with a 2-inch-round cutter, and place on an ungreased baking sheet.

BAKE at 400 degrees for 10 minutes, or until golden.
YIELD: 1 1/2 dozen

# Jalapeño-Corn Bread

Butter-flavored vegetable cooking spray
2   teaspoons vegetable oil
1   cup yellow cornmeal
3/4 cup all-purpose flour
1   tablespoon sugar
2   teaspoons baking powder
1   teaspoon salt
1   cup frozen whole-kernel corn, thawed
    and drained
1   cup low-fat buttermilk
1/3 cup nonfat sour cream
1/4 cup chopped fresh cilantro
1   tablespoon seeded, chopped jalapeño
    pepper
1   tablespoon vegetable oil
2   eggs, lightly beaten

PREHEAT oven to 400 degrees.
COAT a 9-inch cast iron skillet with cooking spray;
add 2 teaspoons oil and place skillet in oven for 8
minutes.
COMBINE cornmeal, flour, sugar, baking powder
and salt in a large bowl.
COMBINE corn and next 6 ingredients in a bowl;
stir well with a wire whisk; add to cornmeal mixture, stirring until dry ingredients are moistened.
SPOON into preheated skillet.
BAKE at 400 degrees for 25 minutes, or until a
wooden pick inserted in center comes out clean.
YIELD: 9 servings (serving size: 1 wedge)

PER serving:
CALORIES 174
(24% from fat)
PROTEIN 6g
FAT 4.6g
(saturated 1.2g,
    mono 1.3g, poly 1.5g)
CARBOHYDRATE 27.5g
FIBER 1.6g
CHOLESTEROL 49mg
IRON 1.6mg
SODIUM 297mg
CALCIUM 105mg

# Make-Ahead Yeast Rolls

2   packages active dry yeast
1/4 cup warm water (105 to 115 degrees)
4 1/2 cups bread flour, divided
1 3/4 cups nonfat buttermilk
1/3 cup sugar
2   tablespoons margarine, softened
1 1/2 teaspoons salt
Vegetable cooking spray

COMBINE yeast and warm water in a 1-cup liquid measuring cup; let stand 5 minutes.

COMBINE yeast mixture, 2 cups flour, and next 4 ingredients in a large bowl; beat with a wooden spoon 2 minutes.

GRADUALLY stir in enough remaining flour to make a soft dough.

COVER and let rise in a warm place (85 degrees), free from drafts, 1 hour; punch down dough and cover. Chill at least 8 hours.

PUNCH dough down; turn dough out onto a lightly-floured surface and knead 3 or 4 times.

DIVIDE dough in half; shape each portion into 16 (2-inch) balls.

PLACE balls in two 9-inch square pans coated with cooking spray.

COVER and let rise in a warm place (85 degrees) free from drafts, 1 1/2 hours, or until dough is doubled in bulk.

BAKE at 375 degrees for 12 minutes, or until golden.
YIELD: 32 rolls

# Mexican Spoon Bread

3 (12-ounce) cans refrigerated buttermilk
    biscuits
1 (16-ounce) jar chunky salsa
Vegetable cooking spray
1 cup (4 ounces) shredded reduced-fat
    Monterey Jack cheese
1/2 cup sliced green onions
1 small green bell pepper, chopped

CUT each biscuit into 8 pieces.
COMBINE biscuits and salsa in a 13x9x2-inch baking
dish coated with cooking spray, tossing gently to
coat; top with cheese and remaining ingredients.
BAKE, uncovered, at 350 degrees for 45 minutes, or
until edges are golden and center is set; let stand 10
minutes. CUT into squares and serve with soup or
salad.
YIELD: 15 biscuits

PER biscuit:
CALORIES 234
(40% from fat)
FAT 10.5g
(saturated 2.8g)
PROTEIN 6.3g
FIBER 0.2g
CARBOHYDRATE 30.5g
CHOLESTEROL 5mg
SODIUM 974mg

# Mini Swiss Cheese Loaves

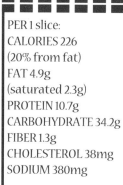

PER 1 slice:
CALORIES 226
(20% from fat)
FAT 4.9g
(saturated 2.3g)
PROTEIN 10.7g
CARBOHYDRATE 34.2g
FIBER 1.3g
CHOLESTEROL 38mg
SODIUM 380mg

1   package active dry yeast
1/4 cup warm water (105 to 115 degrees)
2 1/3 cups all-purpose flour, divided
2   tablespoons sugar
1   teaspoon salt
1/4 teaspoon baking soda
1   (8-ounce) carton plain nonfat yogurt
1   large egg
1   cup (4 ounces) shredded reduced-fat
        Swiss cheese
Vegetable cooking spray
2   teaspoons sesame seeds, toasted

COMBINE yeast and warm water in a 1-cup liquid measuring cup; let stand 5 minutes.
COMBINE yeast mixture, 1 cup flour, and next 5 ingredients in a large mixing bowl; beat at low speed with an electric mixer 30 seconds, then beat at high speed 2 minutes.
STIR in remaining flour and Swiss cheese, mixing well.
DIVIDE batter evenly among eight 5x3x2-inch loaf pans coated with cooking spray; sprinkle evenly with sesame seeds.
COVER and let rise in a warm place (85 degrees), free from drafts, one hour (batter may not double in bulk).
BAKE at 350 degrees for 25 minutes, or until golden; remove from pans; serve warm, or cool on a wire rack.
YIELD: 8 loaves

# Onion-Sesame Rolls

1 1/2 tablespoons grated Parmesan cheese
1  tablespoons instant minced onion
1/2 teaspoon garlic powder
1  (10-ounce) can refrigerated pizza dough
Butter-flavored vegetable cooking spray
2  tablespoons fat-free Italian salad dressing
1  tablespoon sesame seeds

COMBINE first 3 ingredients; set cheese mixture aside.
UNROLL pizza dough and pat into a 10x8-inch rectangle.
COAT dough with cooking spray and brush with salad dressing.
SPRINKLE cheese mixture over dough, leaving a 1/2-inch border.
ROLL UP jellyroll fashion, starting with short side; pinch seams to seal.
CUT into 10 (1-inch-thick) slices and place on an ungreased baking sheet.
COAT tops of rolls with cooking spray and sprinkle with sesame seeds.
BAKE at 400 degrees for 10 to 12 minutes, or until rolls are lightly browned; serve immediately.
YIELD: 10 rolls

PER 1 roll:
CALORIES 87
(20% from fat)
FAT 1.9g
(saturated 0.4g)
PROTEIN 3.1g
FIBER 0.5g
CARBOHYDRATE 14.4g
CHOLESTEROL 1mg
SODIUM 204mg

# Parmesan Bread

This bread calls for semolina flour, it is found in the grocery store on the same aisle as the all-purpose flour. If you have trouble locating this flour, you may increase the bread flour to 2 1/4 cups, and add 1/2 cup cornmeal. I always try to find the semolina flour because of the fine texture.

1   package dry yeast
1/2 teaspoon sugar
1   cup warm water (105 to 115 degrees)
1 3/4 cups bread flour
1   cup semolina or pasta flour
3/4 cup finely-shredded Parmesan cheese
1   teaspoon salt
2   teaspoons olive oil
Vegetable cooking spray
1   tablespoon semolina or pasta flour

SPRINKLE yeast and sugar over warm water in a small bowl; let yeast mixture stand 5 minutes.
PLACE bread flour, 1 cup semolina flour, cheese and salt in a food processor; pulse 3 times or until blended.
WITH processor on, slowly add yeast mixture and olive oil through food chute; process until dough forms a ball.
PROCESS 40 additional seconds; turn dough out onto a lightly-floured surface and knead 3 or 4 times.
PLACE dough in a large bowl coated with cooking spray, turning to coat top; cover and let rise in a warm place (85 degrees), free from drafts, 1 hour and 15 minutes, or until doubled in bulk.
PUNCH dough down, and divide into 2 equal portions; shape each portion into a 6-inch round loaf.
PLACE loaves on a large baking sheet coated with

Continued on following page.

Continued from preceding page.

cooking spray and sprinkled with 1 tablespoon semolina flour.

MAKE 2 (1/8-inch-deep) diagonal cuts across the top of each loaf; cover loaves and let rise 30 minutes, or until doubled in bulk.

PREHEAT oven to 425 degrees.

LIGHTLY spray loaves with water.

BAKE at 425 degrees for 20 minutes, or until loaves sound hollow when tapped, misting loaves every 7 minutes during baking time.

REMOVE loaves from baking sheets; let cool on a wire rack.

YIELD: 2 loaves, 8 servings per loaf (serving size: 1 slice)

PER 1 slice:
CALORIES 81
(18% from fat)
PROTEIN 3.5g
FAT 1.6g
(saturated 0.7g,
     mono 0.6g, poly 0.2g)
CARBOHYDRATE 12.9g
FIBER 0.4g
CHOLESTEROL 1mg
IRON 0.8mg
SODIUM 154mg
CALCIUM 45mg

# Parmesan Cheese Twists

PER serving:
CALORIES 68
(15% from fat)
PROTEIN 2.7g
FAT 1.1g
(saturated 0.5g,
    mono 0.1g, poly 0g)
CARBOHYDRATE 11.9g
FIBER 0.6g
CHOLESTEROL 1mg
IRON 0.3mg
SODIUM 189mg
CALCIUM 25mg

1/4 cup Parmesan cheese
1   teaspoon paprika
1/8 teaspoon ground red pepper
1   (10-ounce) can refrigerated pizza
        crust dough
Butter-flavored vegetable spray

PREHEAT oven to 425 degrees.

COMBINE Parmesan cheese, paprika and red pepper in a small bowl; stir well and set aside.

UNROLL pizza dough and roll into a 12x8-inch rectangle; lightly coat surface of dough with cooking spray, and sprinkle with 2 tablespoons cheese mixture.

FOLD dough in half to form an 8x6-inch rectangle; roll dough into a 12x8-inch rectangle. Lightly coat surface of dough with cooking spray, and sprinkle with remaining cheese mixture; using finger-tips, press cheese mixture into dough.

CUT the dough into 16 (8-inch-long) strips; gently pick up both ends of each strip, and twist the dough.

PLACE the twisted strips of dough 1/2-inch apart on a large baking sheet coated with cooking spray.

BAKE at 425 degrees for 8 minutes, or until lightly browned; remove from baking sheet and let cool on wire racks.

YIELD: 16 breadsticks (serving size: 1 breadstick)

# Roasted Red Bell Pepper Bread

1  (7-ounce) jar roasted red bell peppers
1  package active dry yeast
1  teaspoon sugar
1 1/3 cups warm water (105 to 115 degrees)
3 1/2 cups bread flour
1  cup grated nonfat Parmesan cheese
2  tablespoons chopped fresh rosemary
1  teaspoon salt
1  tablespoon cracked pepper
Vegetable cooking spray

PER slice:
CALORIES 93
(4% from fat)
FAT 0.4g
(saturated 0.1g)
PROTEIN 2.5g
CARBOHYDRATE (18.7g)
FIBER 0.2g
CHOLESTEROL 0mg
SODIUM 191mg

DRAIN bell peppers on paper towels; chop and set aside.

COMBINE yeast, sugar and warm water in a 2-cup liquid measuring cup; let stand 5 minutes and set aside.

COMBINE flour, bell peppers, Parmesan cheese and next 3 ingredients in a large bowl, gradually add yeast mixture, stirring until blended.

TURN dough out onto a well-floured surface and knead until smooth and elastic (about 10 minutes).

PLACE dough in a bowl coated with cooking spray, turning to coat top.

COVER and let rise in a warm place (85 degrees), free from drafts, one hour, or until doubled in bulk.

PUNCH dough down; turn out onto a lightly floured surface and knead 4 or 5 times; divide dough in half.

SHAPE each portion into a 12-inch loaf; place loaves on a large baking sheet coated with cooking spray.

LET rise in a warm place (85 degrees), free from drafts, 45 minutes or until doubled in bulk.

BAKE at 450 degrees for 25 minutes, or until loaves sound hollow when tapped, covering with aluminum foil after 15 minutes to prevent excessive browning.

REMOVE from baking sheet immediately; cool on wire racks.

YIELD: 2 loaves

# Rosemary Biscuits

4 cups reduced-fat biscuit and baking mix
1 1/2 teaspoons dried rosemary, crushed
1 1/3 cups skim milk
Butter-flavored vegetable cooking spray

COMBINE biscuit mix and rosemary in a large bowl; add milk, stirring with a fork until dry ingredients are moistened.

TURN dough out onto a lightly-floured surface, and knead lightly 3 or 4 times.

ROLL dough to 1/2-inch thickness; cut with a 2-inch round biscuit cutter, and place on a baking sheet coated with cooking spray.

COAT tops of biscuits with cooking spray.

BAKE at 450 degrees for 8 to 10 minutes, or until lightly browned.

YIELD: 2 1/2 dozen

# Sour Cream Corn Muffins

1   cup self-rising yellow cornmeal
1   (8.5-ounce) can cream-style corn
1   (8-ounce) carton reduced-fat sour cream
1/4 cup egg substitute
2   tablespoons vegetable oil
Vegetable cooking spray

COMBINE first 5 ingredients, stirring until smooth.
SPOON into a muffin pan coated with cooking
spray, filling two-thirds full.
BAKE at 400 degrees for 25 minutes, or until golden.
REMOVE muffins from pan immediately.
YIELD: 1 dozen

PER muffin:
CALORIES 90
(52% from fat)
FAT 5.2g
(saturated 1.9)
PROTEIN 2.1g
CARBOHYDRATE 11.0g
FIBER 4.3g
CHOLESTEROL 7mg
SODIUM 209mg

# Spoonbread

1 1/2 cups boiling water
1 cup cornmeal
3/4 teaspoon salt
2 tablespoons reduced-calorie margarine
1 cup skim milk
1 egg, separated
1 teaspoon baking powder
1 egg white
Vegetable cooking spray

POUR boiling water over cornmeal gradually, stirring until smooth.

ADD salt and margarine, stirring until blended; cool 10 minutes.

GRADUALLY stir in milk and egg yolk; add baking powder, stirring until blended.

BEAT egg whites at high speed with an electric mixer until stiff peaks form.

GENTLY fold beaten egg whites into cornmeal mixture.

POUR mixture into a 1 1/2-quart baking dish coated with cooking spray.

BAKE at 375 degrees for 45 minutes, or until lightly browned.

YIELD: 6 servings

# Sweet Potato Spoon Bread

3 small sweet potatoes (about 1 3/4-pound)
3   cups 1% low-fat milk, divided
2   cups yellow cornmeal
1/2 teaspoon salt
3   tablespoons brown sugar
2   teaspoons baking powder
1   teaspoon butter, melted
1/2 teaspoon baking soda
1   large egg
2   large egg whites
Vegetable cooking spray

PREHEAT oven to 375 degrees.
WRAP potatoes in aluminum foil; bake at 375 degrees for 1 hour, or until tender.
LET cool; peel potatoes, mash and set aside.
COMBINE 2 cups milk, cornmeal and salt in a large saucepan; stir well with a whisk.
COOK over medium heat 4 minutes, or until thick, stirring constantly.
REMOVE from heat; stir in sweet potato and sugar.
COMBINE potato mixture, remaining cup of milk, baking powder, butter, baking soda and 1 egg in a large bowl; stir well, and set aside.
BEAT 2 egg whites in a bowl, at high speed of an electric mixer, until stiff peaks form; gently fold into potato mixture.
SPOON into an 11x7-inch baking dish coated with cooking spray.
BAKE at 375 degrees for 50 minutes.
YIELD: 8 servings (serving size: 3/4 cup)

PER serving:
CALORIES 270
(10% from fat)
PROTEIN 86.g
FAT 2.9g
(saturated 1.2g,
      mono 0.8g, poly 0.5g)
CARBOHYDRATE 52.1g
FIBER 3.7g
CHOLESTEROL 33mg
IRON 2.2mg
SODIUM 309mg
CALCIUM 203mg

# Zucchini Bread

2   cups coarsely-shredded zucchini
3   cups all-purpose flour
1 3/4 cups sugar
1   teaspoon salt
1   teaspoon baking soda
1   teaspoon ground cinnamon
1/4 teaspoon baking powder
3/4 cup applesauce
1/2 cup egg substitute
1/3 cup vegetable oil
1   tablespoon vanilla extract
Vegetable cooking spray

PREHEAT oven to 350 degrees.
PLACE zucchini on several layers of paper towels, and cover with additional paper towels.
LET stand 5 minutes, pressing down occasionally; set zucchini aside.
COMBINE flour and next 5 ingredients in a large bowl and stir well; make a well in center of mixture.
COMBINE zucchini, applesauce, egg substitute, oil and vanilla; add to dry ingredients, stirring just until ingredients are moistened.
SPOON batter evenly into 2 (7 1/2 x 3-inch) loaf pans coated with cooking spray.
BAKE at 350° for 1 hour and 15 minutes, or until a wooden pick inserted in center comes out clean.
LET cool in pans 10 minutes on a wire rack; remove from pans and let cool completely on wire rack.
YIELD: 2 loaves, 28 servings (serving size: 1 slice)

# Suggestions When Using Your Bread Machine

ADD ingredients to your bread machine according to the manufacturer's instructions. Different machines necessitate adding ingredients in varying orders, depending on whether the machine features a yeast dispenser.

VARIOUS machines make different amounts of bread, ranging from 1- to 2-pound loaves. Look at the amount of flour called for in your instruction book, and scale these recipes accordingly.

BREAD flour is a high-protein flour that stands up to lots of kneading; you may substitute bread flour with all-purpose flour.

EXPERIMENT with flavor combinations that appeal to you. You may add herbs and spices to your taste, and substitute many ingredients.

ALWAYS be sure to include a sweetener, such as honey or sugar, for tenderness, and salt to enhance flavor.

YEAST makes the most difference in your bread. You can use a rapid-rise yeast, but dry yeast seems to work the best in bread machines. You can substitute 2 1/4 teaspoons of bread-machine yeast for 1 packet of dry yeast.

YOU may find that occasionally bread-machine yeast causes the bread to rise too high, so that it touches the top of the machine and burns. If you find this problem, reduce the amount of yeast by 25%, then by one-third, if needed.

# When Shopping for A Bread Machine

MAKE sure the machine will fit on your counter when the lid is open. Smaller households may prefer a smaller machine that makes 1-pound loaves, where larger families may prefer the machine that makes 1 1/2- to 2-pound loaves.

CHECK the time cycles on the machines; some take two hours from beginning to end, while others have four-hour cycles.

BREAD machines come in different sizes, with a variety of settings and timers. They have a large range of prices; some can be quite expensive.

WHEN you have chosen a machine, be sure to allow some time to get used to it; some brown more than others, and some produce a taller loaf. It may take several bakings until you adjust to your machine.

FOR slicing bread from the bread machine, an electric knife works best, or you may use a serrated knife.

# Cornmeal Bread for Bread Machine

1   cup boiling water
1/2 cup yellow cornmeal
1/4 cup molasses
3   tablespoons margarine, melted
2   tablespoons sugar
1   egg, lightly beaten
3   cups bread flour
1/2 teaspoon salt
1   teaspoon dry yeast

COMBINE boiling water, cornmeal, molasses, melted margarine and sugar in a medium bowl; stir well to combine.
LET mixture cool slightly, and stir in beaten egg.
FOLLOW manufacturer's instructions for placing cornmeal mixture, bread flour, salt and dry yeast into bread pan; select bake cycle and start bread machine.
YIELD: 1 (1 3/4-pound) loaf, 14 servings

PER 1 slice:
CALORIES 174
(18% from fat)
PROTEIN 4.5g
FAT 3.4g
(saturated 0.7g,
    mono 1.3g, poly 1.1g)
CARBOHYDRATE 31g
FIBER 0.3g
CHOLESTEROL 16mg
IRON 1.9mg
SODIUM 120mg
CALCIUM 19mg

# Oatmeal Bread for Bread Machine

3/4 cup boiling water
1/2 cup quick-cooking oats
1/4 cup firmly-packed brown sugar
3 tablespoons margarine, melted
1 teaspoon salt
3 cups bread flour
1/4 cup water
1 egg, lightly beaten
1 package dry yeast

COMBINE first 5 ingredients in a bowl; stir well, and let cool slightly.

FOLLOW manufacturer's instructions for placing oat mixture and remaining ingredients into bread pan; select bake cycle, and start bread machine.

YIELD: 1 (1 3/4-pound) loaf, 14 servings

THIS bread is really a nice change from wheat or rye bread, and good with a sandwich, or toasted.

# Onion-Dill Bread for Bread Machine

3 1/2 cups bread flour
1   cup water
1/2 cup chopped onion
3   tablespoons sugar
1   tablespoon dried dill
2   tablespoons vegetable oil
2   teaspoons salt
2   teaspoons paprika
1   package dry yeast

FOLLOW manufacturer's instructions for placing all ingredients into bread pan; select bake cycle and start machine.

YIELD: 1 (1 3/4-pound) loaf, 14 servings

PER 1 slice:
CALORIES 137
(16% from fat)
PROTEIN 3.8g
FAT 2.5g
(saturated 0.4g,
    mono 0.6g, poly, 1.2g)
CARBOHYDRATES 24.6g
FIBER 0.3g
CHOLESTEROL 0mg
IRON 1.6mg
SODIUM 336mg
CALCIUM 11mg

# Romano Cheese and Oregano Bread for Bread Machine

PER 1 slice:
CALORIES 181
(21% from fat)
PROTEIN 6.6g
FAT 4.2g
(saturated 1.5g,
   mono 1.8g, poly 0.5g)
CARBOHYDRATES 28.7g
FIBER 0.2g
CHOLESTEROL 7mg
IRON 1.8mg
SODIUM 281mg
CALCIUM 87mg

3   cups bread flour
1   cup water
3/4 cup (3 ounces) grated fresh Romano cheese
3   tablespoons sugar
1   tablespoon dried oregano
1 1/2 tablespoons olive oil
1   teaspoon salt
1   package dry yeast

FOLLOW manufacturer's instructions for placing all ingredients into bread pan; select bake cycle and start bread machine.
YIELD: 1 (1 1/2-pound loaf), 12 servings

# Rye Bread for Bread Machine

2   cups bread flour
1 1/4 cups rye flour
1   cup water
1   tablespoon caraway seeds
3   tablespoons honey
2   tablespoons vegetable oil
1   teaspoon salt
1   package dry yeast

FOLLOW manufacturer's instructions for placing all ingredients into bread pan; select bake cycle, and start bread machine.
YIELD: 1 (1-pound) loaf, 8 servings

PER 1 slice:
CALORIES 214
(18% from fat)
PROTEIN 5.1g
FAT 4.2g
(saturated 0.7g,
    mono 1.2g, poly 2g)
CARBOHYDRATES 39.3g
FIBER 2.4g
CHOLESTEROL 0mg
IRON 1.8mg
SODIUM 294mg
CALCIUM 14mg

# Wheat Bread for Bread Machine

1 2/3 cups bread flour
1 1/2 cups whole wheat flour
1    cup water
3    tablespoons sugar
1    tablespoon vegetable oil
1 1/2 teaspoons dry yeast
1 1/4 teaspoons salt

FOLLOW manufacturer's instructions for placing all ingredients into bread pan; select bake cycle and start bread machine.
YIELD: 1 (1 1/2-pound) loaf, 12 servings
THIS bread is great for toast.

# Yeast Rolls

This recipe calls for you to use your bread machine to mix the dough and allows it to rise. You handle the final shaping and baking of these rolls.

4   cups bread flour
1   cup water
6   tablespoons sugar
3   tablespoons vegetable oil
1 1/4 teaspoons salt
1   egg, lightly beaten
1   package dry yeast
Vegetable cooking spray

FOLLOW manufacturer's instructions for placing first 7 ingredients into bread pan; select dough cycle and start bread machine.
REMOVE dough from bread machine (Do Not Bake). TURN dough out onto a lightly-floured surface, and knead dough 30 seconds; cover dough and let rest 10 minutes.
PUNCH dough down and divide into 18 equal portions.
SHAPE each portion into a ball and place on baking sheets coated with cooking spray.
COVER and let rise in a warm place (85 degrees), free from drafts, 20 minutes.
PREHEAT oven to 400 degrees.
UNCOVER rolls, and bake at 400 degrees for 13 minutes, or until browned.
REMOVE rolls from pans, and serve warm or at room temperature.
YIELD: 1 1/2 dozen (serving size: 1 roll)

PER 1 roll:
CALORIES 152
(18% from fat)
PROTEIN 4.1g
FAT 3.1g
(saturated fat 0.6g,
    mono, 0.8g, poly 1.4g)
CARBOHYDRATE 26.4g
FIBER 0.1g
CHOLESTEROL 12mg
IRON 1.5mg
SODIUM 167mg
CALCIUM 6mg

# Notes & Recipes

# Breakfast,
# Breakfast Breads
# and Muffins

# List Your Favorite Recipes

| Recipes | Page |
| --- | --- |
| | |
| | |
| | |
| | |
| | |
| | |
| | |
| | |
| | |
| | |
| | |
| | |
| | |
| | |
| | |
| | |
| | |
| | |

# Ambrosia Breakfast Fruit

1 (20 ounce) can unsweetened pineapple
   tidbits
1/4 cup packed brown sugar
1/2 teaspoon grated orange peel
2 medium oranges
2 medium unpeeled apples, diced
1 tablespoon shredded coconut

DRAIN pineapple, reserving 1/4 cup juice in a sauce-
pan; set pineapple aside.
ADD brown sugar and orange peel to the juice;
heat until sugar dissolves.
PEEL and section oranges into a large bowl; add
the apples and pineapple.
ADD the pineapple juice mixture and stir gently;
chill.
JUST before serving, sprinkle with coconut.
YIELD: 6 servings

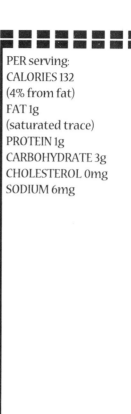

PER serving:
CALORIES 132
(4% from fat)
FAT 1g
(saturated trace)
PROTEIN 1g
CARBOHYDRATE 3g
CHOLESTEROL 0mg
SODIUM 6mg

# Apple Pancakes

1   cup whole wheat flour
1   cup all-purpose flour
2   teaspoons baking soda
2   teaspoons baking powder
1   teaspoon cinnamon
1/2 teaspoon salt
Dash of ground nutmeg
2   cups low-fat buttermilk
1   tablespoon honey
1   tablespoon molasses
1   tablespoon margarine, melted
2   teaspoons lemon juice
2   eggs
2   cups finely-chopped Granny Smith apples
Vegetable cooking spray

COMBINE first 7 ingredients in a large bowl; stir well.

COMBINE buttermilk and next 5 ingredients in a small bowl; stir well.

ADD to flour mixture, stirring until smooth; fold in apple, and let stand 5 minutes.

SPOON about 1/4 cup batter for each pancake onto a hot nonstick griddle, or nonstick skillet coated with cooking spray.

TURN pancakes when tops are covered with bubbles and edges look cooked.

YIELD: 14 pancakes (serving size: 2 pancakes)

# Apple and Spice Muffins

1 1/4 cups all-purpose flour
1/2 cup cornmeal
1/3 cup sugar
1   teaspoon baking powder
1   teaspoon ground cinnamon
1/2 teaspoon baking soda
1/4 teaspoon salt
1/4 teaspoon ground ginger
1 3/4 cups shredded Golden Delicious apple
3/4 cup low-fat buttermilk
2   tablespoons vegetable oil
1   large egg, lightly beaten
Vegetable cooking spray
2   teaspoons sugar
1/4 teaspoon ground cinnamon

PREHEAT oven to 400 degrees.
COMBINE first 8 ingredients in a large bowl; make
a well in center of mixture.
COMBINE apple, buttermilk, oil and egg; stir well.
ADD to dry ingredients, stirring just until moist.
DIVIDE batter evenly among 12 muffin cups coated
with vegetable cooking spray or paper liners.
COMBINE 2 teaspoons sugar and 1/4 teaspoon cin-
namon; sprinkle over muffins.
BAKE at 400 degrees for 20 minutes or until golden.
REMOVE from pans immediately.
SERVE warm.
YIELD: 1 dozen

PER 1 muffin:
CALORIES 139
(23% from fat)
FAT 3.5g
(saturated 0.8g)
PROTEIN 3g
CARBOHYDRATE 24.2g
FIBER 1.2g
CHOLESTEROL 18mg
IRON 1.1mg
SODIUM 115mg

# Blueberry Waffles

1 3/4 cups all-purpose flour
1   tablespoon baking powder
Dash of salt
1 3/4 cup skim milk
3   tablespoons vegetable oil
2   egg whites, lightly beaten, and 2 egg yolks
Vegetable cooking spray
1   cup fresh or frozen blueberries
Additional blueberries (optional)

COMBINE all-purpose flour, baking powder and salt in a medium bowl; stir well.
COMBINE milk, oil, egg whites and egg yolks in a small bowl; stir well.
ADD milk mixture to flour mixture, stirring until mixtures are well blended.
COAT a waffle iron with cooking spray and pre-heat.
SPOON about 1/3 cup of batter per waffle onto hot waffle iron, spreading batter to edges.
SPOON 2 tablespoons blueberries per waffle evenly over batter.
COOK 6 to 7 minutes or until steaming stops; repeat procedure with remaining batter and blueberries. (Serve with syrup, if desired.)
GARNISH with additional blueberries, if desired.
YIELD: 8 (4-inch) waffles (serving size: 1 waffle)

# Bran Muffins

5 cups all-purpose flour
1 2/3 cups sugar
1 tablespoon + 2 teaspoons baking soda
1 tablespoon + 1 teaspoon ground cinnamon
1 1/2 teaspoons salt
1 quart nonfat buttermilk
1/2 cup vegetable oil
1/2 cup unsweetened applesauce
3 large eggs
1 (16-ounce) can fruit cocktail in juice,
   undrained
1 (15-ounce) package wheat bran flakes cereal
   with raisins
Vegetable cooking spray

COMBINE all ingredients except vegetable cooking spray in a large mixing bowl; beat at medium speed of an electric mixer 2 minutes.
SPOON into muffin pans coated with cooking spray, or lined with paper liners; filling two-thirds full.
BAKE at 400 degrees for 16 to 18 minutes, or until muffins spring back when pressed lightly with fingertip.
REMOVE muffins from pans immediately.
YIELD: 4 dozen

PER 1 muffin:
CALORIES 142
(20% from fat)
FAT 3.2g
(saturated 0.6g)
PROTEIN 3.1g
CARBOHYDRATE 26.4g
FIBER 1.6g
CHOLESTEROL 14mg
SODIUM 278mg

# Breakfast Burritos

Egg substitute, equivalent to 8 eggs
2   tablespoons finely-chopped onion
2   tablespoons finely-chopped green pepper
1   drop hot pepper sauce
1/2 cup shredded reduced-fat Cheddar cheese
1/2 cup cooked taco-seasoned ground round
4   (6-inch) fat-free flour tortillas, warmed
Salsa (optional)

IN a bowl, combine egg substitute, onion, green peppers, hot pepper sauce and cheese.
COOK and stir in a nonstick skillet until eggs begin to set.
ADD taco meat; cook until eggs are completely set.
SPOON onto a warmed tortilla and roll up; top with salsa if desired.
YIELD: 4 servings

# Breakfast Pizzas

Egg substitute equivalent to 4 eggs
3   tablespoons finely-chopped green pepper
3   tablespoons skim milk
1/2 teaspoon dried oregano
4   English muffins
4   tablespoons pizza sauce
1/2 cup bulk turkey sausage, cooked and
       drained
2   tablespoons grated Parmesan cheese

IN a bowl, combine egg substitute green pepper,
milk and oregano.
IN a skillet coated with nonstick cooking spray,
cook and stir egg mixture over medium heat until
eggs are completely set; remove from heat.
SPLIT and toast English muffins; spread with pizza
sauce.
SPOON the egg mixture onto muffins, sprinkle with
sausage and cheese.
PLACE under broiler for a few minutes to heat
through.
YIELD: 4 servings

PER serving:
CALORIES 278
(31% from fat)
FAT 10g
(saturated 2g)
PROTEIN 15g
CARBOHYDRATE 32g
CHOLESTEROL 13mg
SODIUM 588mg

# Chocolate Cinnamon Rolls

1 package active dry yeast
2 tablespoons sugar
1 1/4 cups warm skim milk (105 to 115 degrees)
1/4 cup stick margarine, melted
1/2 teaspoon vanilla extract
1 egg, lightly beaten
4 cups bread flour, divided
1/3 cup cocoa
1/2 teaspoon salt
Vegetable cooking spray
1 egg white, lightly beaten
1/4 cup sugar
1 teaspoon ground cinnamon
1 cup sifted powdered sugar
2 tablespoons skim milk
1 teaspoon vanilla extract

DISSOLVE yeast and 2 tablespoons sugar in 1 1/4 cups warm milk in a large bowl; let stand 5 minutes.
ADD melted margarine, 1/2 teaspoon vanilla and egg; stir well.
STIR in 3 1/2 cups flour, cocoa and salt to form a soft dough.
TURN dough out onto a lightly floured surface and knead until smooth and elastic (about 10 minutes); add enough of the remaining flour, 1 tablespoon at a time, to keep dough from sticking to hands.
PLACE dough in a large bowl coated with cooking spray, turning to coat top; cover and let rise in a warm place (85 degrees), free from drafts, 45 minutes or until doubled in bulk.
PUNCH down dough.
TURN onto a lightly-floured surface; roll into a 16x8-inch rectangle.
BRUSH egg white over entire surface of dough.
COMBINE 1/4 cup sugar and ground cinnamon;

Continued on following page.

Continued from preceding page.

sprinkle evenly over dough.

STARTING at long side, roll up dough tightly, jellyroll fashion; pinch seam to seal (do not seal ends of roll).

CUT roll into 16 (1-inch-thick) slices, using string or dental floss.

ARRANGE slices, cut-sides up, in a 13x9-inch baking pan coated with cooking spray.

COVER and let rise 30 minutes, or until doubled in bulk.

PREHEAT oven to 350 degrees, bake rolls at 350 degrees for 20 minutes.

COMBINE powdered sugar, 2 tablespoons milk and 1 teaspoon vanilla, stir well, and drizzle over rolls.

YIELD: 16 servings (serving size: 1 roll)

PER 1 roll:
CALORIES 221
(17% from fat)
FAT 4.1g
(saturated 0.9g)
PROTEIN 6.2g
CARBOHYDRATE 39.3g
FIBER 0.2g
CHOLESTEROL 14mg
IRON 2mg
SODIUM 126mg

# Cinnamon Streusel Coffeecake

1/3 cup chopped walnuts
1/3 cup firmly-packed brown sugar
3 tablespoons all-purpose flour
1 tablespoon ground cinnamon
Vegetable cooking spray
1 1/4 cups sugar
1/3 cup vegetable oil
2 large eggs
3 cups all-purpose flour
1 teaspoon baking powder
1 teaspoon baking soda
1/2 teaspoon salt
1 1/2 cups low-fat buttermilk
1 tablespoon vanilla extract

PREHEAT oven to 350 degrees.
COMBINE first 4 ingredients in small bowl; stir well.
COAT a 12-cup bundt pan with cooking spray; sprinkle 1/3 cup walnut mixture into pan and set remaining mixture aside.
COMBINE 1 1/4 cups sugar and vegetable oil in a large bowl; beat at medium speed of an electric mixer until well blended.
ADD eggs, one at a time, beating well after each addition.
COMBINE flour, baking powder, baking soda and salt; stir well.
ADD flour mixture to creamed mixture alternately with buttermilk, beginning and ending with flour mixture; mix after each addition. Stir in vanilla.
MEASURE 2 cups batter; set aside.
POUR remaining batter into prepared pan; sprinkle remaining walnut mixture over batter.
POUR reserved 2 cups batter over walnut mixture.
BAKE at 350 degrees for 45 minutes or until a wooden pick inserted in center comes out clean.
LET cool in pan 10 minutes on a wire rack; remove from pan.
LET cool completely on wire rack.
YIELD: 16 servings

# Cinnamon-Sugar Cake

2   packages active dry yeast
1/2 teaspoon sugar
1/2 cup warm water (105 to 115 degrees)
1/2 cup margarine, melted and divided
1/4 cup water
1/2 cup sugar
1/4 cup instant potato flakes
2   tablespoons instant nonfat dry milk
        powder
1/2 teaspoon salt
1   large egg
1   egg white
3   cups all-purpose flour, divided
Vegetable cooking spray
1/2 cup firmly-packed brown sugar
1/2 teaspoon ground cinnamon

PER serving:
CALORIES 215
(28% from fat)
FAT 6.7g
(saturated 1.4g)
PROTEIN 4.1g
CARBOHYDRATE 34.7g
FIBER 1.0g
CHOLESTEROL 15mg
SODIUM 167mg

COMBINE first 3 ingredients in a large mixing bowl;
let stand 5 minutes.
ADD 1/4 cup melted margarine, 1/4 cup water and
next 6 ingredients.
ADD 1 cup flour; beat at low speed with an electric
mixer 2 minutes.
STIR in remaining 2 cups flour to make a soft dough.
COVER and let rise in a warm place (85 degrees),
free from drafts, 45 minutes or until double in
bulk.
PUNCH dough down, spread in a 10x15x1-inch
jellyroll pan, coated with cooking spray.
COVER and let rise in a warm plate (85 degrees),
free from drafts, 30 minutes.
MAKE shallow indentations in dough at 1-inch in-
tervals, using the handle of a wooden spoon.
DRIZZLE with remaining 1/4 cup melted marga-
rine.
COMBINE brown sugar and cinnamon; sprinkle
over dough.
BAKE at 375° for 12 to 15 minutes; cut into squares.
YIELD: 15 servings

# Coconut Muffins

2   cups all-purpose flour
1/2 cup sugar
2   teaspoons baking powder
1/4 teaspoon salt
1/4 cup flaked coconut
1   large egg, lightly beaten
1   egg white, lightly beaten
1   (8-ounce) carton vanilla low-fat yogurt
1/4 cup vegetable oil
1/4 teaspoon coconut extract
Vegetable cooking spray

COMBINE first 5 ingredients in a large bowl; make a well in center of mixture.
COMBINE egg and next 4 ingredients; add to dry ingredients, stirring just until moistened.
SPOON into muffin pan coated with cooking spray, or paper liners; filling three-fourths full.
BAKE at 400 degrees for 19 to 20 minutes or until lightly browned.
REMOVE muffins from pan immediately.
YIELD: 1 dozen

# Crumb-Topped French Toast

1/2 cup skim milk
1/2 teaspoon vanilla extract
1/4 teaspoon salt
2   eggs
1   cup cornflake crumbs
9   (1-ounce) diagonally-cut slices French bread
      (about 1-inch thick)
1/4 cup margarine, melted

PREHEAT oven to 450 degrees.
COMBINE first 4 ingredients in a medium bowl; stir
well with a wire whisk.
PLACE cornflake crumbs in a shallow dish.
DIP bread slices into milk mixture and dredge in
cornflake crumbs.
PLACE bread slices on a baking sheet and drizzle
with margarine.
BAKE at 450 degrees for 15 minutes or until golden
brown.
YIELD: 8 servings (serving size: 1 bread slice)

PER 1 slice:
CALORIES 212
(32% from fat)
FAT 6g
(saturated 1.7g)
PROTEIN 5.8g
CARBOHYDRATE 29g
FIBER 0.8g
CHOLESTEROL 56mg
IRON 1.7mg
SODIUM 468mg

# Egg Casserole

1    pound fresh mushrooms, sliced
1/4 cup dry sherry, divided
1    (10 3/4-ounce) can reduced-sodium cream
of chicken soup, undiluted
1    (8-ounce) carton nonfat sour cream
2    tablespoons all-purpose flour
1/2 teaspoon salt
1/2 teaspoon pepper
1    tablespoon finely-chopped onion
1    (2-ounce) jar chopped pimiento, drained
1    (10-ounce) package frozen peas, thawed,
        and drained
7    large hard-cooked eggs, cut lengthwise into
        4 wedges
1    (8-ounce)can sliced water chestnuts,
        drained
Butter-flavored vegetable cooking spray
1    cup soft bread crumbs
11/2 teaspoons reduced-calorie margarine, melted

COOK mushrooms and 2 tablespoons sherry in a large nonstick skillet over medium heat 5 minutes or until mushrooms are tender, stirring occasionally. Drain well; set aside.

COMBINE remaining 2 tablespoons sherry, soup and next 6 ingredients in a medium saucepan. Cook over medium-high heat 2 minutes or until mixture is bubbly; stir in mushrooms and peas.

ARRANGE egg wedges and water chestnuts in bottom of an 11 x 7 x 1 1/2-inch baking dish coated with cooking spray. Pour soup mixture evenly over top.

COMBINE bread crumbs and melted margarine. Sprinkle over soup mixture.

BAKE, uncovered, at 375 degrees for 30 minutes or until top is golden.

YIELD: 8 servings

# English Muffin Breakfast

6 boneless chicken breast halves
1/2 cup all-purpose flour
1 teaspoon paprika
1/4 teaspoon pepper, divided
6 slices Canadian bacon, trimmed
1/2 cup light sour cream
1/2 cup light mayonnaise
1 tablespoon lemon juice
1 teaspoon prepared mustard
3 English muffins, split and toasted

PER 1 English muffin half:
CALORIES 372
(34% from fat)
FAT 14g
(saturated 4g)
PROTEIN 36g
CARBOHYDRATE 23g
CHOLESTEROL 103mg
SODIUM 699 mg

POUND chicken to 1/4-inch thickness.
IN a large resealable plastic bag, combine flour, paprika and 1/8 teaspoon pepper; add chicken, one piece at a time, and shake to coat.
IN a large skillet coated with nonstick cooking spray, cook chicken until browned and juices run clear. Transfer to a platter and keep warm; brown bacon in the same skillet, turning once. Remove and keep warm.
FOR SAUCE: Combine sour cream, mayonnaise, lemon juice, mustard and remaining pepper in a small saucepan. Cook, stirring constantly, until heated through. Keep warm over low heat (do not boil).
PLACE English muffin halves on a baking sheet; top each with a slice of bacon, one chicken breast half and 2 tablespoons sauce.
BROIL until bubbly.
YIELD: 6 servings

# French Toast

1 1/2 cups commercial refrigerated eggnog
1/2 teaspoon freshly-ground nutmeg
8   (1-inch-thick) slices of French bread
Vegetable cooking spray
Rum Syrup (see recipe below)

COMBINE eggnog and nutmeg in a large shallow dish.
PLACE bread slices in dish, turning to coat evenly.
COAT a large nonstick skillet or griddle with cooking spray; place over medium-high heat until hot.
REMOVE bread slices from eggnog mixture, allowing excess to drain.
COOK in skillet 3 minutes on each side or until golden.
SERVE immediately with Rum Syrup.
YIELD: 4 servings

RUM SYRUP:
1   cup light maple syrup
1/2 teaspoon rum extract

PER 2 slices:
CALORIES 313
(23% from fat)
FAT 8.1g
(saturated 4.2g)
PROTEIN 8.2g
CARBOHYDRATE 52.2g
FIBER 1.3g
CHOLESTEROL 58mg
SODIUM 404mg

# German Pancake

1/2 cup all-purpose flour
1 tablespoon sugar
3/4 cup skim milk
1 egg
Vegetable cooking spray
6 tablespoons apricot preserves
Orange slices (optional)
Raspberries (optional)
1 1/2 teaspoons powdered sugar (optional)

COMBINE first 3 ingredients in a medium bowl; stir well.

COMBINE milk and egg in a small bowl; stir well. Add to flour mixture, stirring well with a wire whisk.

COAT 10-inch nonstick skillet with cooking spray, and place over medium-high heat until hot.

REMOVE pan from heat and pour a scant 1/4 cup batter into pan; quickly tilt pan in all directions so batter covers pan with a thin film.

COOK about 1 minute.

LIFT edge of pancake carefully with a spatula to test for doneness (pancake is ready to turn when it can be shaken loose from pan and the underside is lightly browned).

TURN pancake over, and cook an additional 30 seconds.

PLACE pancake on a towel; let cool.

REPEAT procedure with remaining batter; stack pancakes between single layers of waxed paper or paper towels to prevent sticking.

SPREAD 1 tablespoon preserves over each pancake, and roll up.

GARNISH with orange slices and raspberries, if desired.

SPRINKLE with powdered sugar, if desired.

YIELD: 3 servings (serving size: 2 pancakes)

PER 2 pancakes:
CALORIES 238
(9% from fat)
FAT 2.3g
(saturated 0.7g)
PROTEIN 6.7g
CARBOHYDRATE 49g
FIBER 1g
CHOLESTEROL 75mg
IRON 4mg
SODIUM 164mg

# Ham and Egg Muffins

2 teaspoons reduced-calorie margarine,
    divided
4  (1-ounce) slices turkey ham
1  cup egg substitute
4  (3/4-ounce) slices reduced-fat American
    cheese
4  whole wheat English muffins, split and
    toasted

MELT 1 teaspoon margarine in a large nonstick skillet over medium heat; add turkey ham and cook 1 minute on each side or until lightly browned. REMOVE from skillet; set aside and keep warm.
MELT remaining 1 teaspoon margarine in skillet over medium heat.
ADD egg substitute; cook 45 seconds or until set, stirring occasionally.
PLACE 1 cheese slice on each of 4 muffin halves.
SPOON egg substitute mixture evenly over cheese; top with turkey ham and remaining muffin halves.
SERVE immediately.
YIELD 4 servings

PER 1 muffin:
CALORIES 300
(21% from fat)
FAT 7g
(2.9g saturated 2.9g)
PROTEIN 21.5g
CARBOHYDRATE 38.2g
FIBER 0g
CHOLESTEROL 10mg
IRON 3.2mg
SODIUM 864mg

# Ham-Potato-Egg Scramble

1/3 cup chopped onion
1/4 cup chopped green chilies
2   medium potatoes, peeled, cooked and
     cubed
1 1/2 cups fully-cooked low-fat ham, cut into
     strips 1/4-inch wide
Egg substitute equivalent to 6 eggs
2   tablespoons water
Dash of pepper

IN a large skillet coated with nonstick cooking
spray, cook onion and chilies (you may use green
peppers) until onions are tender.
ADD potatoes and ham; cook and stir for 5 minutes.
IN a bowl, combine egg substitute, water and pepper; pour over ham mixture.
COOK over low heat, stirring occasionally, until
eggs are set.
YIELD: 6 servings

PER serving:
CALORIES 141
(25% from fat)
FAT 4g
(saturated 1g)
PROTEIN 15g
CARBOHYDRATE 11g
CHOLESTEROL 17mg
SODIUM 614mg

# Lemon-Ginger Muffins

1   cup sugar, divided
1/4 teaspoon ground ginger
1/4 teaspoon ground cinnamon
1/4 cup peeled, chopped fresh gingerroot
1   tablespoon grated lemon rind
2   cups plus 2 tablespoons all-purpose flour
3/4 teaspoon baking soda
1/4 teaspoon salt
3/4 cup low-fat buttermilk
1/3 cup prune butter (available in groceries, by
       Sunsweet)
1   tablespoon vegetable oil
1   large egg
1   large egg white
Vegetable cooking spray

PREHEAT oven to 375 degrees.
COMBINE 1 tablespoon sugar, ground ginger and cinnamon in a bowl; stir well, and set aside.
PLACE 1/2 cup sugar, gingerroot and lemon rind in a food processor; process until finely chopped and set aside.
COMBINE remaining 1/4 cup plus 3 tablespoons sugar, flour, baking soda and salt in a large bowl; make a well in center of mixture.
COMBINE gingerroot mixture, buttermilk and next 4 ingredients; stir with a wire whisk.
ADD to flour mixture, stirring just until moist.
DIVIDE batter evenly among 12 muffin cups coated with cooking spray or lined with paper muffin cups; sprinkle 1/4 teaspoon cinnamon mixture over each muffin.
BAKE at 375 degrees for 20 minutes or until golden.
REMOVE from pans immediately; let cool on a wire rack.
YIELD: 1 dozen (serving size: 1 muffin)

# Lemon-Glazed Cranberry Rolls

1 (10-ounce) can refrigerated pizza crust
dough
1/2 cup orange marmalade
2/3 cup dried cranberries
Vegetable cooking spray
1/2 cup sifted powdered sugar
1 1/2 teaspoons lemon juice
1 teaspoon hot water

PREHEAT oven to 375 degrees.
UNROLL pizza dough and pat into a 12x9-inch rectangle.
SPREAD marmalade over dough, leaving a 1/2-inch
border; sprinkle dried cranberries over marmalade, pressing gently into dough.
BEGINNING with a long side, roll up dough jellyroll
fashion; pinch seam to seal (do not seal ends of
roll).
CUT roll into 12 (1-inch) slices; place slices, cut-sides
up, into muffin cups coated with cooking spray.
BAKE at 375 degrees for 15 minutes or until golden;
remove rolls from pan and place on a wire rack.
COMBINE powdered sugar, lemon juice and hot
water in a small bowl, stirring until smooth.
DRIZZLE icing over warm rolls.
YIELD: 12 rolls

PER 1 roll:
CALORIES 155
(6% from fat)
FAT 1g
(saturated .3g)
PROTEIN 2.9g
CARBOHYDRATE 34.7g
FIBER 3g
CHOLESTEROL 0mg
IRON 0.3mg
SODIUM 229mg

# Lemon-Poppy Seed Muffins

2   cups all-purpose flour
1/2 cup sugar
2   tablespoons poppy seeds
1   teaspoon baking powder
1   teaspoon baking soda
1/4 teaspoon salt
3   tablespoons vegetable oil
1   teaspoon grated lemon rind
2   tablespoons fresh lemon juice
1   (8-ounce) carton lemon low-fat yogurt
1   large egg, lightly beaten
Vegetable cooking spray

PREHEAT OVEN to 400 degrees.
COMBINE first 6 ingredients in a medium bowl;
make a well in center of mixture.
COMBINE oil, rind, juice, yogurt and egg; stir well.
ADD to dry ingredients, stirring just until moist.
SPOON batter evenly into 12 muffin cups coated
with cooking spray or lined with paper baking
cups.
BAKE at 400 degrees for 14 minutes or until golden
REMOVE muffins from pan immediately; place on
a wire rack.
YIELD: 1 dozen

# Nutty French Toast

3 egg whites, lightly beaten
2 large eggs, lightly beaten
1/4 cup sugar
1/4 teaspoon ground nutmeg
2/3 cup orange juice
1/3 cup skim milk
1/2 teaspoon extract
1 (16-ounce) loaf Italian bread, cut into
    12 (1-inch) slices
Vegetable cooking spray
1/4 cup macadamia nuts, pecans, or slivered
    almonds, chopped and toasted
Garnish: ground nutmeg

COMBINE first 7 ingredients; stir well.
FIT bread slices in a single layer into a 13x9x2-inch
baking dish coated with cooking spray.
POUR egg mixture over bread slices; cover and chill
at least 8 hours, turning bread once.
PLACE bread in a single layer in a 15x10x1-inch
jellyroll pan coated with cooking spray.
BAKE at 400 degrees for 10 minutes; sprinkle with
nuts.
BAKE 10 additional minutes.
GARNISH, if desired.
SERVE immediately.
YIELD 6 servings

PER serving:
CALORIES 345
(21% from fat)
FAT 7.9 g
(saturated 1.4g)
PROTEIN 11.9g
CARBOHYDRATE 56.0g
FIBER 2.2g
CHOLESTEROL 75mg
SODIUM 498mg

# O'Brien Frittata

1   cup peeled, diced baking potato
1/2 cup (2 ounces) shredded fat-free Cheddar
      cheese, divided
4   egg whites, lightly beaten, and 1 egg yolk
2   teaspoons reduced-calorie margarine
1/2 cup diced red onion
1/2 cup diced red bell pepper
1/2 cup diced lean Canadian bacon
2   garlic cloves, minced
1/4 cup fat-free sour cream

PLACE potato in a small saucepan; cover with water.
BRING to a boil and cook 10 minutes or until tender; drain.
PREHEAT oven to 450 degrees.
COMBINE 1/4 cup cheese, egg whites and egg yolk in a bowl; stir well.
MELT margarine in a 10-inch nonstick skillet over medium heat.
ADD potato, onion and next 3 ingredients; sauté 5 minutes.
STIR in egg mixture; spread evenly in bottom of skillet; cook over medium-low heat 5 minutes or until almost set.
WRAP handle of skillet with aluminum foil; place skillet in oven and bake at 450 degrees for 5 minutes or until set.
SPRINKLE with remaining 1/4 cup cheese; bake an additional minute or until cheese melts.
TOP each serving with sour cream.
YIELD: 2 servings

NOTE: Substitute 2/3 cup egg substitute for 4 egg whites and 1 egg yolk, if desired.

# Onion-Bacon-Spinach Frittata

2  turkey bacon slices, chopped
1/8 teaspoon pepper
1/.8 teaspoon ground nutmeg
6  large egg whites, lightly beaten
1  large egg yolk, lightly beaten
1 1/2 cups thinly-sliced sweet onion, separated
      into rings
2  tablespoons water
1/4 teaspoon sugar
4 cups fresh spinach
1/4 cup (1 ounce) shredded part-skim
      Mozzarella cheese

PREHEAT oven to 450 degrees.
COOK bacon slices in a 10-inch nonstick skillet over medium heat until crisp.
COMBINE bacon slices and next 4 ingredients in a bowl and stir.
ADD onion to skillet; cover and cook 5 minutes or until crisp-tender, stirring occasionally.
ADD water and sugar; sauté 5 minutes or until onion is tender and golden.
ADD spinach; cover and cook 2 minutes or until spinach wilts.
STIR in bacon mixture; spread evenly in bottom of skillet.
COOK over medium-low heat 5 minutes or until almost set.
WRAP handle of skillet with aluminum foil; place skillet in oven and bake at 450 degrees for 5 minutes or until set.
SPRINKLE with cheese. Bake an additional minute or until cheese melts.
YIELD: 2 servings

NOTE: You may substitute 1 cup egg substitute for 6 egg whites and 1 egg yolk, if desired.

PER serving:
CALORIES 205
(33% from fat)
FAT 7.5g
(saturated 2.6g)
CARBOHYDRATE 13.6g
FIBER 6.1g
CHOLESTEROL 127mg
IRON 3.6mg
SODIUM 659mg

# Orange-Nut Coffee Cake

1/2 cup sugar
1/4 cup finely-chopped pecans
2 teaspoons grated orange rind
1/2 (8-ounce) package nonfat cream cheese
2 (12-ounce) cans refrigerated buttermilk
   biscuits
Butter-flavored vegetable cooking spray
1/2 cup sifted powdered sugar
1 tablespoon fresh orange juice

COMBINE first 3 ingredients; set aside.
PLACE about 1 teaspoon cream cheese on half of each biscuit; fold biscuit over cheese, pressing edges to seal.
COAT biscuits with cooking spray; dredge in sugar mixture.
PLACE, curved-side down, in a 12-cup bundt pan coated with cooking spray, spacing evenly.
COAT tops with cooking spray; sprinkle with remaining sugar mixture.
BAKE at 350 degrees for 35 minutes or until done.
IMMEDIATELY invert onto a serving plate.
COMBINE powdered sugar and orange juice, stirring well; drizzle over warm coffee cake.
SERVE immediately.
YIELD: 10 servings

# Quick Baked Applesauce

2   large tart apples, peeled and sliced
3   tablespoons sugar
1/4 teaspoon ground cinnamon
1/4 teaspoon vanilla extract

PLACE apples in a 1-quart baking dish coated with nonstick cooking spray.
IN a small bowl, combine sugar, cinnamon and vanilla; mix well.
SPRINKLE cinnamon mixture over apples.
COVER and bake at 350 degrees for 40 to 45 minutes or until apples are tender.
UNCOVER and mash apples with a fork; serve warm.
YIELD: 2 servings

NOTE: YOU may increase this recipe as desired, it's a great dish for a brunch.

PER serving:
CALORIES 194
(5% from fat)
FAT 1g
(saturated trace)
PROTEIN trace
CARBOHYDRATE 50gm
CHOLESTEROL 0mg
SODIUM trace

# Quiche

1   cup egg substitute
1   cup water
1/2 cup low-fat buttermilk biscuit and baking
      mix
1/2 cup instant nonfat dry milk powder
1/2 cup plain yogurt
2   tablespoons grated fresh Parmesan cheese
1/2 teaspoon dry mustard
1/4 teaspoon hot sauce
1   cup (4 ounces) shredded reduced-fat sharp
      Cheddar cheese
3/4 cup diced low-salt reduced-fat ham
1/2 cup chopped green onions
Vegetable cooking spray
Green onion slices (optional)
Cherry tomatoes (optional)

PREHEAT oven to 350 degrees.
POSITION knife blade in food processor bowl; add
first 8 ingredients to bowl and process 1 minute or
until mixture is smooth.
COMBINE egg substitute mixture, Cheddar cheese,
ham and chopped green onion in a medium bowl
and stir well.
POUR egg substitute mixture into a 9-inch pie plate
coated with cooking spray.
BAKE at 350 degrees for 40 minutes or until set; let
stand 5 minutes before serving.
GARNISH with green onion slices and cherry tomatoes, if desired.
YIELD: 6 servings

# Raisin Scones

2 cups all-purpose flour
1/4 cup firmly-packed brown sugar
1 1/2 teaspoons baking powder
1/2 teaspoon baking soda
1/4 teaspoon salt
1/3 cup chilled stick margarine, cut into small
    pieces
1/2 cup chopped raisins or pitted, chopped
    dates
1'/2 cup 1% low-fat milk
3 tablespoons maple syrup
Vegetable cooking spray

PREHEAT oven to 400 degrees.
COMBINE first 5 ingredients in a bowl; cut in margarine with a pastry blender or 2 knives until mixture resembles coarse meal.
ADD raisins (or dates); toss well.
COMBINE milk and syrup; add to flour mixture, stirring just until moist.
TURN dough out onto a lightly floured surface; knead 4 or 5 times.
PAT dough into an 8-inch circle on a baking sheet coated with vegetable spray.
CUT dough into 12 wedges, cutting into, but not through, dough. (Do not separate wedges!)
BAKE at 400 degrees for 15 minutes or until golden.
SERVE warm.
YIELD: 1 dozen

PER 1 scone:
CALORIES 176
(28% from fat)
FAT 5.5g
(saturated 1.1g)
PROTEIN 2.7g
CARBOHYDRATE 29.8g
FIBER 1.2g
CHOLESTEROL 0mg
IRON 1.3mg
SODIUM 168mg

# Sausage and Egg Casserole

1   pound bulk turkey breakfast sausage
3   cups (1/2-inch) cubed white bread (about 6
      [1 ounce] slices)
2   cups skim milk
1 1/2 cups egg substitute
1/2 cup (2 ounces) shredded reduced-fat sharp
      Cheddar cheese
1   teaspoon dry mustard
Vegetable cooking spray

PREHEAT oven to 350 degrees.
COOK sausage in a nonstick skillet over medium-high heat until browned, stirring to crumble; drain well.
COMBINE sausage and next 5 ingredients in a 13x9-inch baking dish coated with cooking spray; stir well.
BAKE at 350 degrees for 45 minutes, or until wooden pick inserted in center comes out clean.
YIELD: 9 servings

# Sunny Fruit Breakfast

1    cantaloupe melon, halved and seeded
1/2 honeydew melon, seeded
1/4 cup superfine or granulated sugar
1/4 cup fresh lime juice
2    tablespoons fresh lemon juice
1    tablespoon orange-flavored liqueur
        (optional)
1 1/2 teaspoons grated lime peel
1    cup sliced fresh strawberries
1    cup black or red seedless grapes

PER serving:
CALORIES 105
(3% from fat)
FAT 0g
PROTEIN 1g
CARBOHYDRATE 27g
CHOLESTEROL 0mg
SODIUM 19mg

USING a melon baller, scoop flesh from cantaloupe and honeydew into balls; set aside.

IN a large glass or ceramic bowl, combine the sugar, lime juice, lemon juice, orange liqueur, and lime peel.

STIR well to dissolve the sugar; add the cantaloupe and honeydew balls, strawberries and grapes, and toss gently to combine.

COVER the bowl with plastic wrap and refrigerate for at least 1 hour to blend flavors, stirring once or twice.

SPOON the fruit mixture into serving bowls or hollowed-out melon halves, dividing evenly.

SERVE immediately. 1/2-cup per serving.

FOR A REALLY GOOD TROPICAL VARIATION: Substitute kiwi slices, pineapple chunks, papaya slices, or mango cubes for some of the melon balls. Add a little grated fresh ginger or ground ginger. A dash of coconut extract would also enhance the flavor. You could serve this in a hollowed-out pineapple half.

# Sweet Kugel

1   cup low-fat cottage cheese
4   (8-ounce cartons egg substitute
1   (8-ounce carton low-fat sour cream
1   cup raisins
1/2 cup sugar
2   tablespoons reduced-calorie stick margarine, melted
1   teaspoon ground cinnamon
1/4 teaspoon salt
1   (16-ounce) can sliced peaches in juice, drained and coarsely chopped
8   cups cooked egg noodles (about 12 ounces uncooked)
Vegetable cooking spray
1/3 cup coarsely-crushed cornflakes

PREHEAT oven to 350 degrees.
COMBINE First 9 ingredients in a large bowl; stir well.
ADD noodles; toss gently to coat.
SPOON mixture into a 13x9-inch baking dish coated with cooking spray.
SPRINKLE crushed cornflakes over noodle mixture; cover and bake for 30 minutes; uncover and bake an additional 10 minutes.
YIELD: 12 servings

# Vegetable Frittata

2   tablespoons vegetate oil, divided
1/2 cup chopped onion
1/2 cup chopped green pepper
1/2 cup chopped sweet red pepper
1   garlic clove, minced
Dash of pepper
2   medium red potatoes, cooked and cubed
1   small zucchini, cubed
Egg substitute equivalent to 6 eggs

HEAT 1 tablespoon of oil in a 10-inch cast-iron skillet; sauté onion, peppers and garlic until tender; remove vegetables with a slotted spoon; set aside.
IN the same skillet, over medium-high heat, lightly brown potatoes in remaining oil. Add vegetable mixture and zucchini; cook for 4 minutes.
IN a bowl, combine egg substitute and pepper; pour over vegetables.
COVER and cook for 8 to 10 minutes, or until eggs are completely set.
CUT into wedges.
YIELD: 6 servings

PER serving:
CALORIES 115
(52% from fat)
FAT 7g
(saturated 1g)
PROTEIN 8g
CARBOHYDRATE 6g
SODIUM 112mg

# Vegetable-Ground Round-Egg Bake

1   pound ground round
1/2 pound fresh mushrooms, sliced
1/2 pound fresh spinach, torn
6   green onions, sliced
1/4 cup chopped celery
1/4 cup chopped sweet red pepper
1/4 teaspoon garlic powder
1/2 teaspoon pepper
Egg substitute equivalent to 6 eggs

IN a large skillet, brown beef and mushrooms; drain.
ADD spinach, onions, celery, red pepper, garlic powder and pepper.
COOK and stir for 1 minute.
ADD egg substitute; cook and stir until the eggs are completely set.
SERVE immediately.
YIELD: 6 servings

# Walnut-Maple Muffins

2 1/4 cups all-purpose flour
1   cup sugar
1   teaspoon baking powder
1/2 teaspoon baking soda
1/4 teaspoon salt
1/2 cup chilled reduced-calorie stick margarine, cut into small pieces
2   tablespoons maple syrup
1   teaspoon imitation maple flavoring
3   egg whites, lightly beaten
1   (8-ounce) carton plain nonfat yogurt
Vegetable cooking spray
1/4 cup chopped walnuts

PREHEAT oven to 350 degrees.
COMBINE first 5 ingredients in a large bowl; cut in margarine with a pastry blender or 2 knives until mixture resembles coarse meal.
COMBINE maple syrup, maple flavoring, egg whites and yogurt; add to dry ingredients, stirring just until dry ingredients are moistened.
SPOON batter evenly into 18 muffin cups coated with cooking spray, or paper liners; sprinkle walnuts evenly over batter.
BAKE at 350 degrees for 25 minutes or until muffins spring back when touched lightly in center.
REMOVE from pans immediately; let cool on a wire rack.
YIELD: 1 1/2 dozen (serving size: 1 muffin)

PER 1 muffin:
CALORIES 148
(27% from fat)
FAT 4.4g
(saturated 0.8g)
PROTEIN 3g
CARBOHYDRATE 24.9g
FIBER 0.5g
CHOLESTEROL 0mg
IRON 0.8mg
SODIUM 124mg

# Notes & Recipes

# Desserts

# List Your Favorite Recipes

| Recipes | Page |
|---|---|
| | |
| | |
| | |
| | |
| | |
| | |
| | |
| | |
| | |
| | |
| | |
| | |
| | |
| | |
| | |
| | |
| | |

# Angel Food Cake with Vanilla Custard Sauce

1 1/2 cups 2% low-fat milk
1/4 cup sugar
4   large egg yolks
1   tablespoon vanilla extract
8   (2-ounce) slices angel food cake

PLACE milk in a 1-quart glass measure. Microwave on HIGH 3 minutes.
COMBINE sugar and egg yolks in a medium bowl; stir with a wire whisk.
GRADUALLY add hot milk to egg mixture, stirring constantly with a whisk.
RETURN milk mixture to a glass measure. Microwave at HIGH for 2 1/2 minutes, stirring after 1 1/2 minutes; stir in vanilla.
COVER and cool to room temperature.
SERVE over angel food cake.
YIELD: 8 servings

PER serving:
CALORIES 228
(15% from fat)
FAT 3.7g
(saturated 1.4g,
    mono 1.3g, poly 0.5g)
PROTEIN 6.4g
CARBOHYDRATE 42.1g
FIBER 0g
CHOLESTEROL 113mg
IRON 0.5mg
SODIUM 315mg
CALCIUM 115mg

# Apple-Bourbon Pie

1/3 cup currants
1/3 cup bourbon
3   pounds cooking apples
1/2 cup sugar
2   tablespoons all-purpose flour
1   teaspoon ground cinnamon
1/4 teaspoon salt
1/8 teaspoon ground nutmeg
1/4 cup finely-chopped pecans or walnuts, toasted
1   (15-ounce) package refrigerated pie crusts
2   teaspoons low-sugar apricot spread
1   teaspoon nonfat buttermilk
1   teaspoon sugar

COMBINE currants and bourbon and let soak 2 hours.
PEEL apples, and cut into 1/2-inch slices; arrange apple slices in a steamer basket over boiling water.
COVER and steam 10 minutes, or until apples are tender.
COMBINE 1/2 cup sugar and next 4 ingredients in a large bowl; add apple slices, currant mixture and pecans, stirring to combine.
FILL 1 pie crust into a 9-inch pie plate according to package directions; brush apricot spread over pie crust, and spoon apple mixture into pie crust.
UNFOLD remaining pie crust and press out fold lines; cut pie crust in half.
RESERVE remaining half of pie crust for another use.
CUT remaining half into 2 leaves and an apple with a 3-inch leaf-shaped cutter and apple-shaped cutter. Mark veins on leaves with a pastry wheel or sharp knife.
ARRANGE leaves and apple cut-outs over apple mixture; brush with buttermilk and sprinkle with 1 teaspoon sugar.
BAKE at 450 degrees on lower rack of oven for 15 minutes.
COVER edges of pastry with strips of aluminum foil to prevent excess browning.
BAKE at 350 degrees for 30 minutes.
LET cool 1 hour before serving.
YIELD: 8 servings

# Apple-Currant Bars

1   cup all-purpose flour
1   teaspoon ground cinnamon
3/4 teaspoon baking powder
1/4 teaspoon baking soda
1/4 teaspoon salt
1/4 teaspoon ground nutmeg
1/3 cup margarine
3/4 cup firmly-packed dark brown sugar
1   large egg
1   teaspoon vanilla extract
1   cup peeled, diced Rome apple
3/4 cup regular oats, uncooked
1/2 cup dried currants (you may use
       chopped raisins)
1   tablespoon powdered sugar

PREHEAT oven to 350 degrees.
COMBINE first 6 ingredients. Stir well and set aside.
CREAM margarine in a large bowl; gradually add
brown sugar, beating at medium speed of an elec-
tric mixer until light and fluffy.
ADD egg; beat well.
ADD flour mixture to creamed mixture; beat just
until dry ingredients are moist.
STIR in vanilla, apple, oats and currants. (You may
substitute chopped raisins.)
SPOON batter into a 9-inch square baking pan
coated with cooking spray.
BAKE at 350°for 40 minutes, or until a wooden pick
inserted in center comes out clean.
COOL completely in pan on a wire rack; sprinkle
powdered sugar over top.
YIELD: 16 squares

PER 1 square:
CALORIES 141
(29% from fat)
FAT 4.6g
(saturated 0.9g,
    mono 1.9g, poly 1.4g)
PROTEIN 2g
CARBOHYDRATE 23.4g
FIBER 0.9g
CHOLESTEROL 14mg
IRON 1mg
SODIUM 111mg
CALCIUM 34mg

# Apple Pie

1/4 cup packed light-brown sugar
1/4 cup granulated sugar
1   tablespoon all-purpose flour
1   teaspoon grated lemon peel
1/4 teaspoon ground cinnamon
1/4 teaspoon ground nutmeg
6   medium baking apples, peeled, cored and
        thinly sliced (about 2 pounds)
1   cup dark raisins
1   unbaked, ready-made 9-inch pie crust.

GLAZE (optional):
1   large egg, beaten
1   teaspoon granulated sugar

PREHEAT oven to 425 degrees.
SPRAY a 9-inch deep-dish pie plate with vegetable cooking spray.
IN a large bowl, combine brown sugar, granulated sugar, flour, lemon peel, cinnamon and nutmeg; mix well.
ADD apples to sugar mixture; stir until coated.
STIR in raisins; spoon into prepared pie plate.
PLACE pie crust on top of filling.
TRIM edges, pressing against edge of pan.
USING a sharp knife, cut steam vents in pie crust.
TO glaze, lightly brush pie crust with beaten egg; sprinkle with sugar.
BAKE until pie crust is golden brown, about 35 to 40 minutes.
PLACE on a wire rack and cool for 30 minutes; serve warm.
YIELD: 10 slices

# Apple Upside-Down Banana Cake

1 tablespoon stick margarine, melted
1/4 cup packed brown sugar
1 1/2 cups peeled, thinly-sliced Granny Smith apple
1 1/4 cups all-purpose flour
1 teaspoon baking powder
3/4 teaspoon ground cinnamon
1/2 teaspoon baking soda
1/4 teaspoon ground nutmeg
1/8 teaspoon salt
1/4 cup stick margarine, softened
1/3 cup granulated sugar
1/3 cup firmly-packed brown sugar
1/2 cup mashed ripe banana
1 teaspoon vanilla extract
1 large egg
1/4 cup orange juice
2 tablespoons finely-chopped pecans, toasted
       (you may use walnuts)

PREHEAT oven to 350 degrees.
COAT bottom of 9-inch round cake pan with melted margarine. Sprinkle 1/4 cup brown sugar over margarine.
ARRANGE apple slices spoke-like, working from center of pan to the edges.
COMBINE flour and next 5 ingredients in a bowl; stir well, and set aside.
BEAT 1/4 cup margarine, 1/3 cup sugar and 1/3 cup brown sugar at medium speed of an electric mixer until well blended.
ADD banana, vanilla and egg; beat well.
ADD flour mixture to creamed mixture alternately with orange juice, beginning and ending with flour mixture; beat well after each addition.
STIR in pecans; pour batter over apple slices.
BAKE at 350 degrees for 30 minutes, or until a wooden pick inserted in center comes out clean.
LET cool in pan 5 minutes on a wire rack; loosen cake from around sides of pan, using a narrow metal spatula.
INVERT onto cake plate; cut into wedges; serve warm.
YIELD: 8 servings

PER 1 slice:
CALORIES 280
(30% from fat)
FAT 9.4g
(saturated 1.8g,
       mono 4.2g, poly 2.8g)
PROTEIN 3.3g
CARBOHYDRATE 47g
FIBER 1.8g
CHOLESTEROL 28mg
IRON 1.6mg
SODIUM 214mg
CALCIUM 63mg

# Apricot-Almond Tart

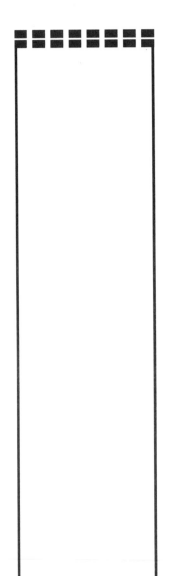

1 1/3 cups all-purpose flour, divided
1/4 cup plus 1 tablespoon ice water
1   tablespoon sugar
1/4 teaspoon salt
1/4 cup vegetable shortening
Vegetable cooking spray
1/3 cup sliced almonds, divided
3   tablespoons flour
2   pounds apricots, halved and pitted
       (about 12 large)
3/4 cup sugar
1/2 teaspoon pumpkin pie spice
2   teaspoons water

PREHEAT oven to 400 degrees.
COMBINE 1/3 cup flour and ice water, stirring with
a whisk until well-blended; set aside.
COMBINE remaining 1 cup flour, 1 tablespoon sugar
and salt in a bowl; cut in shortening with a pastry
blender, or two knives until mixture resembles
coarse meal.
ADD ice water mixture, and mix with a fork until
dry ingredients are moist.
ROLL dough into a 14-inch circle on a lightly-floured
surface.
PLACE dough on a large baking sheet coated with
cooking spray.
COMBINE 3 tablespoons almonds and 3 tablespoons
flour in a food processor; process 30 seconds, or
until almonds are finely chopped.
SPRINKLE almond-flour mixture over dough.
ARRANGE apricot halves, cut-sides down, over
dough, leaving a 2-inch border.
COMBINE 3/4 cup sugar and pie spice in a bowl; stir
well, and reserve 1 tablespoon of sugar-spice mixture; set aside.
SPRINKLE remaining sugar-spice mixture over

Continued on following page.

Continued from preceding page.

apricots and top with remaining 2 1/2 tablespoons almonds.

FOLD 2 inch border of dough over apricots, pressing gently to seal (it will only partially cover apricots).

BRUSH border of dough with 2 teaspoons water, and sprinkle with reserved sugar-spice mixture.

BAKE at 400 degrees for 45 minutes, or until lightly browned; let cool on baking sheet 5 minutes.

CAREFULLY slide tart onto a serving platter using a spatula; cut into 8 wedges and serve warm.

YIELD: 8 servings

PER 1 wedge:
CALORIES 284
(26% from fat)
FAT 8.1g
(saturated 1.8g, mono,
    3.1g, poly 2.6g)
CARBOHYDRATE 50.4g
FIBER 3.4g
CHOLESTEROL 4mg
IRON 1.8mg
SODIUM 76mg
CALCIUM 31mg

# Apricot Pinwheels

1   cup apricot preserves
3/4 cup minced dried apricots
2 1/2 tablespoons orange juice
2 3/4 cups all-purpose flour
3/4 teaspoon baking powder
1/4 teaspoon baking soda
1/4 teaspoon salt
1/4 cup stick margarine, softened
1   cup granulated sugar
1/2 cup firmly-packed brown sugar
2 1/2 tablespoons vegetable oil
1/2 teaspoon vanilla extract
3   egg whites
Vegetable cooking spray

COMBINE first three ingredients in a small saucepan; bring to a boil.
REDUCE heat to medium-low and cook 10 minutes,
stirring occasionally.
REMOVE from heat; cover and let cool completely.
COMBINE flour, baking powder, baking soda and
salt in a large bowl; stir well and set aside.
PLACE margarine in a large mixing bowl; beat at
medium speed of an electric mixer until light and
fluffy.
GRADUALLY add sugars, beating at medium speed
until well blended.
ADD oil, vanilla and egg whites; beat well. Add flour
mixture and beat until well blended.
DIVIDE dough in half; working with one half at a
time (cover remaining half to keep from drying),
gently press dough into a 4-inch square on a heavy-
duty plastic wrap, and cover with additional plastic wrap.
ROLL each half of dough, still covered, into a 12-
inch square. Chill 30 minutes.

Continued on following page.

Continued from preceding page.

REMOVE top sheet of plastic wrap, and divide apricot mixture evenly between dough squares.

ROLL up each square jelly-roll fashion, peeling plastic wrap from bottom of dough while rolling (dough may be soft).

WRAP each roll individually in plastic wrap and freeze 8 hours.

PREHEAT oven to 350 degrees.

CUT each roll into 24 (1/2-inch) slices, and place 1 inch apart on baking sheets, coated with cooking spray.

BAKE at 350 degrees for 10 minutes.

REMOVE from baking sheets; let cool on wire racks.

YIELD: 4 dozen

PER serving:
CALORIES 89
(18% from fat)
FAT 1.8g
(saturated 0.3g,
      mono 0.6g, poly 0.7g)
PROTEIN 1.1g
CARBOHYDRATE 17.7g
FIBER 0.3g
CHOLESTEROL 0mg
IRON 0.5mg
SODIUM 39mg
CALCIUM 10mg

# Banana Cream Pie

PER 1 slice:
CALORIES 200
FAT 6g
PROTEIN 32 g
SODIUM 298mg

2   cups sliced banana (2 medium)
1   (6-ounce) chocolate-flavored pie crust
1   (4-serving) package of Jello sugar-free
        instant banana pudding mix
2/3 cup Carnation nonfat dry milk powder
1 1/3 cups water
1   cup Cool Whip Lite
1   tablespoon chocolate syrup

LAYER bananas on bottom of pie crust.
IN a medium bowl, combine dry pudding mix and
dry milk powder.
ADD water; mix well, using a wire whisk.
BLEND in 1/4 cup Cool Whip Lite.
POUR mixture over bananas.
REFRIGERATE for about 15 minutes.
SPREAD remaining 3/4 cup Cool Whip Lite evenly
over filling.
DRIZZLE chocolate syrup over top.
REFRIGERATE until ready to serve.
YIELD: 8 servings

# Bananas Foster

1/3 cup maple syrup
1/3 cup dark rum
3 1/2 cups diagonally-sliced firm, ripe bananas
1/3 cup chopped walnuts, toasted
3   cups vanilla nonfat frozen yogurt

COMBINE syrup and rum in a large nonstick skillet;
bring to a simmer over medium-low heat.
ADD banana; cook 3 minutes, stirring occasionally.
ADD walnuts; cook 1 minute.
DO Not overcook this mixture, as it will turn dark.
SERVE immediately over frozen yogurt.
YIELD: 6 servings (serving size: 1/2 cup banana mix-
ture and 1/2 cup frozen yogurt)

PER serving:
CALORIES 296
(13% from fat)
FAT 4.4g
(saturated 0.4g,
    mono 0.9g, poly 2.7g)
PROTEIN 6.2g
CARBOHYDRATE 51.9g
FIBER 3g
CHOLESTEROL 0mg
IRON 0.7mg
SODIUM 65mg
CALCIUM 156mg

# Fresh Blueberry Cobbler

4   cups blueberries
1   teaspoon lemon juice
Vegetable cooking spray
1   cup all-purpose flour
1/2 cup sugar
1   teaspoon baking powder
1/8 teaspoon ground nutmeg
Dash of salt
1   tablespoon vegetable oil
1/2 teaspoon vanilla extract
2   egg whites, lightly beaten
3   tablespoons sugar
1/2 teaspoon ground cinnamon

PREHEAT oven to 350 degrees.
COMBINE blueberries and lemon juice in a 9-inch square baking dish, coated with cooking spray; set aside.
COMBINE flour and next 4 ingredients in a bowl; make a well in center of mixture.
COMBINE oil, vanilla and egg whites; stir well with a whisk.
ADD to flour mixture, stirring just until moist.
DROP dough by spoonfuls onto blueberry mixture to form 8 dumplings.
COMBINE 3 tablespoons sugar and cinnamon; sprinkle over dumplings.
BAKE at 350 degrees for 35 minutes, or until filling is bubbly and dumplings are lightly browned.
YIELD: 8 servings

# Brownies

6  tablespoons vegetable oil spread
1  cup granulated sugar
1/3 cup cocoa
1  teaspoon vanilla extract
2  egg whites, slightly beaten
1/2 cup all-purpose flour
2  tablespoons finely-chopped walnuts
1/2 cup reduced-fat semi-sweet baking chips

HEAT oven to 350 degrees.
LIGHTLY spray 8-inch square baking pan with non-stick cooking spray.
MELT vegetable oil spread in medium saucepan over low heat.
ADD sugar; stir until well blended.
REMOVE from heat; stir in cocoa and vanilla.
ADD egg whites; stir to blend.
STIR in flour and walnuts.
ADD chips; stir just to blend.
SPREAD batter into prepared pan.
BAKE at 350 degrees for 25 minutes, or until edges begin to pull away from sides of pan.
COOL in pan on wire racks; cut into bars.
YIELD: 16 brownies (1 brownie per serving)

PER 1 brownie:
CALORIES 140
FAT 5g

# Brownies

■ ■ ■ ■ ■ ■ ■

PER 1 square:
CALORIES 112
(30% from fat)
FAT 4g
PROTEIN 2g
CARBOHYDRATE 18g
SODIUM 60mg
CHOLESTEROL 18mg

1/2 cup cake flour, sifted
1/2 cup unsweetened cocoa
1/4 teaspoon salt
2 egg whites
1 large egg
3/4 cup granulated sugar
6 tablespoons unsweetened applesauce
2 tablespoons vegetable oil
1 1/2 teaspoons vanilla extract
1 tablespoon chopped walnuts (optional)

PREHEAT oven to 350 degrees.
SPRAY an 8-inch square baking pan with vegetable cooking spray and set aside.
IN a medium bowl, combine flour, cocoa and salt; mix well.
IN a large bowl, whisk together egg whites, egg, sugar, applesauce, oil and vanilla.
STIR in flour mixture until just blended; do not overmix.
POUR batter into prepared pan; sprinkle with walnuts.
BAKE until just set and a toothpick inserted in center comes out clean, about 25 minutes.
PLACE pan on a wire rack and cool for at least 15 minutes.
CUT brownies into squares and place on a serving plate.
FOR slightly chewier brownies, replace the 1/2 cup of the cake flour with 7 tablespoons of all-purpose flour. Sifting is not necessary. Proceed with recipe as directed. Also, instead of walnuts, try sprinkling brownie batter with pecans or almonds.
YIELD: 12 squares.

FRUIT purées, such as pear or applesauce, add sweetness and moistness to baked goods. Use one-quarter of the oil called for, and substitute purée for the rest.

# Brownie Cheesecake

1   (10.25 ounce) package fudge brownie mix
1   tablespoon water
1   teaspoon vegetable oil
1   (2 1/2-ounce) jar prune baby food
1   egg white
Vegetable cooking spray
1   cup nonfat cottage cheese
2   (8-ounce) blocks Neufchatel cheese,
       softened
1   (8-ounce) block nonfat cream cheese,
       softened
1 1/2 cups sugar
1   tablespoon vanilla extract
1/4 teaspoon salt
3   eggs
1/4 cup semi-sweet chocolate morsels

PREHEAT oven to 350 degrees.
COMBINE first 5 ingredients in a bowl; stir well.
SPREAD into bottom of a 9-inch square baking pan
coated with cooking spray.
BAKE at 350 degrees for 25 minutes; let cool on a
wire rack.
TEAR brownies into small pieces.
PRESS half of pieces into bottom of a 9-inch
springform pan, coated with cooking spray.
SET aside pan and remaining brownie pieces.
PREHEAT oven to 300 degrees.
ADD cheeses; beat until smooth.
ADD sugar, vanilla and salt; beat well.
ADD eggs, one at a time, beating well after each
addition. Stir in chocolate.
POUR half of cheese mixture over brownie pieces.
BAKE at 300 degrees for 40 minutes, or until al-
most set.
TURN oven off, and let cheesecake stand 40 min-
utes in oven with door closed.
REMOVE cheesecake from oven, and let cool to
room temperature.
COVER and chill at least 8 hours.
YIELD: 16 servings (serving size: 1 wedge)

PER 1 wedge:
CALORIES 271
(30% from fat)
FAT 9.1g
(saturated 5.3g,
    mono 0.6g, poly 0.3g)
PROTEIN 9.6g
CARBOHYDRATE 37.7g
FIBER 0.8g
CHOLESTEROL 65mg
IRON 0.2mg
SODIUM 373mg
CALCIUM 69mg

# Brownie Snack Mix

3/4 cup sugar
1/4 cup vegetable oil
1/4 cup plain nonfat yogurt
1    teaspoon vanilla extract
3    large egg whites, or 2/3 cup egg substitute
1/2 cup all-purpose flour
1/3 cup unsweetened cocoa
1/4 teaspoon salt
1/4 teaspoon baking powder
Vegetable cooking spray
1 1/2 cups powdered sugar
2 1/2 tablespoons skim milk
1    teaspoon unsweetened cocoa

PREHEAT oven to 375 degrees.
COMBINE first 5 ingredients in a bowl; beat at medium speed of an electric mixer until well blended.
COMBINE flour and next 3 ingredients; stir well.
ADD flour mixture to sugar mixture, beating just until blended.
POUR batter into a 9-inch round pan coated with cooking spray.
BAKE at 375 degrees for 25 minutes, or until a wooden pick inserted into center comes out clean.
COOL in pan 10 minutes; remove from pan and let cool completely on a wire rack.
COMBINE powdered sugar and milk; beat at low speed until glaze is smooth.
SPREAD 1/2 cup glaze over cake.
ADD 1 teaspoon cocoa to remaining glaze, stirring with a wire whisk until blended.
SPOON into a zip-top plastic bag; snip off 1 corner of bag, making a small hole.
STARTING at the center of cake, pipe glaze in 5 concentric circles.
STARTING at center circle, pull a wooden pick or the top of a knife through circles at regular intervals to edge of cake to form a "web" design.
YIELD: 12 servings

# Cappuccino Pudding Mix

1   cup all-purpose flour
2/3 cup sugar
2   tablespoons unsweetened cocoa
2   teaspoons baking powder
1/4 teaspoon salt
1/2 cup evaporated skim milk
1   teaspoon vegetable oil
1   teaspoon vanilla extract
1/4 cup semi-sweet chocolate morsels
1   cup firmly-packed dark brown sugar
1/4 cup unsweetened cocoa
1 3/4 cups hot water
2   (.77-ounce) envelopes instant cappuccino
       coffee mix, or 1/4 cup other instant
       flavored coffee mix
1/2 cup plus 1 tablespoon frozen vanilla yogurt

PREHEAT oven to 350 degrees.
COMBINE first 5 ingredients in a 9-inch square baking pan and stir well.
ADD milk, oil and vanilla, stirring until smooth.
STIR in chocolate morsels.
COMBINE brown sugar and 1/4 cup cocoa; sprinkle over batter.
COMBINE water and coffee mix, stirring to dissolve.
POUR coffee mixture over batter; do not stir.
BAKE at 350 degrees for 40 minutes, or until cake springs back when touched lightly in center.
SERVE warm with frozen yogurt.
YIELD: 9 servings

PER serving:
CALORIES 247
(11% from fat)
FAT 3.0g
(saturated 1.5g,
    mono 0.5g, poly 0.4g)
PROTEIN 4.2g
CARBOHYDRATE 52.4g
FIBER 0.3g
CHOLESTEROL 1mg
IRON 2mg
SODIUM 123mg
CALCIUM 175mg

# Caramel Swirl-and-Apple Cheesecake

1   (32-ounce) carton vanilla low-fat yogurt
1/4 cup sugar
1   tablespoon stick margarine, softened
1   egg white
1 1/4 cups graham cracker crumbs
1   teaspoon ground cinnamon
Vegetable cooking spray
1/4 cup firmly-packed brown sugar
1/4 cup orange juice
3   cups peeled, cubed Golden Delicious apples
1/2 cup sugar
3   tablespoons cornstarch
1   tablespoon vanilla extract
1/4 teaspoon salt
1   (8-ounce) block Neufchatel cheese, softened
1   (8-ounce) block nonfat cream cheese, softened
2   eggs
1/3 cup fat-free caramel-flavored sundae syrup
2   tablespoons fat-free caramel-flavored sundae syrup
    Cinnamon stick (optional)

PLACE colander in a 2-quart glass measure or bowl. Line colander with 4 layers of cheesecloth, allowing cheesecloth to extend over edge of bowl. Spoon yogurt into colander. COVER colander loosely with plastic wrap; refrigerate 12 hours. Spoon yogurt cheese into a bowl; discard liquid. Cover and refrigerate.
PREHEAT oven to 350 degrees.
COMBINE 1/4 cup sugar, margarine and egg white in a bowl; beat at medium speed of an electric mixer until blended.
ADD crumbs and ground cinnamon; stir well.
FIRMLY press crumb mixture into bottom and 1 1/2

Continued on following page.

Continued from preceding page.

inches up sides of a 9-inch springform pan coated with cooking spray.

BAKE at 350 degrees for 10 minutes; let cool on a wire rack.

PREHEAT oven to 300 degrees.

COMBINE brown sugar and orange juice in a large nonstick skillet; bring to a boil.

ADD apple; cook 8 minutes, or until apple is tender and liquid evaporates, stirring occasionally; set aside.

COMBINE yogurt cheese, 1/2 cup sugar, and next 5 ingredients in a bowl; beat at medium speed of mixer until smooth.

ADD eggs, one at a time, beating well after each addition.

SPOON apple mixture into prepared pan.

POUR cheese mixture over apples; top with 1/3 cup sundae syrup, and swirl with a knife to create a marbled effect.

BAKE at 300 degrees for 1 hour until almost set.

TURN oven off; loosen cake from sides of pan using a narrow metal spatula or knife.

LET cheesecake stand 40 minutes in oven with door closed.

REMOVE cheesecake from oven and let cool to room temperature.

COVER and chill at least 8 hours.

DRIZZLE 2 tablespoons sundae syrup over top.

YIELD: 12 servings

PER serving:
CALORIES 286
(25% from fat)
FAT 8g
(saturated 3.7g,
mono 1.3g, poly 0.5g)
PROTEIN 10.4g
CARBOHYDRATE 44.2g
FIBER 0.9g
CHOLESTEROL 55mg
IRON 0.7mg
SODIUM 384mg
CALCIUM 160mg

# Carrot Spice Cake

PER serving:
CALORIES 180
(1% from fat)
FAT trace
(saturated trace)
SODIUM 309mg
CHOLESTEROL trace
CARBOHYDRATE 42g
PROTEIN 4g

1 1/4 cups sugar
3/4 cup light corn syrup
3/4 cup skim milk
8  egg whites
2  cups all-purpose flour
2  teaspoons baking powder
2  teaspoons baking soda
2  teaspoons ground cinnamon
1/4 teaspoon salt
2  cups grated carrots

IN a large mixing bowl, beat sugar, corn syrup, milk and egg whites.
COMBINE dry ingredients; add to batter and beat well.
PAT carrots dry with paper towels; stir into batter.
POUR into a 10-inch fluted tube pan that has been coated with nonstick cooking spray and floured.
BAKE at 350 degrees for 1 hour, or until a toothpick inserted near the center comes out clean.
COOL in pan for 10 minutes; invert onto a wire rack and cool completely.
YIELD: 16 servings (serving size: 1/16 of recipe)

# Cherry Cobbler

5   cups pitted canned tart red cherries
1/3 cup sugar
1/3 cup packed brown sugar
1 1/2 tablespoons cornstarch
1   teaspoon ground cinnamon
1/4 teaspoon ground nutmeg
2 1/2 tablespoons lemon juice

TOPPING:
1   cup all-purpose flour
1   tablespoon sugar
1   teaspoon baking powder
1/4 teaspoon salt
2   tablespoons margarine
1/3 to 1/2 cup skim milk

DRAIN cherries, reserving 1/4 cup juice; set aside.
IN a saucepan, combine sugars, cornstarch, cinnamon and nutmeg; stir in cherry and lemon juices.
BRING to a boil, stirring occasionally; boil for 2 minutes.
ADD cherries; pour into an ungreased 9-inch square baking dish.

FOR TOPPING: Combine flour, sugar, baking powder and salt; cut in margarine until crumbly.
STIR in enough milk to moisten; drop by rounded tablespoonfuls over cherries.
BAKE at 450 degrees for 10 to 13 minutes, or until golden brown.
YIELD: 9 servings

PER serving:
CALORIES 176
(12% from fat)
FAT 3g
(saturated 1g)
CHOLESTEROL trace
SODIUM 253mg
CARBOHYDRATE 37g
PROTEIN 3mg

# Chocolate Chews

1 3/4 cups all-purpose flour
2/3 cup sifted powdered sugar
1/3 cup unsweetened cocoa
2 1/4 teaspoons baking powder
1/8 teaspoon salt
1   cup semi-sweet chocolate mini-morsels,
     divided
3   tablespoons vegetable oil
1   cup firmly-packed brown sugar
2 1/2 tablespoons light-colored corn syrup
1   tablespoon water
2 1/2 teaspoons vanilla extract
3   egg whites
Vegetable cooking spray

PREHEAT oven to 350 degrees.
COMBINE first 5 ingredients in a bowl; stir well and set aside.
COMBINE 3/4 cup chocolate morsels and oil in a small saucepan; cook over low heat until chocolate melts, stirring constantly.
POUR melted chocolate mixture into a large bowl, and let cool 5 minutes.
ADD brown sugar and next 4 ingredients to chocolate mixture; stir well.
STIR in flour mixture and remaining chocolate morsels.
DROP dough by level tablespoons, 2 inches apart, onto baking sheets coated with cooking spray.
BAKE at 350 degrees for 8 minutes; let cool 2 minutes or until firm.
REMOVE cookies from baking sheets; let cool on wire racks.
YIELD: 4 dozen

# Chocolate Angel Food Cake

1   cup cake flour
1/2 cup baking cocoa
2   cups egg whites (14 eggs)
2   teaspoons cream of tartar
2   cups sugar
1   teaspoon vanilla extract

SIFT flour and cocoa together 3 times; set aside.
IN a large mixing bowl, beat the egg whites until foamy; sprinkle with cream of tartar and beat until soft peaks form. GRADUALLY add sugar, about 2 tablespoons at a time, beating until stiff peaks form; blend in vanilla.
SIFT about a fourth of the flour mixture over egg white mixture; fold in gently.
REPEAT, folding in remaining flour mixture by fourths; pour into an ungreased 10-inch tube pan.
BAKE at 325 degrees for 1 hour.
TURN off the oven, but let cake sit in the oven for 5 minutes.
REMOVE from the oven and immediately invert pan; cool.
LOOSEN sides of cake from pan and remove.
YIELD: 12 servings

PER serving:
CALORIES 190
(2% from fat)
FAT trace
(saturated trace)
CHOLESTEROL 0
SODIUM 65mg
CARBOHYDRATE 42 g
PROTEIN 5g

# Chocolate Chiffon Cake with Coffee Buttercream

Butter-flavored vegetable cooking spray
6   egg whites
3/4 teaspoon cream of tartar
1 1/3 cups sugar
1   cup unsweetened cocoa
1/2 cup water
1/3 cup vegetable oil
1/4 cup margarine, melted
3   egg yolks
2   cups sifted cake flour
2   teaspoons baking soda
1/8 teaspoon salt
1   cup reduced-fat sour cream
2   teaspoons vanilla extract
Coffee Buttercream
1/3 cup chocolate-covered coffee beans,
        coarsely chopped

COAT three 9-inch round cake pans with cooking spray; line with waxed paper.
SPRAY waxed paper; set aside.
BEAT egg whites and cream of tartar at high speed with an electric mixer until stiff peaks form; set aside.
COMBINE sugar and next 4 ingredients in a large mixer bowl. Beat at low speed of an electric mixer until smooth.
ADD egg yolks, one at a time, beating just until blended after each addition.
COMBINE flour, baking soda and salt; add to cocoa mixture alternately with sour cream, beginning and ending with flour mixture; mix at low speed after each addition until blended. STIR in vanilla.
FOLD 1/3 of egg white into batter; fold in remaining egg white.

Continued on following page.

Continued from preceding page.

POUR batter into prepared pans.

BAKE at 350 degrees for 18 minutes or until a wooden toothpick inserted in center comes out clean.

COOL in pans on wire racks 18 minutes; remove cake layers from pans.

COOL cake layers completely on wire racks.

SPREAD Coffee Buttercream between cake layers and on top and sides of cake.

SPRINKLE chocolate-covered coffee beans on top of cake.

YIELD: 12 servings

COFFEE BUTTERCREAM:

2   teaspoons boiling water
1/4 cup instant coffee granules
1   cup light butter, softened
7   cups sifted powdered sugar

COMBINE water and coffee granules, stirring until coffee dissolves.

BEAT butter at medium speed with an electric mixer until creamy; gradually add powdered sugar, beating until blended.

GRADUALLY add coffee mixture; beat until spreading consistency.

YIELD 3 1/3 cups

PER serving:
CALORIES 679
(31% from fat)
FAT 23.6g
(10.1g saturated)
PROTEIN 7.0g
FIBER 0.2g
CARBOHYDRATE 113.1g
CHOLESTEROL 79g
SODIUM 413mg

# Chocolate-Cola Cake

1   (18.25 ounce) package light devils food cake mix
1   (3.8 ounce) package fat-free chocolate-
        flavored instant pudding mix
1   cup egg substitute
1/3 cup vegetable oil
1   (10-ounce) bottle diet cola-flavored
        carbonated drink
Vegetable cooking spray
Chocolate-Cola Frosting
1/2 cup finely-chopped pecans, toasted

COMBINE first 4 ingredients in a mixing bowl; beat at medium speed with an electric mixer until blended.
POUR cola gradually into cake batter, beating at low speed. Increase speed to medium; beat 2 minutes.
POUR batter into a 13x9x2-inch pan coated with cooking spray.
BAKE at 350 degrees for 30 minutes. Cool in pan on a wire rack 10 minutes.
SPREAD Chocolate-Cola Frosting over top of warm cake; sprinkle with pecans.
COOL cake completely on wire rack.
YIELD: 15 servings

I USED Betty Crocker Reduced-Fat Sweet Rewards devils food cake mix.

CHOCOLATE-COLA FROSTING
1/3 cup reduced-calorie margarine
3   tablespoons diet cola-flavored carbonated
        beverage
3   tablespoons unsweetened cocoa
1   (16-ounce) package powdered sugar, sifted
1   teaspoon vanilla extract

COMBINE first 3 ingredients in a large saucepan; cook over medium heat, stirring constantly, until margarine melts (Do Not Boil).
REMOVE from heat; add powdered sugar and vanilla until smooth.
YIELD: 1 3/4 cups

# Chocolate Macaroon Tunnel Cake

1 1/4 cups sugar
1/4 cup plus 2 tablespoons vegetable oil
2   large eggs
3   cups all-purpose flour
1 1/4 teaspoons baking soda
1/4 teaspoon salt
1 1/2 cups low-fat buttermilk
2   teaspoons vanilla extract
1/2 cup flaked sweetened coconut
1 1/2 teaspoons coconut flavoring, divided
1/3 cup unsweetened cocoa
Vegetable cooking spray
3/4 cup sifted powdered sugar
1   tablespoon skim milk

PREHEAT oven to 350 degrees.
COMBINE 1 1/4 cups sugar and oil in a large bowl, beating well at medium speed of an electric mixer.
ADD eggs, one at a time, beating well after each addition.
COMBINE flour, baking soda and salt; add flour mixture to sugar mixture alternately with buttermilk, beginning and ending with flour mixture; mix after each addition. Stir in vanilla.
COMBINE one cup batter, coconut and 1 teaspoon coconut flavoring in a small bowl; stir well and set aside.
ADD cocoa to remaining batter in a large bowl; stir well.
RESERVE one cup chocolate batter and set aside.
POUR remaining chocolate batter over center of batter to form ring, making sure not to touch sides of pan.
TOP with reserved chocolate batter, spreading evenly to cover.
BAKE at 350 degrees for 40 minutes, or until a wooden toothpick inserted in center comes out clean.
COOL in pan 10 minutes; remove from pan.
COOL on a wire rack.
COMBINE remaining 1/2 teaspoon coconut flavoring, powdered sugar and skim milk; stir well.
DRIZZLE over cake.
YIELD: 16 servings

PER slice:
CALORIES 258
(27% from fat)
FAT 7.7g
(saturated 2.2g,
    mono 1.8g, poly 2.7g)
CARBOHYDRATE 42.6g
FIBER 0.8g
CHOLESTEROL 28mg
SODIUM 164mg
FIBER 0.8g
IRON 1.6mg
CALCIUM 38mg

# Chocolate-Mint Pie

1   (4-serving) package Jello sugar-free
    instant vanilla pudding mix
2/3 cup Carnation nonfat dry milk powder
1 1/4 cups water
1/2 teaspoon mint extract
2 to 3 drops green food coloring
1   cup Cool Whip Lite
2   tablespoons (1/2 ounce) mini chocolate
    chips
1   (6-ounce) Keebler chocolate-flavored
    pie crust

IN a medium bowl, combine dry pudding mix, dry milk powder and water; mix well, using a wire whisk.
FOLD in mint extract, green food coloring and Cool Whip Lite.
STIR in chocolate chips.
POUR mixture into pie crust.
REFRIGERATE until ready to serve.

# Chocolate Nuggets

1 3/4 cups all-purpose flour
1/3 cup unsweetened cocoa
1/4 cup sugar
Dash of salt
1/2 cup reduced-calorie stick margarine
1/4 cup plus 2 tablespoons strongly-brewed coffee
Vegetable cooking spray
3 tablespoons skim milk
1 tablespoons reduced-calorie stick margarine
2 cups (12 ounces) reduced-fat semi-sweet
    chocolate baking chips, melted
1/4 cup sugar
1/2 cup egg substitute
1/4 cup finely-chopped pecans
1/2 cup reduced-calorie frozen whipped topping, thawed
2 teaspoons strongly-brewed coffee

PER 1 cookie:
CALORIES 73
(46% from fat)
FAT 3.7g
(1.9g saturated)
PROTEIN 1.0g
FIBER 0.2g
CHOLESTEROL 0mg
CARBOHYDRATE 10.7g
SODIUM 29mg

COMBINE first 4 ingredients; cut in 1/2 cup margarine with pastry blender until mixture is crumbly.
SPRINKLE 1/4 cup plus 2 tablespoons coffee, 1 tablespoon at a time, over flour mixture. Stir with a fork until dry ingredients are moistened.
TURN dough out, and knead 2 or 3 times; wrap in waxed paper and chill 2 hours.
SHAPE dough into 3/4-inch balls; press into miniature (1 3/4-inch) muffin pans coated with cooking spray, using a tart tamper or back of spoon.
COVER and chill slightly.
COMBINE milk and 1 tablespoon margarine in a small saucepan; cook over low heat until margarine melts, stirring often.
COMBINE margarine mixture, melted baking chips and 1/4 cup sugar in a medium mixing bowl.
BEAT at medium speed with an electric mixer until smooth; add egg substitute and pecans; beat well.
SPOON 1 rounded teaspoonful mixture into each shell.
BAKE at 350 degrees for 20 minutes; cool in pans on wire racks for 15 minutes.
REMOVE from pans and cool completely on wire racks.
COMBINE whipped topping and 2 teaspoons coffee; dollop onto each cookie just before serving.
YIELD: 4 dozen

# Chocolate Pound Cake

3/4 cup stick margarine, softened
1 1/2 cups sugar
2   large eggs
2   large egg whites
1 1/2 cups low-fat buttermilk
1   teaspoon baking soda
3 1/2 cups all-purpose flour
3/4 cups unsweetened cocoa
1   teaspoon baking powder
1/4 teaspoon salt
2   teaspoons vanilla extract
1   teaspoon powdered sugar

PREHEAT oven to 350 degrees.
PREPARE bundt pan with cooking spray, and dust with 1 teaspoon of flour (if available, you may use baking spray with flour).
BEAT margarine at medium speed of an electric mixer until creamy.
GRADUALLY add 1 1/2 cups sugar; beat well.
ADD eggs and egg whites, one at a time, beating well after each addition.
COMBINE buttermilk and baking soda; stir well.
COMBINE flour, cocoa, baking powder and salt; stir well.
ADD flour mixture to margarine mixture alternately with buttermilk mixture, beginning and ending with flour mixture; stir in vanilla.
POUR batter into the 12-cup Bundt pan that has been prepared.
BAKE at 350 degrees for 45 minutes, or until a wooden pick inserted in center of cake comes out clean.
LET cake cool completely on wire rack.
SIFT powdered sugar over top of cake.
YIELD: 18 servings

# Chocolate Pudding

2   egg whites
2/3 cup unsweetened cocoa powder
2   tablespoons cornstarch
2 1/4 cups skim milk, divided
1/2 cup granulated sugar
1/8 teaspoon salt
1   teaspoon vanilla extract
Fresh strawberries, mint leaves and
        unsweetened cocoa powder for garnish

PER serving:
CALORIES 210
(11% from fat)
FAT 3g
CARBOHYDRATE 43g
PROTEIN 9g
SODIUM 100mg
CHOLESTEROL 3mg

IN a small bowl, lightly beat egg whites and set aside.
IN a large bowl, combine 2/3 cup of cocoa and corn-
starch.
WHISK 3/4 cup of milk into cocoa mixture until
completely smooth.
IN a large heavy saucepan, combine remaining
milk, sugar and salt; mix well.
BRING to a boil over high heat, whisking constantly.
REMOVE pan from heat.
WHISK cocoa mixture into hot milk mixture.
BRING to a boil over medium-high heat; boil for 2
minutes, whisking constantly.
REMOVE pan from heat.
GRADUALLY whisk 1 cup of hot cocoa mixture into
the egg whites; pour mixture back into pan.
COOK over medium-low heat for 2 minutes, whisk-
ing constantly; Do Not Boil.
REMOVE pan from heat.
ADD vanilla; blend well.
POUR pudding into serving dishes. Cool to room
temperature; cover and chill for 1 hour.
GARNISH with berries, mint leaves and cocoa.
YIELD: 4 servings

HINTS: When making pudding, stir the mixture
constantly as it cooks. This helps release steam;
which, if it condenses, may result in watery pudding.
TO prevent "skin" from forming on the top of pudding, cover with waxed paper or plastic wrap
placed directly on pudding surface. Cool as directed.

# Chocolate Pudding

1 cup sugar
1/2 cup baking cocoa
1/4 cup all-purpose flour
2 cups water
3/4 cup evaporated skim milk
1 tablespoon vanilla extract

IN a saucepan, combine sugar, cocoa and flour.
ADD water and milk; stir until smooth.
COOK over medium heat, stirring constantly, until mixture comes to a boil.
COOK until thick, about 1 minute.
REMOVE from heat; stir in vanilla.
COOL to room temperature, stirring several times.
POUR into a serving bowl or individual dishes.
SERVE warm or chilled.
YIELD: 6 servings

PER serving:
CALORIES 194
(1% from fat)
FAT 1g
(1g saturated fat)
CHOLESTEROL 0
SODIUM 42mg
CARBOHYDRATE 45g
PROTEIN 4g

# Cream Cheese Bruleé Raspberries

1/3 cup firmly-packed light brown sugar
2  tablespoons cornstarch
3  egg whites, lightly beaten
1  egg, lightly beaten
1  (12-ounce) can evaporated skimmed milk
1  teaspoon vanilla
1  (8-ounce) container reduced-fat cream
    cheese
1 1/2 cups fresh raspberries
2  tablespoons plus 2 teaspoons light
    brown sugar

COMBINE first 5 ingredients in the top of a double boiler; stir well.

COOK over simmering water for 4 minutes, or until thickened, stirring constantly with a wire whisk.

REMOVE from heat; add vanilla and cream cheese, stirring until smooth.

GENTLY fold in raspberries.

SPOON 1/2 cup cheese mixture into each of 8 (6-ounce) custard cups.

COVER and chill at least 4 hours.

SPRINKLE each serving with 1 teaspoon brown sugar.

PLACE custard cups on a baking sheet; broil 1 minute, or until sugar melts.

SERVE immediately.

YIELD: 8 servings

PER serving:
CALORIES 177
(28% from fat)
FAT 5.6g
(saturated 3.1g,
    mono 2g, poly 0.3g)
PROTEIN 8.4g
CARBOHYDRATE 23.4g
FIBER 1.7g
CHOLESTEROL 46mg
IRON 0.6mg
SODIUM 242mg
CALCIUM 181mg

# Cocoa Berry Cake

Vegetable cooking spray
2/3 cup water
1   cup dried cranberries
1/3 cup orange juice
1   tablespoon orange juice
1   tablespoon margarine
1 1/2 cups sugar
1   cup unsweetened cocoa
1/2 cup all-purpose flour
1/4 cup boiling water
1   teaspoon vanilla
1   tablespoon Grand Mariner (orange-
      flavored liqueur)
5   ounces unsweetened chocolate, melted
2   large egg yolks
1   teaspoon cream of tartar
10  large egg whites
1/4 cup sugar
Chocolate Glaze

PREHEAT oven to 350 degrees.
COAT bottom of two (9-inch) round cake pans with
cooking spray; line bottoms with waxed paper.
COAT waxed paper with cooking spray, and set
pans aside.
COMBINE 2/3 cup water, cranberries, orange juice
and margarine in a small saucepan. BRING mixture to a boil; cook 5 minutes.
COMBINE 1 1/2 cups sugar, cocoa and flour in a large
bowl. Add cranberry mixture and boiling water;
stir until well-blended. ADD Grand Marnier, vanilla, chocolate and egg yolks to cranberry mixture; stir until well-blended. Set batter aside.
BEAT cream of tartar and egg whites at high speed
of an electric mixer until foamy.
GRADUALLY add 1/4 cup sugar, 1 tablespoon at a
time, beating until stiff peaks form.

Continued on following page.

Continued from preceding page.

GENTLY stir 1/4 of egg white mixture into batter; gently fold in remaining egg white mixture.

POUR batter into prepared pans.

BAKE at 350 degrees for 35 minutes or until cake springs back when touched lightly in center.

LET cool in pans 10 minutes on a wire rack; remove from pans. Peel off waxed paper; let cool completely.

PLACE 1 cake layer on a plate; spread with half of Chocolate Glaze, and top with other cake layer.

SPREAD remaining glaze over top of cake.

YIELD: 16 servings (serving size: 1 slice)

CHOCOLATE GLAZE:

1/3 cup sugar
1/3 cup unsweetened cocoa
3 tablespoons hot water
1 teaspoon instant espresso or 2 teaspoons instant coffee granules

YIELD: 1/2 cup

PER 1 slice:
CALORIES 249
(27% from fat)
FAT 7.1g
(saturated 3.7g,
mono 2.1g, poly 0.5g)
PROTEIN 6.3g
CARBOHYDRATE 43.6g
FIBER 0.8g
CHOLESTEROL 28mg
IRON 2.4mg
SODIUM 47mg
CALCIUM 29mg

excluding Chocolate Glaze

# Coconut-Lemon Cake

Vegetable cooking spray
3/4 cup skim milk
1/2 cup vegetable oil
1   teaspoon vanilla extract
2 2/3 cups sifted flour
1 1/2 cups fine sugar
1   tablespoon baking powder
1/8 teaspoon salt
8   egg whites
1/2 teaspoon cream of tartar
Lemon Filling
Fluffy White Frosting
1/2 cup flaked coconut

COAT three 9-inch round cake pans with cooking spray; line with waxed paper. Spray waxed paper and set aside.
COMBINE milk, oil and vanilla in a large mixing bowl, stirring well.
COMBINE flour, sugar, baking powder and salt.
GRADUALLY add flour mixture to milk mixture, beating at medium speed with an electric mixer just until blended.
BEAT egg whites and cream of tartar at high speed with an electric mixer until stiff peaks form.
FOLD about one-third of beaten egg white into batter; fold in remaining egg white.
POUR batter into prepared pans.
BAKE at 350 degrees for 15 minutes.
COOL in pans on wire racks 10 minutes; remove from pans; cool completely on racks.
SPREAD Lemon Filling between layers. Immediately spread Fluffy White Frosting on top and sides of cake.
SPRINKLE top of cake with coconut.
YIELD: 12 servings

Continued on following page.

Continued from preceding page.

LEMON FILLING:
1/2 cup sugar
2 1/2 tablespoons cornstarch
1   cup boiling water
2   tablespoons egg substitute
1/3 cup fresh lemon juice
1   tablespoon reduced-calorie margarine

COMBINE sugar and cornstarch in a medium sauce-pan; stir in water. Cook over medium heat, stirring constantly, until mixture boils. Boil 1 minute.
GRADUALLY stir about 1/4 of hot mixture into egg substitute; add to remaining hot mixture, stirring constantly with a wire whisk. ADD lemon juice and margarine, stirring until margarine melts.
REMOVE from heat. Let cool.
YIELD: 1 1/2 cups

FLUFFY WHITE FROSTING
1 1/2 cups water
1   cup sugar
2   tablespoons light corn syrup
4   egg whites
1/4 teaspoon cream of tartar
1   teaspoon coconut extract

COMBINE first 3 ingredients in a small heavy sauce-pan; cook over medium heat, stirring constantly, until clear.
COOK, without stirring, until mixture reaches soft ball stage or candy thermometer registers 240 degrees (15 to 20 minutes).
BEAT egg whites and cream of tartar at high speed of an electric mixer until soft peaks form; slowly add syrup mixture, stirring constantly.
ADD coconut extract; continue beating just until stiff peaks form and frost is desired consistency.
YIELD: 7 1/2 cups

PER slice:
CALORIES 421
(24% from fat)
FAT 11.4g
(3.0 saturated)
PROTEIN 6.1g
FIBER 0.2g
CHOLESTEROL 0mg
CARBOHYDRATE 74.6g
SODIUM 115mg

Desserts    347

# Coffee Napoleons

2   teaspoons instant coffee granules
1   tablespoon hot water
1   (8-ounce) package Neufchatel cheese, softened
1 1/4 cups skim milk
1   (3.8-ounce) package fat-free chocolate-
      flavored instant pudding mix
1   cup frozen reduced-calorie whipped topping,
      thawed
36 wonton wrappers
Butter-flavored vegetable cooking spray
1/2 cup sugar
1 1/2 tablespoons skim milk
1   teaspoon instant coffee granules
1/2 cup (3 ounces) reduced-fat semi-sweet
      chocolate baking chips
1   tablespoon powdered sugar

DISSOLVE 2 teaspoons coffee granules in 1 tablespoon hot water.
BEAT Neufchatel cheese at medium speed with an
electric mixer until creamy; add coffee mixture, 1 1/
4 cups skim milk, and pudding mix.
BEAT at low speed until thickened; fold in whipped
topping; cover and chill.
COAT both sides of each wonton wrapper with
cooking spray; dredge in 1/2 cup sugar.
PLACE on two 15x10x1-inch jellyroll pans lined with
parchment paper.
BAKE at 375 degrees for 3 1/2 minutes; turn wrappers, and bake an additional 1 1/2 minutes, or until
edges are golden.
TRANSFER to wire racks to cool.
COMBINE 1 1/2 tablespoons skim milk, 1 teaspoon
coffee granules and baking chips in a heavy saucepan; cook over low heat, stirring constantly, until
chips melt.
COOL slightly, and spoon into a small zip-lock plas-

Continued on following page.

Continued from preceding page.

tic bag; seal bag.

SNIP a tiny hole in one corner of bag, using scissors.

DRIZZLE mixture evenly over 12 wonton wrappers; set aside.

PIPE or spoon half of filling evenly on 12 plain wonton wrappers; top each with a plain wonton wrapper.

SPOON remaining half of filling on top of plain wrappers; top with drizzled wrappers.

SPRINKLE evenly with powdered sugar, and serve immediately.

YIELD: 12 servings

PER serving:
CALORIES 217
(26% from fat)
FAT 6.3g
 (3.1g saturated)
PROTEIN 5.4g
FIBER 0.0g
CARBOHYDRATE 34.7g
CHOLESTEROL 17mg
SODIUM 348mg

# Key Lime Pie

1   teaspoon unflavored gelatin
2   tablespoons cold water
1/2 cup fresh lime juice, may use bottled
2   egg yolks
1   (14-ounce) can fat-free sweetened
        condensed milk
3   egg whites
1/4 teaspoon cream of tartar
1/8 teaspoon salt
1/3 cup sugar
Lime slices (optional)
Graham Cracker Crust (see below)

PREHEAT oven to 325 degrees.
SPRINKLE gelatin over cold water in a small bowl;
set aside.
COMBINE lime juice and egg yolks in a small heavy
saucepan; cook over medium-low heat 10 minutes,
or until slightly thick and very hot (180 degrees),
stirring constantly (do not boil). Be sure to use
nonaluminum saucepan.
ADD softened gelatin to lime juice mixture; cook 1
minute, stirring until gelatin dissolves.
PLACE in a large ice-filled bowl; stir gelatin mixture
3 minutes, or until mixture reaches room temperature (do not allow gelatin mixture to set).
STRAIN gelatin mixture into a medium bowl; discard any solids.
GRADUALLY add milk; stirring with a whisk until
blended (mixture will be very thick); spoon mixture into Graham Cracker Crust and spread evenly.
BEAT egg whites, cream of tartar and salt at high
speed of an electric mixer until foamy.
GRADUALLY add sugar, 1 tablespoon at a time, beating until stiff peaks form.
SPREAD evenly over filling, sealing to edge of crust.

Continued on following page.

Continued from preceding page.

BAKE at 325 degrees for 25 minutes; let cool 1 hour
on a wire rack.
CHILL 3 hours, or until set.
CUT with a sharp knife dipped in hot water.
GARNISH with lime slices, if desired.
YIELD: 8 servings (serving size: 1 wedge)

GRAHAM CRACKER CRUST:
2   tablespoons sugar
1   tablespoon chilled stick margarine,
        softened
1   egg white
1 1/4 cups graham cracker crumbs
1   teaspoon ground cinnamon
Vegetable cooking spray

PREHEAT oven to 325 degrees.
COMBINE first 3 ingredients in a bowl; beat at me-
dium speed of an electric mixer until blended.
ADD crumbs and cinnamon; toss with a fork until
moistened.
PRESS crumb mixture into a 9-inch pie plate coated
with cooking spray.
BAKE at 325 degrees for 20 minutes, or until lightly
browned. Let cool on a wire rack.
YIELD: 1 (9-inch) crust

PER 1 wedge:
CALORIES 290
(14% from fat)
FAT 4.4g
(saturated 1.1g,
    mono 1.7g, poly 1.1g)
PROTEIN 7.5g
CARBOHYDRATE 65.1g
FIBER 0.1g
CHOLESTEROL 61mg
IRON 0.9mg
SODIUM 230mg
CALCIUM 118mg

# Lemon Cookies

PER 1 cookie:
CALORIES 44
(29% from fat)
FAT 1.4g
(saturated 0.3g,
    mono 0.6g, poly 0.4g)
PROTEIN 0.6g
CARBOHYDRATE 7.4g
FIBER 0.1g
CHOLESTEROL 4mg
IRON 0.2mg
SODIUM 21mg
CALCIUM 11mg

2   cups all-purpose flour
2   teaspoons baking powder
1/4 teaspoon baking soda
1   cup sugar
1   tablespoon grated lemon rind, divided
1/2 teaspoon ground ginger
1/4 cup plus 2 1/2 tablespoons stick margarine,
        softened
2   teaspoons light-colored corn syrup
2   teaspoons vanilla extract
1   egg
3   tablespoons sugar
Vegetable cooking spray

COMBINE first 3 ingredients in a bowl; stir well and set aside.

PLACE 1 cup sugar, 2 teaspoons lemon rind and ginger in a food processor; process 1 minute, or until the sugar mixture is lemon-colored, scraping the sides of the processor bowl once.

SPOON sugar mixture into a large bowl; add margarine to the sugar mixture and beat at medium speed of an electric mixer until light and fluffy.

ADD corn syrup, vanilla extract and egg; beat well. Stir in flour mixture (dough will be stiff).

COMBINE remaining 1 teaspoon lemon rind and 3 tablespoons sugar in a small bowl; stir well. Set lemon-sugar aside.

PREHEAT oven to 375 degrees. Coat hands lightly with cooking spray, and shape dough into 60 (1-inch) balls.

ROLL balls in lemon-sugar, and place 2 inches apart on baking sheets coated with cooking spray; flatten balls with the bottom of a glass.

BAKE at 375 degrees for 7 minutes, and let cool 5 minutes.

REMOVE cookies from baking sheets, and let cool on wire racks.

YIELD: 5 dozen

# Light Chocolate Cake

2   cups sugar
1 3/4 cups all-purpose flour
3/4 cup baking cocoa
1 1/2 teaspoons baking soda
1 1/2 teaspoons baking powder
1   teaspoon salt
1   cup skim milk
Egg substitute equivalent to 2 eggs
1/2 cup unsweetened applesauce
2   teaspoons vanilla extract
1   cup boiling water

PER 1 slice:
CALORIES 139
(4% from fat)
TOTAL FAT 1g
(saturated trace)
CHOLESTEROL trace
SODIUM 256mg
CARBOHYDRATE 32g
PROTEIN 3g

IN a large mixing bowl, combine dry ingredients.
BEAT in milk, egg substitute, applesauce and vanilla.
ADD water; beat on medium speed for 2 minutes (batter will be very thin).
POUR into a 13x9x2-inch baking pan coated with nonstick cooking spray.
BAKE at 350 degrees for 30 minutes, or until a toothpick inserted near center comes out clean; cool.
YIELD: 20 servings

# Mandarin Orange Rice Pudding

PER serving:
CALORIES 142
FAT ‹1g
PROTEIN 4g
SODIUM 266mg

1   (4-serving) package Jello sugar-
      free banana instant pudding mix
2/3 cup Carnation nonfat dry milk powder
1 1/2 cups water
1   teaspoon vanilla extract
1   teaspoon cinnamon
1/4 cup Cool Whip Lite
1 1/2 cups cooked rice
1/2 cup raisins
1   cup (11-ounce can) canned mandarin
      oranges, rinsed and drained

IN a large bowl, combine dry pudding mix, dry milk powder and water; mix well, using a wire whisk.
BLEND in vanilla extract, cinnamon and Cool Whip Lite.
ADD rice, raisins and mandarin oranges; mix gently to combine.
SPOON mixture evenly into 6 dessert dishes.
REFRIGERATE for at least 30 minutes.
YIELD: 6 servings

*1 cup uncooked rice makes 1 1/2 cups cooked rice. To plump up raisins, place in glass measuring cup and microwave on HIGH for 30 seconds.

# Maple-Pecan Cheesecake

This cheesecake is very easy to make, mix the crust in a springform pan, then press to form crust. It can be made in advance, frozen, then thawed before serving.

2/3 cup graham cracker crumbs, about 8 cookie squares
2    tablespoons sugar
1    tablespoon margarine, melted
1/2 teaspoon ground cinnamon
Vegetable cooking spray
2    (8-ounce) blocks Neufchatel cheese, softened
2    (8-ounce) blocks fat-free cream cheese, softened
2    tablespoons cornstarch
1/4 teaspoon salt
1 1/4 cups maple syrup
3    large egg whites
1/4 cup chopped pecans, toasted
1    pecan half (optional)

PREHEAT oven to 400 degrees.
COMBINE first 4 ingredients in an 8-inch springform pan coated with cooking spray; toss with a fork until blended.
PRESS crumb mixture into bottom of pan.
BAKE at 400 degrees for 8 minutes; let cool on wire rack.
INCREASE oven temperature to 525 degrees.
COMBINE cheeses, cornstarch and salt in a large bowl; beat at high speed of an electric mixer until smooth. Gradually add maple syrup; beat well. Add egg whites, and beat just until combined.
POUR half of cheese mixture into prepared pan, and sprinkle with chopped pecans.
TOP with remaining cheese mixture.
BAKE at 525 degrees for 7 minutes.
REDUCE oven temperature to 200 degrees and bake 45 minutes, or until almost set.
REMOVE from oven, and let cool to room temperature.
COVER and chill at least 8 hours.
GARNISH with pecan half, if desired.
YIELD: 12 servings (serving size: 1 wedge)

PER 1 wedge:
CALORIES 282
(39% from fat)
FAT 12.2g
(saturated 5.9g,
    mono 4g, poly 1g)
PROTEIN 10.5g
CARBOHYDRATE 32.6g
FIBER 0.2g
CHOLESTEROL 35mg
IRON 0.8mg
SODIUM 489mg
CALCIUM 162mg

# Marble Pound Cake

Vegetable cooking spray
2   teaspoons all-purpose flour
3   cups sifted cake flour
1 1/2 cups sugar
1   tablespoon baking powder
1   teaspoon salt
3/4 cup vegetable oil
3/4 cup skim milk
2   teaspoons vanilla extract
2   eggs
4   egg whites
1/2 cup reduced-calorie chocolate syrup

COAT a 12-cup Bundt or 10-inch tube pan with cooking spray; dust pan with 2 teaspoons flour and set aside.

COMBINE cake flour and next 7 ingredients in a large mixing bowl; beat at low speed with an electric mixer until blended.

BEAT egg whites at high speed with an electric mixer until stiff peaks form; gently fold into batter.

COMBINE 1 cup batter and chocolate syrup; set aside.

DIVIDE remaining batter in half; pour 1 portion into prepared pan.

SPOON half of reserved chocolate batter on top; repeat layers. Gently swirl batter with a knife to create a marbled effect.

BAKE at 350 degrees for 50 minutes. Cover loosely with aluminum foil after 40 minutes to prevent excessive browning.

COOL in pan on wire rack 10 to 15 minutes, remove from pan; cool completely on wire rack.

YIELD: 16 servings

# Marinated Strawberries in Orange Liqueur

3   cups quartered strawberries
1   tablespoon sugar
2   tablespoons Grand Mariner or other
      orange-flavored liqueur, divided
1   teaspoon lemon juice
3/4 cup vanilla low-fat frozen yogurt, softened
1   cup frozen reduced-calorie whipped
      topping, thawed

COMBINE strawberries, sugar and 1 tablespoon liqueur in a bowl; toss gently.
COVER and chill.
PLACE frozen yogurt in a bowl and stir until smooth; fold in whipped topping.
ADD remaining liqueur and lemon juice; stir well.
SPOON 1/2 cup strawberry mixture into each of 6 dessert dishes; top with 1/4 cup yogurt mixture.
YIELD: 6 servings

PER serving:
CALORIES 93
(21% from fat)
FAT 2.2g
(saturated 1.3g,
  mono 0g, poly 0.7g)
PROTEIN 1.5g
CARBOHYDRATE 15.4g
FIBER 1.9g
CHOLESTEROL 2mg
IRON 0.3mg
SODIUM 16mg
CALCIUM 41mg

# Minty Peach Sorbet

4   cups peeled, chopped peaches (about 2
      pounds), or 4 cups frozen sliced peaches
1   cup water
1/2 cup sugar
2   tablespoons fresh lime juice
2   (4-inch) mint sprigs, crushed

COMBINE all ingredients in a large saucepan; bring
to a boil.
REDUCE heat and simmer 7 minutes; discard mint.
PLACE mixture in a blender or food processor; cover
and process until smooth.
POUR into a bowl; cover and chill.
POUR chilled mixture into the freezer can of an ice
cream freezer; freeze according to manufacturer's
instructions.
YIELD: 8 servings (serving size: 1/2 cup)

# Molasses Cookies

2 2/3 cups all-purpose flour
1 1/4 teaspoons baking powder
1   teaspoon ginger
1/4 teaspoon baking soda
2 1/4 teaspoons ground cinnamon
3/4 teaspoon ground cloves
1/8 teaspoon salt
1/2 cup dark molasses
1/4 cup plus 3 tablespoons dark corn syrup
1/4 teaspoon grated orange rind
1 1/3 cups sifted powdered sugar, divided
1   egg
Vegetable cooking spray

COMBINE first 7 ingredients in bowl; stir well and set aside.

COMBINE molasses and next 3 ingredients in a large bowl; beat at medium speed of an electric mixer until blended.

ADD 1 cup powdered sugar and egg; beat until well blended.

STIR in flour mixture; cover and freeze 1 hour.

PREHEAT oven to 375 degrees. Coat hands with cooking spray, and shape dough into 48 (1-inch) balls.

ROLL balls in remaining powdered sugar, and place 2 inches apart on baking sheets coated with cooking spray.

BAKE at 375 degrees for 8 minutes; let cool 2 minutes or until firm.

REMOVE cookies from baking sheets, and let cool on wire racks.

YIELD: 4 dozen

PER 1 cookie:
CALORIES 69
(29% from fat)
FAT 2.2g
(saturated 0.4g,
    mono 0.6g, poly 1g)
PROTEIN 0.9g
CARBOHYDRATE 11.7g
FIBER 0.2g
CHOLESTEROL 5mg
IRON 1mg
SODIUM 17mg
CALCIUM 40mg

# Oatmeal-Coconut Cookie

1   cup regular oats
1   cup all-purpose flour
1   cup firmly-packed brown sugar
1/2 cup shredded sweetened coconut
1/2 teaspoon baking soda
1/4 cup stick margarine, melted
3   tablespoons water
2   tablespoons golden cane sugar or light-
        colored corn syrup
Vegetable cooking spray

PREHEAT oven to 325 degrees.
COMBINE first 5 ingredients in a bowl; stir well.
ADD margarine, water and syrup; stir well.
DROP by level tablespoons, 2 inches apart, onto
baking sheets coated with cooking spray.
BAKE at 325 degrees for 12 minutes, or until almost
set; remove from oven and let stand 2 to 3 minutes,
or until firm.
REMOVE cookies from baking sheets; place on wire
racks, and let cool completely.
YIELD: 2 dozen

# Oatmeal-Raisin Cookies

1 1/2 cups all-purpose flour
3/4 teaspoon baking powder
3/4 teaspoon baking soda
1/2 teaspoon ground cinnamon
1/4 teaspoon salt
1/8 teaspoon ground nutmeg
1 1/4 cups firmly-packed brown sugar
1/4 cup plus 2 tablespoons stick margarine,
    melted
2   tablespoons light-colored corn syrup
1   tablespoon vanilla extract
1   tablespoon water
3   egg whites
1 2/3 cups regular oats
1/2 cup raisins
1 2/3 cups chopped pecans, toasted
Vegetable cooking spray

PREHEAT oven to 350 degrees.
COMBINE first 6 ingredients in a large bowl; stir
well and set aside.
COMBINE brown sugar and next 5 ingredients in a
large bowl; beat at medium speed of an electric
mixer until well-blended; stir in oats, raisins and
pecans. Let stand for 5 minutes and stir in flour
mixture.
DROP dough by level tablespoons, 2 inches apart,
onto baking sheets coated with cooking spray.
BAKE at 350°for 12 minutes, or until almost set.
LET cool 2 minutes, or until firm.
REMOVE cookies from baking sheets; let cool on
wire racks.
YIELD: 3 1/2 dozen

PER 1 cookie:
CALORIES 97
(24% from fat)
FAT 2.6g
(saturated 0.4g,
    mono 1.2g, poly 0.8g)
PROTEIN 1.5g
CARBOHYDRATE 17.5g
FIBER 0.8g
CHOLESTEROL 0mg
IRON 0.6mg
SODIUM 64mg
CALCIUM 17mg

# Orange Eclair Miniatures

PER serving:
CALORIES 53
(15% from fat)
FAT 0.9g
(0.5g saturated)
PROTEIN 1.0g
FIBER 0.3g
CARBOHYDRATE 9.4g
CHOLESTEROL 13mg
SODIUM 72mg

1 1/4 cups reduced-calorie whipped topping, thawed
2   drops yellow liquid food coloring
2   drops red liquid food coloring
24 ladyfingers
1/4 cup Grand Marnier or other orange-flavored liqueur
1/2 cup fat-free chocolate fudge sauce

Garnishes: orange rind strips (optional), fresh mint sprigs (optional)

COMBINE first 3 ingredients with a wire whisk; set aside.
SEPARATE ladyfinger halves. Brush inside of ladyfingers with Grand Marnier.
SPREAD whipped topping mixture evenly over bottom halves. Cover with top halves of ladyfingers.
SPOON fudge sauce into a small ziplock plastic bag. Snip a tiny hole in one corner of bag, using scissors.
PIPE about 2 teaspoons fudge sauce on top of each eclair.
GARNISH, if desired.
YIELD: 2 dozen

# Orange Soufflé

Vegetable cooking spray
1   tablespoon sugar
3   tablespoons all-purpose flour
3/4 cup 2% low-fat milk
1/4 cup sugar
1   teaspoon grated orange rind
1/4 cup fresh orange juice
5   large egg whites
1/4 teaspoon cream of tartar
Dash of salt
2   tablespoons sugar
1   teaspoon powdered sugar

PREHEAT oven to 375 degrees.
COAT a 1 1/2-quart soufflé dish with cooking spray;
sprinkle with 1 tablespoon sugar. Set aside.
PLACE flour in a small saucepan. Gradually add
milk, stirring with a whisk until blended.
ADD 1/4 cup sugar and rind; stir well. Bring to a boil
over medium heat; cook 1 minute, or until thick-
ened, stirring constantly.
STIR in juice; set aside.
BEAT egg whites, cream of tartar and salt at high
speed of an electric mixer until soft peaks form.
Gradually add 2 tablespoons sugar, 1 tablespoon at
a time, beating until stiff peaks form.
GENTLY fold one-fourth egg white mixture into
orange mixture; gently fold in remaining egg white
mixture.
SPOON mixture into prepared soufflé dish.
BAKE soufflé at 375 degrees for 30 minutes, or until
puffy and set.
SPRINKLE with powdered sugar.
SERVE immediately.
YIELD: 4 servings

PER serving:
CALORIES 160
(6% from fat)
FAT 1.1g
(saturated 0.6g,
    mono, 0.3g poly 0.1g)
PROTEIN 6.4g
CARBOHYDRATE 31.5g
FIBER 0.2g
CHOLESTEROL 4mg
SODIUM 96mg
CALCIUM 62mg

# Peach-Apple Crisp

2 1/3 cups peeled, sliced, fresh or thawed
    frozen peaches
1 3/4 cups peeled, sliced Granny Smith
    apple
1/4 cup honey
1   tablespoon peach brandy
1/2 teaspoon vanilla extract
1/4 teaspoon ground cinnamon
Vegetable cooking spray
1/2 cup all-purpose flour
1/4 cup firmly-packed brown sugar
1/8 teaspoon salt
3   tablespoons chilled reduced-calorie
    margarine, cut into small pieces
2   tablespoons chopped nut of choice

PREHEAT oven to 375 degrees.
COMBINE first 6 ingredients in a 2-quart casserole
coated with cooking spray; toss well.
COMBINE flour, sugar and salt in a bowl; cut in
margarine with a pastry blender until the mixture
resembles coarse meal.
STIR in nuts.
SPRINKLE flour mixture over peach mixture.
BAKE at 375 degrees for 30 minutes, or until lightly
browned and bubbly.
YIELD: 6 servings (serving size: 1/2 cup)

# Peanut Butter Cake

Vegetable cooking spray
1   tablespoon all-purpose flour
1/2 cup reduced-calorie stick margarine,
        softened
1 1/4 cups firmly-packed brown sugar
1   teaspoon vanilla extract
3   large egg whites
1   large egg
1 1/2 cups all-purpose flour
1/2 teaspoon baking powder
1/4 cup unsweetened cocoa
1/4 cup reduced-fat creamy peanut butter

PREHEAT oven to 350 degrees.
COAT a 9-inch square baking pan with cooking spray; dust with 1 tablespoon flour; set aside.
BEAT margarine at medium speed of an electric mixer until creamy.
GRADUALLY add sugar; beat until well-blended.
ADD vanilla, egg whites and egg; mix until blended.
COMBINE 1 1/2 cups flour and baking powder; with mixer at low speed, add flour mixture to creamed mixture. Reserve 1 1/2 cups batter; pour remaining batter into a bowl.
STIR cocoa into reserved batter; stir peanut butter into remaining batter.
SPOON cocoa batter alternately with peanut butter batter into prepared pan.
SWIRL together, using the tip of a knife.
BAKE at 350 degrees for 30 minutes, or until a wooden pick inserted in center comes out clean.
YIELD: 16 servings

PER serving:
CALORIES 156
(33% from fat)
FAT 5.8g
(saturated 1.2g,
    mono 2.5g, poly 1.7g)
PROTEIN 3.7g
CARBOHYDRATE 23.1
FIBER 0.3g
CHOLESTEROL 14mg
IRON 1.1mg
SODIUM 93mg
CALCIUM 24mg

# Peanut Butter Cookies

PER 1 cookie:
CALORIES 59
(31% from fat)
FAT 2g
(saturated 0.4g,
mono 0.7g, poly 0.8g)
PROTEIN 1g
CARBOHYDRATE 9.5g
FIBER 0.2g
CHOLESTEROL 5mg
IRON 0.3mg
SODIUM 23mg
CALCIUM 14mg

1 1/2 cups all-purpose flour
1 1/2 tablespoons cornstarch
1 3/4 teaspoons baking powder
1/2 teaspoon baking soda
3/4 cup firmly-packed brown sugar
1/4 cup vegetable oil
1/4 cup sugar
1/4 cup creamy peanut butter
1 1/2 tablespoons light-colored corn syrup
2 1/2 teaspoons vanilla extract
1    egg
Vegetable cooking spray
3    tablespoons granulated sugar

COMBINE first 4 ingredients in a bowl; stir well and set aside.
COMBINE brown sugar and next 3 ingredients in a large bowl; beat at medium speed of an electric mixer until well-blended.
ADD corn syrup, vanilla and egg; beat well. Stir in flour mixture.
PREHEAT oven to 375 degrees.
COAT hands lightly with cooking spray and shape dough into 48 (1-inch) balls; roll balls in 3 tablespoons granulated sugar, and place 2 inches apart on baking sheets coated with cooking spray.
FLATTEN balls with the bottom of a glass.
BAKE at 375 degrees for 7 minutes, or until lightly browned.
REMOVE cookies from baking sheets, and let cool on wire racks.
YIELD: 4 dozen

# Pear Cake with Blue Cheese

2/3 cup sugar
1   cup crumbled blue cheese, divided
2   tablespoons stick margarine, softened
1/3 cup skim milk
2   egg whites
1   teaspoon vanilla extract
1 1/3 cups all-purpose flour
2   teaspoons baking powder
Vegetable cooking spray
2   cups peeled, thinly-sliced pear,
      about 3 medium
1/4 cup all-purpose flour
3   tablespoons sugar

PREHEAT oven to 350 degrees.

COMBINE 2/3 cup sugar, 1/2 cup blue cheese and margarine in a bowl; beat at high speed of an electric mixer until smooth.

ADD milk, egg whites and vanilla; beat well.

COMBINE 1 1/3 cups flour and baking powder; add to cheese mixture, stirring just until moistened.

SPREAD batter into a 9-inch square baking pan coated with cooking spray.

ARRANGE pear slices in a single layer in 3 rows on top of batter, pressing pear slices gently into batter.

COMBINE 1/4 cup flour and 3 tablespoons sugar in a bowl; cut in remaining cheese with a pastry blender or 2 knives until mixture resembles coarse meal; sprinkle over pears.

BAKE at 350 degrees for 45 minutes, or until browned. Serve warm.

YIELD: 9 servings

PER 1 slice:
CALORIES 252
(24% from fat)
FAT 6.6g
(saturated 2.9g,
   mono 2.2g, poly 1g)
PROTEIN 6.2g
CARBOHYDRATE 42.6g
FIBER 1.5g
CHOLESTEROL 10mg
IRON 1.3mg
SODIUM 222mg
CALCIUM 147mg

# Pineapple Upside-Down Cake with Cheese

1   (20-ounce) can unsweetened pineapple
        slices, undrained
1/2 cup firmly-packed brown sugar
2   tablespoons margarine
Vegetable cooking spray
3/4 cup sugar
1/4 cup reduced-fat cream cheese, softened
2   tablespoons stick margarine, softened
2   egg whites
1   egg
3/4 cup all-purpose flour
1   teaspoon baking powder
1/4 teaspoon salt
3/4 cup (3 ounces) finely-shredded sharp
        Cheddar cheese
1/2 teaspoon vanilla extract

PREHEAT oven to 350 degrees.
DRAIN pineapple, reserving 1/4 cup juice. Place reserved juice and 3 pineapple slices in a blender;
cover and process until smooth, and set aside.
COMBINE brown sugar and 2 tablespoons margarine
in a saucepan; cook over medium-low heat until melted.
REMOVE from heat; add 1/4 cup puréed pineapple,
stirring until blended.
POUR brown sugar mixture into a 9-inch round
cake pan coated with cooking spray.
CUT remaining pineapple slices in half crosswise,
and arrange in a single layer over brown sugar
mixture; set aside.
COMBINE 3/4 cup sugar, cream cheese and 2 tablespoons margarine in a large bowl; beat at medium
speed of an electric mixer until blended.

Continued on following page.

Continued from preceding page.

ADD 2 egg whites and egg, one at a time, beating after each addition.
COMBINE flour, baking powder and salt; add to cream cheese mixture, beating until blended.
STIR in remaining puréed pineapple, Cheddar cheese and vanilla.
POUR batter evenly over pineapple slices.
BAKE at 350 degrees for 45 minutes, or until a wooden pick inserted in center comes out clean.
LET cool in pan 10 minutes; invert cake onto a serving plate.
SERVE warm.
YIELD: 12 servings

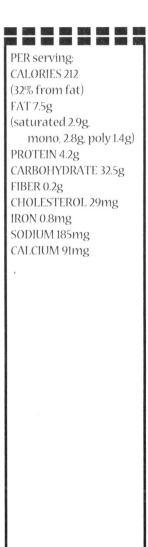

PER serving:
CALORIES 212
(32% from fat)
FAT 7.5g
(saturated 2.9g,
     mono, 2.8g, poly 1.4g)
PROTEIN 4.2g
CARBOHYDRATE 32.5g
FIBER 0.2g
CHOLESTEROL 29mg
IRON 0.8mg
SODIUM 185mg
CALCIUM 91mg

# Pumpkin Chiffon Pie

PER 1 slice:
CALORIES 206
FAT 8g
PROTEIN 4g
CALCIUM 30g
SODIUM 350mg

2   cups (one 16-ounce can) canned pumpkin
1   (4-serving) package Jello sugar-free
        instant vanilla pudding mix
2/3 cup nonfat dry milk powder
1   teaspoon pumpkin pie spice
3/4 cup water
1   cup Cool Whip Lite
1   (6-ounce) graham cracker pie crust
2   tablespoons pecans, chopped

IN a medium bowl, combine canned pumpkin, dry
pudding mix, dry milk powder, pumpkin pie spice
and water.
MIX well, using a wire whisk.
BLEND in 1/4 cup Cool Whip Lite.
POUR mixture into pie crust.
REFRIGERATE for about 15 minutes.
SPREAD remaining 3/4 cup Cool Whip Lite over top
of set filling.
SPRINKLE pecans evenly on top.
REFRIGERATE until ready to serve.

# Raspberry Angel Torte

2  cups raspberries
2  tablespoons sugar
2  tablespoons seedless red raspberry jam,
    melted
1  (10 1/2-ounce) loaf angel food cake
1/4 cup plus 2 tablespoons Amaretto, divided
3/4 cup vanilla low-fat yogurt
1/2 cup blueberries
2  tablespoons plus 2 teaspoons sliced
    almonds, toasted

PLACE first 3 ingredients in a food processor, and
pulse 3 times, or until coarsely chopped; set aside.
LINE an 8-inch loaf pan with plastic wrap, allowing
plastic wrap to extend over edge of loaf pan.
CUT cake horizontally into 6 slices (slices will be
very thin).
PLACE 1 cake slice in bottom of loaf pan; brush cake
with 1 tablespoon Amaretto.
SPREAD 3 tablespoons raspberry mixture over cake
slice, and top with another cake slice; repeat layers, ending with cake slice (do not put Amaretto or
raspberry mixture on top of cake layer).
COVER and chill 2 hours. Place a serving plate up-
side-down on top of pan; invert cake onto plate
and remove plastic wrap.
COMBINE yogurt and remaining 1 tablespoon
Amaretto in a small bowl; stir well.
CUT torte crosswise into 8 slices; dollop 1 1/2 tablespoons yogurt mixture onto each slice and sprinkle
with 1 tablespoon blueberries and 1 tablespoon
almonds.
YIELD: 8 servings

PER serving:
CALORIES 207
(7% from fat)
FAT 1.7g
(saturated 0.3g,
    mono 0.8g, poly 0.4g)
PROTEIN 4.1g
CARBOHYDRATE 39.7g
FIBER 2.9g
CHOLESTEROL 1mg
IRON 0.4mg
SODIUM 206mg
CALCIUM 81mg

# Raspberry Cream Cheese Pie

RASPBERRY TOPPING:
6   cups fresh raspberries
1   cup sugar
3   tablespoons cornstarch
1/2 cup water

CREAM FILLING:
1   cup light whipped topping
1   (8-ounce) package fat-free cream
       cheese, softened
1   cup confectioners' sugar
1   (8-inch) reduced-fat graham cracker crust
Fresh mint (optional)

MASH about 2 cups raspberries to measure 1 cup; place in a saucepan, and add sugar, cornstarch and water.
BRING to a boil, stirring constantly; cook and stir 2 minutes longer. (You may strain to remove seeds if you desire.)
COOL to room temperature, about 20 minutes.
MEANWHILE, for filling, beat whipped topping, cream cheese and confectioner's sugar in a mixing bowl; spread into crust.
TOP with remaining raspberries; pour cooled raspberry sauce over top.
REFRIGERATE until set, about 3 hours; store in refrigerator.
GARNISH with mint, if desired.
YIELD: 8 servings

# Strawberry Delight Dessert

1   envelope unflavored gelatin
3/4 cup cold water
1/2 cup sugar
1   (10-ounce) package frozen sliced
       strawberries, thawed
1   (8-ounce) carton frozen light whipped
       topping, thawed
5   cups angel food cake cubes
Fresh strawberries and mint (optional)

IN a saucepan, combine gelatin and cold water; let stand 5 minutes to soften.
STIR over low heat just until gelatin dissolves.
REMOVE from heat; add sugar and stir until dissolved.
STIR in undrained strawberries; chill until partially thickened, and fold in whipped topping.
PLACE cake cubes in a mixing bowl; pour strawberry mixture over cake and mix gently.
POUR into an ungreased 8-inch square baking dish; chill until firm.
GARNISH with strawberries and mint, if desired.
YIELD: 9 servings (serving size: 1/9 recipe)

PER serving:
CALORIES 210
(14% from fat)
FAT 3g
(3g saturated)
SODIUM 144mg
CHOLESTEROL 0
CARBOHYDRATE 42g
PROTEIN 3g

# Strawberry Shortcake

1 3/4 cup all-purpose flour
2   tablespoons granulated sugar
1   tablespoon baking powder
1/2 teaspoon grated orange peel
3   tablespoons unsalted butter or
        margarine, cut into pieces
3/4 cup skim milk

FILLING:
2   pints fresh strawberries, sliced
1   tablespoon orange juice
1   tablespoon granulated sugar
Vanilla nonfat yogurt and mint
        leaves for garnish

PREHEAT oven to 450 degrees.
SPRAY a baking sheet with vegetable cooking spray;
set aside.
IN a large bowl, sift together the flour, sugar and
baking powder. Stir in the orange peel.
USING a pastry blender or 2 knives, cut the butter
into the flour mixture until coarse crumbs form;
quickly stir in the milk until a soft dough forms.
ON a lightly-floured surface, roll out dough to 1/2-
inch thickness; using a 2 1/2-inch biscuit cutter, cut
out biscuits.
GATHER trimmings, reroll, cut out more biscuits;
place on prepared baking sheet.
BAKE until golden, about 12 to 15 minutes; place
biscuits on a wire rack and cool slightly.

FILLING: In a large bowl, combine strawberries,
orange juice and sugar; mix well.
SPLIT warm biscuits in half horizontally; place
bottom halves on serving plates.
TOP with some filling; cover with biscuit tops, and
serve with remaining filling.
GARNISH with yogurt and mint.

PER serving:
CALORIES 216
(21% from fat)
FAT 5g
PROTEIN 6g
CARBOHYDRATE 38g
SODIUM 217mg
CHOLESTEROL 13mg

# Toasted Oatmeal Cookies

Butter-flavored vegetable cooking spray
2   cups quick-cooking oats, uncooked
1/4 cup margarine, softened
3/4 cup firmly-packed brown sugar
1/2 cup egg substitute
1   teaspoon vanilla extract
3/4 cup all-purpose flour
1   teaspoon ground cinnamon
1/2 teaspoon baking soda
1/2 teaspoon salt
1/2 cup pecans, chopped

PER cookie:
CALORIES 57
(36% from fat)
FAT 2.3g
(0.3g saturated)
PROTEIN 1.2g
FIBER 0.5g
CARBOHYDRATE 8.3g
CHOLESTEROL 0mg
SODIUM 56mg

COAT a 15x10x1-inch jellyroll pan with cooking spray;
add oats.
BAKE at 350 degrees for 10 minutes, or until oats
are golden, stirring once.
COOL.
BEAT margarine at medium speed of an electric
mixer; gradually add sugar, beating well.
ADD egg substitute and vanilla, beating well.
COMBINE flour and remaining 4 ingredients; stir
in toasted oats; add oat mixture to sugar mixture,
stirring well.
DROP dough by rounded teaspoonfuls, 3 inches
apart, onto cookie sheets coated with cooking
spray.
BAKE at 350°for 12 minutes, or until golden.
COOL on cookie sheets 5 minutes; remove to wire
racks to cool completely.
YIELD: 3 1/2 dozen.

# Notes & Recipes

**ORDER BLANK**

NAME _____

ADDRESS _____

CITY & STATE _____ ZIP _____

How many copies? _____ Amount enclosed _____
    Price per book ......................................... $18.95
    Postage & handling ................................... 2.50
    Total ...................................................... $21.45
Please make checks payable to:
                Heart of America Restaurants & Inns
Mail orders to:   Heart of America Restaurants & Inns
                1501 River Drive
                Moline, IL 61265

- - - - - - - - - - - - - - - - - - - - - - - - - - - - - - - -

**ORDER BLANK**

NAME _____

ADDRESS _____

CITY & STATE _____ ZIP _____

How many copies? _____ Amount enclosed _____
    Price per book ......................................... $18.95
    Postage & handling ................................... 2.50
    Total ...................................................... $21.45
Please make checks payable to:
                Heart of America Restaurants & Inns
Mail orders to:   Heart of America Restaurants & Inns
                1501 River Drive
                Moline, IL 61265